CAMBRIDGE LIBRARY COLLECTION

Books of enduring scholarly value

History

The books reissued in this series include accounts of historical events and movements by eye-witnesses and contemporaries, as well as landmark studies that assembled significant source materials or developed new historiographical methods. The series includes work in social, political and military history on a wide range of periods and regions, giving modern scholars ready access to influential publications of the past.

A Formula Book of English Official Historical Documents

This 1908 work supplements Hall's *Studies in English Official Historical Documents*. It gives examples of a wide range of English diplomatic documents from the seventh to the nineteenth centuries. These are arranged according to type and purpose, the majority in Latin, but others in French or English. The intention is to assist the user of such archival materials, by familiarising them with the format and language used in each kind of document, and explaining why and how they were written. The 211 transcriptions were made by palaeography students at the London School of Economics and classified and edited with extensive notes by Mr Hall. They are not literal transcriptions, as contractions have been expanded, and the punctuation and capitalisation modernised. To save space, standard formulas have not been repeated each time. Despite the lack of any illustrations of originals, the book filled a need long felt by students of history.

Cambridge University Press has long been a pioneer in the reissuing of out-of-print titles from its own backlist, producing digital reprints of books that are still sought after by scholars and students but could not be reprinted economically using traditional technology. The Cambridge Library Collection extends this activity to a wider range of books which are still of importance to researchers and professionals, either for the source material they contain, or as landmarks in the history of their academic discipline.

Drawing from the world-renowned collections in the Cambridge University Library, and guided by the advice of experts in each subject area, Cambridge University Press is using state-of-the-art scanning machines in its own Printing House to capture the content of each book selected for inclusion. The files are processed to give a consistently clear, crisp image, and the books finished to the high quality standard for which the Press is recognised around the world. The latest print-on-demand technology ensures that the books will remain available indefinitely, and that orders for single or multiple copies can quickly be supplied.

The Cambridge Library Collection will bring back to life books of enduring scholarly value (including out-of-copyright works originally issued by other publishers) across a wide range of disciplines in the humanities and social sciences and in science and technology.

A Formula Book
of English Official
Historical Documents

VOLUME 1:
DIPLOMATIC DOCUMENTS

EDITED BY HUBERT HALL

CAMBRIDGE
UNIVERSITY PRESS

CAMBRIDGE UNIVERSITY PRESS

Cambridge, New York, Melbourne, Madrid, Cape Town, Singapore,
São Paolo, Delhi, Dubai, Tokyo

Published in the United States of America by Cambridge University Press, New York

www.cambridge.org
Information on this title: www.cambridge.org/9781108010221

© in this compilation Cambridge University Press 2010

This edition first published 1908
This digitally printed version 2010

ISBN 978-1-108-01022-1 Paperback

FORMULA BOOK

OF

DIPLOMATIC DOCUMENTS

CAMBRIDGE UNIVERSITY PRESS WAREHOUSE,

C. F. CLAY, Manager.

London: FETTER LANE, E.C.

Edinburgh: 100, PRINCES STREET.

Leipzig: F. A. BROCKHAUS.

Berlin: A. ASHER AND CO.

New York: G. P. PUTNAM'S SONS.

Bombay and Calcutta: MACMILLAN AND CO., Ltd.

A FORMULA BOOK

OF ENGLISH OFFICIAL HISTORICAL DOCUMENTS

PART I

DIPLOMATIC DOCUMENTS

SELECTED AND TRANSCRIBED BY A SEMINAR OF
THE LONDON SCHOOL OF ECONOMICS

EDITED BY

HUBERT HALL, F.S.A.

OF H.M. PUBLIC RECORD OFFICE
READER IN PALÆOGRAPHY IN THE UNIVERSITY OF LONDON

CAMBRIDGE:
AT THE UNIVERSITY PRESS
1908

Cambridge:
PRINTED BY JOHN CLAY, M.A.
AT THE UNIVERSITY PRESS.

PREFACE

THE present work was originally planned as an Appendix to the Diplomatic "Studies" which have been published by the Editor as a separate work[1]. It was suggested, however, that these Formulas might be worthy of publication in an expanded form, and a Seminar of the London School of Economics was prepared to undertake the task of selecting and transcribing the documents required for this purpose. The venture, therefore, was made under conditions which have at least proved interesting and instructive to those who have taken part in it.

In one aspect, however, the scope of the work is strictly limited, for it was quite impracticable to specialize in any one period or to give an exhaustive account of any particular class of instruments in a survey of the whole field of official diplomatic composition from the 7th century to the 19th. The chief claim of this Formula Book upon the attention of historical students and Record workers will be found in its comprehensive design and in the further attempt that it makes, for the first time, to present the several types of official instruments in a connected series. In addition to a serious diplomatic description of the several documents, their *provenance* has also been broadly indicated, together with their bibliographical relations. Thus the student can in most cases ascertain at a glance the position of an original instrument in respect of enrolment or entry, together with its published form as a complete text, abstract, or mere description.

---

[1] *Studies in English Official Historical Documents* (Cambridge, at the University Press, 1908).

It has seemed preferable to present concrete examples of diplomatic composition rather than the abstract forms usually associated with a scientific *Formula Book*. At the same time it must be clearly understood that no attempt has been made to demonstrate the historical or personal interest of the several documents. Incidentally, however, it will be found that several of the original instruments supply gaps in the official series of enrolments, whilst the individual interest of a large proportion of the whole series is considerable.

The arrangement of the documents is based upon the classification adopted by the Editor in the work above referred to. It was intended in the first instance to prefix a brief introductory note to each document in turn, but it was found that a great saving of space could be effected by substituting for this plan a connected introduction to each section.

An equally necessary economy has been made, with some reluctance, by omitting many details from the texts which were not essential to their diplomatic construction. In such cases the omission is indicated by an *etc.* in square brackets.

The dates given in the headings to the individual documents are those actually employed for the purpose of official reference. The distinction between the several systems in use at different times is thus preserved, but the year of Our Lord has been given in the Table of Contents.

As in the case of former academical exercises[1] it has seemed desirable to attempt a full extension of the original Text, except in the case of the more modern State Papers and Departmental Records, the Palæographical aspect of which could scarcely be realized in a modern guise. Following the same precedents, the capitalisation and punctuation of the original documents have been modernized together with the typographical forms of *i* and *u*. In the case of the diphthong *æ*, in deference to certain representations, it was originally intended that the usual mediæval form should be preserved. It was found, however, that, owing to the exceptional scope of the work, not fewer

---

[1] *i.e.* in the publications dealing with the "Exchequer Receipt Roll, 1185" and the "Pipe Roll of the Bishopric of Winchester, 1208," both published by the London School of Economics.

than four systems of indicating this diphthong had to be reckoned with. In the pre-Conquest period, indeed, three of these forms may occur in the same text, whilst the mediæval form of the tagged, or untagged, *e* is replaced before the 18th century by the conventional diphthong. The latter has therefore necessarily been preserved in the earliest and latest documents printed in this collection. The "tagged" *e* has not been reproduced for the same reason that the reproduction of the Old English letters has been eschewed, as far as possible, whilst the diphthong *at the end of* Latin words has been indicated by an accent. This further license has been taken chiefly in the interests of a large body of readers to whom certain printed mediæval texts of our own time are practically closed books. It is hoped that this unusual device will not offend the susceptibilities of those scholars for whose benefit the present work was not primarily intended.

The present volume contains the "Diplomatic Documents" which form the best-known class of official instruments. It is proposed to publish in a Second Part, which is in active preparation, Formulas of Surveys, Inquisitions, Accounts and of such judicial Records as chiefly lend themselves to diplomatic study.

The Formula Book when completed in two Parts will have been the result of three years' work in a Seminar for Advanced Historical Studies[1]. As only one evening weekly has been available for this purpose the progress of the work has necessarily been slow. Following the practice established on former occasions the transcription of the text has been allotted to individual students whilst the palæographical and diplomatic aspects of the whole subject and the selection of the several examples have been considered by the whole class.

The following students have taken part in the above operations: Miss H. Hadley (Archivist, L.C.C.) has transcribed the texts of the Old English charters; Miss S. E. Moffat (certificate in Arts, Edinburgh) those of the Anglo-Norman charters; Miss E. M. Leonard (Historical Tripos, Cambridge, and M.A. Dublin) those of the Royal Charters 1200–1516; Miss L. Drucker, those of the Confirmations, the

---

[1] Provided by and given under the authority of the Committee of the Advanced History Teaching Fund.

Writs under the Great Seal and the semi-official Instruments; Miss A. Raven (Staff of Victoria County History) those of the Missives under the Smaller Seals and the sequence of an ecclesiastical election; Mrs M. E. Maynard (Honours School of Modern History, Oxford) those of the Warrants for Issue of the Great Seal; and Miss P. Steele Hutton (M.A. St Andrews) those of the Royal Letters and Secretarial or Departmental Instruments. The Editor, as previously implied, is solely responsible for the classification of the documents and the introductory matter.

The Documents included in this volume have all been transcribed at the Public Record Office with the exception of the Anglo-Saxon charters and certain mediæval Royal Letters at the British Museum. A key to the abbreviated references employed is appended with a classified Table of Contents.

The transcribers and the editor alike wish to express their sincere appreciation of the courteous assistance rendered by the officials in charge of the Search Rooms at the Public Record Office, as well as by the authorities of the London School of Economics and of the Cambridge University Press. They have also to express their grateful acknowledgement of the kindness of Professor T. F. Tout in reading the proofs.

H. H.

July, 1908.

TABLE OF CONTENTS

C. CONVENTIONAL CHARTERS (1200–1516).

(*a*) *General Forms.*

Contents

B. Later Procedure.

(i) Normal Procedure subsequent to the year 1535.

(ii) Special Procedure (by Immediate Warrant, etc.).

(*c*) *Royal Household.*

3. Departmental Instruments.

ABBREVIATIONS USED IN THE REFERENCES, ETC. OF THIS WORK.

C. S. = *Cartularium Saxonicum* (ed. W. de G. Birch, 1885–93).

C. D. = *Codex Diplomaticus ævi Saxonici* (ed. J. M. Kemble, 1839–48).

A. C. No.— = *Ancient Charters* (ed. J. H. Round in Pipe Roll Society's *Publications*, Vol. x.).

B. M. Facs. = *Facsimiles of Ancient Charters in the British Museum* (ed. E. A. Bond, 1873–78).

Rot. Litt. Pat. = *Rotuli Litterarum Patentium* (ed. T. D. Hardy, 1835).

Cal. = Calendars of Charters, Letters Patènt and Close, etc. (Rolls Series).

D. of L. R. C. = Duchy of Lancaster, Royal Charters.

A. C. Vol.— = Ancient Correspondence (Chancery).

O. L. P. = Original Letters Patent (Exchequer Series).

K. R. and L. T. R. Mem. Roll = King's Remembrancer's or Lord Treasurer's Remembrancer's Memoranda Rolls.

Exch. T. of R. = Exchequer, Treasury of Receipt.

Chanc. Warrts., etc. = Chancery, Warrants for Issue.

F. O. = Foreign Office.

H. O. = Home Office.

S. P. Dom., etc. = State Papers Domestic, etc.

I. INSTRUMENTS UNDER THE GREAT SEAL

I. ROYAL CHARTERS (GRANTS)

A. ANGLO-SAXON CHARTERS (7TH—11TH CENTURIES)

THE specimens of pre-Conquest diplomatic given in the following pages are necessarily limited to a few examples. Of these, one group represents the general form of the Old English Charter in several periods of its development. The other group contains specimens of special forms which are characteristic of this diplomatic era.

The Charters in question have been selected without any further design than to secure specimens which afford credible and accessible examples of their class. That is to say, care has only been taken that these should be either originals sufficiently legible to be collated by a non-expert editor, or copies entered in a cartulary of good repute.

A complete diplomatic description of the Charters being beyond the scope of this work, and the space allotted to the section being strictly limited, such portions of the texts (consisting chiefly of the usual conditions of enjoyment, boundaries and subscriptions) as appeared to be unnecessary for the mere indication of the characteristic formulas, have been omitted to permit of the inclusion of a greater number of examples.

It has appeared desirable, however, to identify these Charters with the several religious houses for which they were presumably composed and by which they were subsequently preserved. This identification in the case of original charters, which contain no internal evidence of ownership, and which have not been entered in any monastic register, is a matter of some difficulty. The Collections in which the Charters are now found have never been assigned to their original sources, and in some cases no identification whatever has been attempted by the editors of the several 'Codices.' Again the identifications proposed by the editors of the official 'Facsimiles' are not always conclusive. More than one of the following identifications must be regarded, therefore, as merely conjectural, whilst the diplomatic descriptions are wholly elementary.

H. F.   1

(a) General Forms of Old English Charters

1. *Suaebraed of Essex* (704).—It may perhaps be suggested that this Charter is connected with the later grant (cf. C.S. 860) of Twickenham to Christ Church, Canterbury, and the 12th century endorsement is characteristic of this house.

This Charter is assigned by the British Museum Editor to the end of the 8th or early 9th century from the handwriting, and its formulas are characteristic of that period. The Invocation and Preamble are well defined; but the Superscription is involved with the rudimentary Exposition, or explanatory clause, and with the Dispositive Clause, as is so frequently found in Old English Charters.

The Boundaries follow the words of concession, but are succeeded by an elaborate Final or Injunctive clause prescribing the nature of the enjoyment of the premises. The announcement of Attestation, and the Subscriptions of the witnesses are in the early style, but the royal Subscriptions have possibly been embellished at the date of making this copy.

2. *Offa of Mercia* (779).—This Charter may perhaps be connected with the interest of the Church of Evesham in Bourton-on-the-Water, co. Gloucester (cf. Bigland, *Gloucestershire*, I. 225), although it is not entered in the cartularies of this Abbey, nor referred to in the Evesham Chronicle. The 'Chrismon' prefixed to the Invocation, and the formulas that occur in a spurious Charter of the same year (C.S. 229), which is entered in the well-known Cartulary (Vesp. B. 24), closely resemble those found in the present Charter, which was probably used as a model for a later forgery.

The Charter given here is characteristic of the official style used by expert 'dictatores' in the reign of King Offa, denoting the high degree of excellence in diplomatic composition attained under this king.

The date, the form of which is interesting, appears to be correct.

3. *Æthelwulf of Wessex* (847).—Some difficulty has been found in identifying the source of this Charter, which has been ascribed by the Editor of the British Museum 'Facsimiles' to the Church of Canterbury. The character of the local Boundaries, however, suggests a connection with the interest of the Church of Sherborne in Wareham, where Marcomb's Lane divided the parishes of St Michael and Holy

Trinity, in the latter of which this Church had lands. King Æthelwulf was also a benefactor of this Church, as appears from Charters dated 841 and 844, which are not now preserved[1]. The Charter is regarded as 'doubtful' by the British Museum Editor from the character of the handwriting, although it can scarcely be regarded as suspicious on diplomatic grounds, in spite of the indifferent repute of the Charters attributed to this king.

4. *Æthelstan* (933).—This is one of the few original charters which have survived for a reign in which the art of diplomatic composition reaches its highest point of consistency. That is to say, we find several recurrent forms in which the essential clauses present characteristic features. Thus in the majority of the ten Charters of the reign in which the Preamble begins with the words 'Flebilia fortiter detestanda,' there is no Invocation; the Superscription gives the style 'per omnipatrantis dexteram'; the florid Exposition begins 'Qua de re' and the grant (in the case of 'landbocs') is expressed by 'tribuo'; whilst the clause announcing the Boundaries is especially characteristic of the 'diplomata' of this reign. The Sanction begins with 'Si autem' and the Dating Clause with 'Hujus namque.' Finally the royal Subscription usually contains the style 'ierarchia praeditus Rex.' This form appears to have been chiefly affected by western Churches, the surviving examples being associated with those of Winchester, Shaftesbury, Sherborne, Crediton and Abingdon. In the case of the Charter printed below, the Grant, being concerned with privileges, is expressed by 'dijudicavi' and the clause announcing the Boundaries is of course absent. The Dating Clause 'Hujus namque' does not occur here and variants are seen in the Sanction and Subscription.

5. *Cnut* (1031).—This Charter, like No. 3 of the present series, is ascribed to the Church of Canterbury by the British Museum Editor, probably from an identification of the grantee with a famous Kentish thegn. The learned editors of the Crawford Charters have, however, incidentally distinguished this Æthelric from a presumably West-Country namesake, and have further identified the locality of this grant with the river Mewy, co. Devon.

This identification is supported by the character of the Boundaries, whilst a resemblance to the style of certain charters granted to the Church of Exeter during this reign might suggest that the Church of

---

[1] *Monasticon*, I. 333, and Hutchins, *History of Dorset*, IV. 228.

Crediton was ultimately interested in the grant. Moreover the Priory of Plimpton, which was founded by the See of Exeter, held Meavy after the Conquest. (Oliver, *Monasticon, Dioc. Exon.* p. 129 sq.; cf. *Transactions*, Devon. Assoc. vol. XXVIII. p. 455)

This is one of the few original and undoubtedly genuine Charters of the reign and may be contrasted with the inflated formulas of certain specimens.

6. *Edward the Confessor* (1045).—The Charter printed below is one of the few original Latin Charters of this reign which contain nothing of a suspicious character. It is in fact characterized by a severe simplicity of style without, however, any affectation of archaism. It will be noticed that the royal Subscription contains no allusion to sealing.

The Charter is of special interest as corroborating in this instance at least the evidence of the Winchester Cartulary, a register which is perhaps justly regarded with some suspicion.

(b) *Special Forms of Old English Charters*

The following Charters are given here as specimens of privileges which were undoubtedly sought for and obtained during the pre-Conquest period, although their alleged concession was frequently the subject of a later forgery. To the types presented here the well-known privileges which characterized a later franchise, namely ' sac ' and ' soc,' ' toll,' ' theam ' and ' infangthef,' might have been added, but the occurrence of these terms in a genuine Latin pre-Conquest Charter is something more than questionable.

It is, however, a striking fact that Charters which purport to grant various privileges and immunities in more or less fantastic terms are to be found in reputable cartularies like those of Rochester and Worcester, whilst in certain cases their authenticity is confirmed by the survival of the original or at least of contemporary instruments, as in the case of No. 8 in the present series. On the other hand an attempted forgery of such privileges will be seen in the case of the Cotton Charter VIII. 35 (C.S. 469) and a sequence of suspicious forms (including No. 7 in the present series) may be noted in the Worcester Cartulary, possibly composed with the intention of expounding the purport of a genuine charter (C.S. 416).

7. *Grant of Privileges.*—Apart from the entry of the Charter in the Worcester Register, we know that this Church had absorbed the above foundation before the Norman Conquest.

The Charter belongs to a class of 'diplomata,' which is generally regarded with suspicion. The short form (C.S. 435) is obviously a 'résumé' composed at a much later date; but another version of this Charter (C.S. 454) is highly suspicious.

The Invocation of the Charter printed here resembles that of C.S. 448, and the general composition may be compared with C.S. 433 and others of the series noticed above as probably based on a genuine contemporary charter (C.S. 416).

8. *Remission of Customs dues.*—This is one of a very interesting and important series of 'diplomata,' dealing with similar concessions, which range between the years 732–3 and 761 (C.S. 149, 150, 171, 173, 177, 188, 189).

The authenticity of this Charter, which is entered in the 'Textus Roffensis,' is established by the survival of the original (Cotton Charter XVII. 1) which was, however, apparently composed at the date of the Confirmation of the reputed Charter of 734, namely, in the year 840. This Charter evidently served as the model for the forged privileges of 732–3 entered in the Register of St Augustine's, Canterbury (C.S. 149, 150), with which we may compare the Old English version of like privileges for the Church of Worcester (C.S. 171).

9. *Exemption from Royal Service.*—This is a specimen of a type of land-boc which is usually regarded with suspicion owing to the non-reservation of the 'Trinoda Necessitas,' and it may be compared with the numerous grants 'in free and perpetual alms' (No. 15) during the post-Conquest period. No original of this Charter is preserved, but its entry in the 'Textus Roffensis,' a register of good repute, as well as the simplicity of its form, are in favour of its authenticity. It may be contrasted with numerous Charters containing a statement of similar immunities in exaggerated terms. It will be noted that the Datal clause is omitted. This should have followed the announcement of validation, and has probably been replaced by the rogatory Final Clause, which is characteristic of the occasional pious interpolations of the compilers of the Rochester and Worcester registers.

10. *Land-boc with Sanction in the form of a 'glacial' curse.*— This Charter is clearly connected with the Church of Wells, though the premises have been identified with Hanham (co. Gloucester) by the learned editor of the *Cartularium Saxonicum.* The recent identification with West Hatch (co. Somerset) in the Historical MSS. Commissioners' *Report* on the Wells 'Liber Albus' (vol. 1) is supported by the vernacular heading printed in that Report (p. 449). The form

of Sanction seen in this Charter was only used between the years 937 and 947 and was chiefly affected by south-western monasteries. It occurs in the following Charters:—C.S. 714, 734, 741, 756, 759, 767, 781, 783, 822, 874. It has been suggested (by Sir F. Pollock) that this formula was invented by a dictator, who had been impressed with the terrors of the dangerous passage of the Alps, which have been so graphically described by William of Malmesbury (*Gesta Pont.* p. 26, cf. Stubbs, *Oxford Lectures*, p. 128).

---

1. *Grant of lands in Twickenham (co. Middlesex) to Walhari, bishop of London* (704).

✠ In nomine domini nostri Jhesu Christi salvatoris.

Quamvis solus sermo sufficeret ad testimonium, attamen pro cautella futurorum temporum, ne quis forte posterum fraudulentam ignorantiæ piaculum perperam incurrat, idcirco scedulis saltim vilibus pro ampliore firmitatis supplimento necessarium reor adnectere. Quapropter ego Sueabræd rex Eastsaxanorum et ego Peogthath, cum licentia Ædelredi regis comis, aliquantulum agri partem, pro remedio animarum nostrarum, Uualdhario episcopo in dominio donare decrevimus, id est xxx cassatorum in loco qui dicitur Tuican Hom in provincia quæ nuncupatur Middelseaxan. Hæc autem terra his locorum limitibus designatur. Ab oriente [*etc.*]. Possessionem autem hujus terræ taliter, ut supradiximus, cum campis sationalibus, pascualibus, pratis, palludibus, piscuariis, fluminibus, clusuris, omnibus quæ ad eam pertinentibus, in dominio supra dicti Episcopi possidendum perpetuale jure tradidimus et liberam habeat potestatem agendi quodcumque voluerit. Porro ut firmior hujus donationis largitio jugiter servaretur, etiam testes adjunximus, quorum nomina subter tenentur inserta. Si quis vero successorum nostrorum hanc donationis nostræ munificentiam augere et amplificare maluerit, augeat Dominus partem ejus in libro vitæ; si quis e diverso, quod absit, tyrannica potestate fretus, infringere temptaverit, sciat se ante tribunal Christi tremibundum rationem redditurum. Maneatque nilhominus in sua firmitate hæc kartala scripta anno ab incarnatione Domini nostri DCC. iiij. indictione ij, tertia decima die mensis Junij, quod est idus Junij.

Ego Coenredus rex Mercensium hanc terram Waldhario episcopo pro remedio animæ meæ in dominio donare decrevi, in loco qui dicitur Tuiccanham, et libenti animo propria manu crucem infixi.

Ego Headda episcopus consensi et subscripsi.

Ego Cotta abbas consensi et subscripsi.

Ego Suebrædus rex Eastsaxonum propria manu.

Ego Peohthat signum manus imposui.

Ego Friodored signum manus. [*Three others sign thus.*]

Eadred signum. [*Two others sign thus.*]

Ego Ciolred [rex] Mercensium hanc donationem, quam ante donavit propinqus meus Coenredus rex et ego, confirmavi in loco Arcencale et signum sancté crucis expressi.

Ælric signum manus. [*Two others sign thus.*]

Eadberht signum. [*Three others sign thus.*]

[*Original Charter, MS. Cott. Aug.* II. 82.
B. M. Facs. I. 3.
C.S. No. 111.]

---

2. *Grant of lands in Salmonnesburg to Duddonus the King's thegn* (779).

$\frac{P}{A|\omega}$ Regnanti in perpetuum domino nostro Jhesu Christo: Universa quippe quæ hic in præsentia visibus humanis corporaliter contemplantur nihil esse nisi vana et caduca transitoriaque, ex sacrorum voluminum testimoniis certissimi verum patet. Et tamen cum istis æternaliter sine fine mansura alta polorum regna et jugiter florentis paradisi amoenitas mercari a fidelibus viris queunt.

Quapropter ego Offa, Deo cuncta pie disponente, in cujus manu sunt omnia jura regnorum, absque ulla antecidente merito, rex Mercionum ; hoc mente precogitans, aliquam ruris partem, pro amore cælestis patriæ et pro remedio animæ meæ, fideli meo ministro Duddono, hoc est quatuor cassatas in jus ecclesiasticæ liberalitatis, in perpetuum possid...libentissime concedens donabo, quatinus ut se vivente [*etc.*]. Et si quis ex heredum ejus, quod absit, maculo majore peccati forte inplicatus fuerit, dign...scilicet pretio se emundet a delicto commisso ; manente tamen hac munificentiæ meæ dono nihilominus in sua stabilitate firmiter, absque ulla commutatione. Est autem portio ruriculi illius attinens urbi illi [*etc.*]. Ad confirmandum vero hujus antedicti telluris donationem, testium et consentientium episcoporum, abbatum ac ducum meorum signa et nomina in hac cartula testimonii infra conscribta adnotabo.

Conscribta est autem hæc munificentia piisimi regis Offan anno ab incarnatione Christi DCCLXXVIIIJ, indictione secunda, anno decennovenali primo, lunari xvij, aet Iorotlaforda (*Hartleford*).

Ego Offa, divina gubernante gratia rex Mercensium, huic donationis meæ signum crucis infixi.

Ego Eadberhtus, Dei dono episcopus, consensi et subscripsi

[*and other bishops, princes and dukes, etc.*].

[*Original Charter, MS. Cott. Aug.* II. 4.
B. M. Facs. I. 10.
C.S. No. 230.]

3. *Grant of lands at Hamme* (? *Wareham, co. Dorset*) *to the King himself* (847).

℥   Regnante domino nostro Jhesu Christo in perpetuum. · Siquidem
Aǀω   sacris insertum voluminibus...[qu]orum preclaris satisque salu-
taribus cotidie instruimur oraculis, hoc solum superesse homini in omni
labore suo quod laborat sub sole, et in cunctis quæ possidet diebus
vanitatis suae, si quid in elemoxsinarum largitate piis intentus operibus
expenderet, proximorumque communicanda necessitatibus, pro possi-
bilitate virium, " faciat sibi," secundum salvatoris preceptum, " amicos
de mamona iniquitatis, qui eum recipiant in æterna tabernacula." Qua
de re ego Ætheluulf, Deo auxiliante occidentalium Saxonum rex, cum
consensu ac licentia episcoporum et principium meorum, aliquantulam
ruris partem, viginti manentium, mihi in hereditatem propriam
describere jusi, id est me ad habendum et ad perfruendum, cum pratis
et pascuis, cum campis et silvis, cum aquis currentium et incurrentium,
et iterum qualicumque, prout me placabilis sit, æternaliter relinquen-
dum. Terra autem predicta liber et securus omnium rerum permaneat, id est regalium et principalium tributum et vi exactorum
operum sive poenalium causarum, furisque conprehensione, et omni
sæculari gravidine, sine expeditione et pontis instructione.

Scripta est autem hujus donationis pagina anno dominici incarnationis, DCCC° XLVIIª, indictione, Xª.

Territoria vero ista sunt orum vigintorum cassatorum qui Æthel-
uulfe regi om Homme senatores ejus concedissent in illo loco qui
nuncupater Dornuuarana ceaster, secunda die Natalis Domini, coram
idoneis testibus quorum nomina infra aspicientium oculis caraxata
liquescunt :—*Ærest on merce cumb* [*etc.*].

Si quis autem hujus munificentia conlationem quovis tempore,
qualibet occasione, cujuslibet etiam dignitates vel professiones vel
gradus, pervertere vel in irritum deducere, sacrilega presumptione,
temptaverit, sit a consortio Christi ecclesiæ et a collegio sanctorum
hic et in futuro dispartitus, parsque ejus cum avaris et rapacibusque
ponatur, et communionem habeat cum Judas Scarioth qui tradidit
dominum. Si quis autem pia intentione potius preditus, hæc roborare
(h)ac defendere curaverit, amplificet Deus portionem ejus in hereditate
justorum, et cum omnibus...sine fine gaudeat.

Ego Ætheluulf rex ad confirmandam hanc donationem venera-
biliter trophei signum sanctæ crucis exarrabi.

Signum manus Æðelbaldi filii regis [*and many others*].

[*Original Charter, Cotton Ch.* VIII. 36.
B. M. Facs. II. 30.
C.S. No. 451.]

4. *Grant of Privileges to the Bishopric of Crediton* (933).

✠ Flebilia fortiter detestanda totillantis sæculi piacula diris obscenæ horrendæque mortalitatis circumsepta latratibus, non nos patria indeptæ pacis securos, sed quasi fetidæ corruptelæ in voraginem casuros provocando ammonent ut ea toto mentis conamine cum casibus suis non solum despiciendo, sed etiam velut fastidiosam melancoliæ nausiam abominando fugiamus, tendentes ad illud evangelicum, " date et dabitur vobis." Qua de re infima quasi peripsema quisquiliarum abiciens, superna ad instar pretiosorum monilium eliens, animum sempiternis in gaudiis fiens ad nanciscendam mellifluæ dulcedinis misericordiam, perfruendamque infinitæ letitiæ jocunditatem, ego Æthelstanus, per omnipatrantis dexteram apice totius Albionis sublimatus, circumquaque basilicas in honore Dei sanctorumque ejus dedicatas prout potero ab antiquo ritu vectigalium redimam, quod sibi mei antecessores usurpative decreverunt habere. Nunc vero, pro Dei omnipotentis amore et beatæ Dei genetricis Mariæ veneratione, sanctorumque omnium auctoritate, necnon pro venerabilis episcopi Eadulfi placabilis pecuniæ datione, id est, LX. librarum argenti, tantam libertatem episcopatui Cridiensis ecclesiæ perdonare dijudicavi, ut sit perpetualiter tutus atque munitus ab omnibus secularibus servitutibus, fiscis regalibus, tributis majoribus et minoribus, atque expeditionalibus videlicet taxationibus, omniumque rerum, nisi sola expeditione et arcis munitione. Si quis autem post hoc, subdola cavillatione deceptus, nostrum non perhorrescat machinari decretum, sciat se novissima ac magna examinationis die classica, archangeli clangente salpice, bustis sponte patentibus, somata jam rediviva propellentibus, cum Juda proditore, infaustoque pecuniarum compilatore, suisque impiissimis fautoribus, sub æternæ maledictionis anathemate edacibus innumerabilium tormentorum flammis sine defectu periturum. Acta est hæc præfatæ libertatis munificentia. DCCCCXXXIIJ. dominicæ incarnationis, anno indictione VI ; his testibus consentientibus signumque crucis Christi adponentibus quorum nomina infra caraxata esse monstrantur.

Ego Æthelstanus, gratia Dei largiente totius Brittanniæ rex, præfatam libertatem cum sigillo sancté crucis confirmavi.

Ego Wulfhelm, Dorobornensis ecclesiæ archiepiscopus, ejusdem regis largitatem cum tropheo sancté crucis consignavi.

Ego Ælfheah, Wintaniensis ecclesiæ episcopus, triumphalem agiæ crucis tropheum impressi.

Ego Theodred, Lundoniensis ecclesiæ episcopus, consignavi.

Ego Coenwald, episcopus, consensi.

Ego Oda, episcopus, confirmavi.

Ego Wulfhun, episcopus, roboravi.

Ego Ælfhere, dux [*and two others*].

Ego Odda, minister [*and six others*].

[*Original Charter, MS. Cott. Aug.* II. 31.
B. M. Facs. III. 4.
C.S. No. 694.]

5. *Grant of lands in Maewi* (?*Mewy, co. Devon*) *to Ætheric, the King's thegn* (1031).

✠ In altithroni onomate, qui nos qui voluit creavit plasmate. Ego, Cnut, rex totius Albionis céterarumque gentium triviatim persistentium basileus, dum plerumque cogitarem de hujus caduci séculi rebus quomodo superni arbitris examine cuncta qué videntur vana et labilia rite censentur. Verbi gratia, qué quasi tenuis venti flatus aut fumigantis ignis vapor ad nihilum redacta evanescunt, secundum illud quod preco gentium in sacris scripturam paginis clara promulgat predicatione; dicens omnia que videntur temporalia sunt; qué autem non videntur, éterna. Idcirco quandam rusculi particulam, dimedié, videlicet, mansé in loco qui a solicolis Maewi vocitatur nomine, cuidam fideli ministro, nomine Ætheric, libens, perpetualiter in éternam hereditatem concedo: quatenus cuicumque, post fragilis vité curriculum, voluerit heredi, liberam habeat, omnibus ad se rite pertinentibus éternaliter in jus proprium, potestatem tradendi. Sit autem predictum rus omni terrené servitutis jugo liberum, tribus exceptis, rata videlicet expeditione, pontis arcisve restauratione. Nunc vero pace nostra conglutinata vigens et florens inter agmina sancta éterné beatitudinis tripudia succedat, qui nostré donationis muniri consentiat. Si quis vero non perhorrescat evertere, machinans, nostrum decretum, sciat se corruentem in profundum barathrum eterni Orci, et éternaliter létalis laquei, in diris flammis cruciatum. Acta est autem héc mea donatio anno ab Incarnatione domini nostri Jesu Christi millesimo xxxi, Indictione iiij.

Istis terminis predicta tellus circumgyrata esse videtur [*etc.*].

Hujus namque nostré munificentié testes extiterunt quorum inferius nomina decusatim, Domino disponente, carraxantur.

Ego Cnut, Britannié totius Anglorum monarchus, hoc agié crucis taumate roboravi.

Ego Æthelnoð, Eboracensis basilicé primas insegnis, hoc donum regale confirmavi.

Ego Ælfgifo, regina humillima, adjuvi.

Ego Aelfsige, Episcopus, assensum prebui.

Ego Byrhtwold, Episcopus, dictando titulavi.

Ego Byrhtwig, Episcopus, dignum duxi.

Ego Ælmær, Episcopus, confirmavi.

Ego Lyfinc, Episcopus, consolidavi.

Ego Aethelric, Episcopus, consensi.

Ego Byrhtwine, Episcopus, conclusi.

Ego Godwine, dux [*and three other dukes*].

Ego Brihtmær, abbas [*and three other abbots*].

Ego Osgod, minister [*and seven other thegns*].

[*Original Charter, MS. Cott. Aug.* II. 69.
B. M. Facs. IV. 18.
C.D. DCCXLIV.]

6. *Grant of lands in Melebroc to Ælfwine, bishop of Winchester* (1045).

✠ In nomine domini nostri Jesu Christi qui cuncta gubernat et regit, quique sua multimoda potentia omnibus, ut voluerit, finem inponit, et de secretis humanae naturae mysteriis docet ut cum his fugitivis et sine dubio transitoriis possessiunculis, jugiter mansura et eternaliter regna mercanda, Dei suffragio, adipiscenda sunt. Qua de re ego Eadweardus divina mihi arridente gratia rex Anglorum, et eque totius Albionis, aliquam ruris partem, septem videlicet cassatos, illo in loco qui vulgariter Melebroc dicitur, cuidam episcoporum meorum perpetualiter trado, Ælfuuino, videlicet, Wentané civitatis episcopo ; ut hoc nostrum donum habeat quamdiu vivat et post se cuicumque voluerit heredi derelinquat, cum campis, pascuis, pratis, silvis. Haec igitur tellus a cuncta sit sequestrata servitute nisi pontis et arcis ac expeditionis juvamine. [Si quis] autem hoc nostrum donum infringere temtaverit, nullius adventant[is] consolationem uspiam repperiat nisi an[te ob]itum suum emendaverit quod hic contra nostrum decretum peregit. Istis namque terminis ambitur predicta tellus. *Dis synd tha landgemaera,* [*etc.*].

Anno dominicae incarnationis millesimo quadragesimo quinto, indictione xiij, et nullis epactis atque uno concurrente rotantibus, haec regalis concessio atque donatio facta est sub astipulatione primatum quorum nomina hic caraxata sunt.

Ego Eadweardus, rex totius Bryttanniae, prefatam meam donationem cum sigillo sanctae crucis regali stabilimento affirmavi.

Ego Eadgyđ, ejusdem regis conlaterana, hanc regalem donationem gaudenter stabilivi.

Ego Siweardus, archiepiscopus, triumphalem agiae crucis tropheum hic regio munere gaudenter inpressi.

Ego Ælfricus, archipresul, hanc territoriam scedulam signo sanctae crucis diligenter adsignare curavi.

Ego Ælfwinus, Wintoniensis episcopus, consolidavi.

Ego Lyfingus, Cridiensis episcopus, coadunavi.

Ego Heremannus, Wiltuniensis episcopus, corroboravi.

Ego Æthelstanus, Herfordensis episcopus, confirmavi.

Ego Eadnođus, Dorcensis episcopus, consensi.

Ego Duduco, Willensis episcopus, consigillavi.

Ego Grimkillus, Australium Saxonum episcopus, conscripsi.

Ego Wulfsinus, Licetfeldensis episcopus, condixi.

Ego Brihtwinus, Scirburnensis episcopus, conclusi.

Ego Godwine, dux [*and five others*].

Ego Ælfwine, Abbas [*and two others*].

Ego Ordgar, minister [*and eight others*].

[*Original Charter, Cotton Ch.* VIII. 9.
MS. Add. 15,350, *fo. 76 b.*
B. M. Facs. IV. 31.
C.D. DCCLXXXI.]

7. *Grant of privileges to the monastery of Bredon* (841).

✠   Aio et alto domino Deo Zabaoth regnanti in ævum. Siquidem humani generis prosapia de primo patre et matre oriundus in hanc seculum venit, et sic per longa vaga temporum spatium diversis nationibus derimuntur. Ut janitor cælestis bibliothecæ et vas electionis predicator egregius apostolus Paulus dixit, "Preteriit enim figura hujus mundi," quoniam in velocitate dies et anni deficiunt. Et iterum sagax sophista, qui quondam Solymis dives regnavit in arvis, katolectico versu cecinit, dicens, "Non semper licet gaudere, fugit hora qua jacemur." Et ideo sunt omnes nostræ series litterarum apicibus confirmandas, ne posteris ex memoria labere possit quicquid facta precedentium patrum ac regum firmiter statuerunt.

Qua de re ego Berhtuulf, Domino disponente, rex Merciorum, mihi et omnibus Mercis in æternam elemosinam, donans donabo Eanmundo venerabili abbati et ejus familiæ on Breodune, cum licentia et testimonia obtimatum gentis Merciorum, hanc libertatis gratiam, id est, ut sit liberatum et obsolutum illud monasterium in æternitatem ab illis incommodiis quam nos Saxonica lingua *foestingmen* dicimus, Christo domino teste et omnibus sanctis in celis, tam diu fides catholica et baptismum Christi in Brittannia servetur. Ob hujus rei gratiam, ipse vero supradictus Eanmund abbas et illius sancta congregatio Breodunensis monasterii dederunt mihi et omnibus Mercis, regaliter perfruendum et possedendum, in famoso vico in Tomeworðie, magnum discum argenteum, valde bene operatum ac faleratum in magno pretio, et c.xx mancusas in auro puro. Similiter etiam decantaverunt duodecim vicibus c psalterios et c.xx missas pro Berhtthulfum regem, et pro illius caros amicos, et pro omnem gentem Merciorum, ut eorum libertas firmior ac stabilior permaneat in eorum, et ut illius regis memoria et amicorum ejus qui hanc pietatem in elemosinam sempiternam omnibus Mercis ille congregatione on Breodune donaverat in eorum sacris orationibus jugiter permaneat usque in evum. Insuper in Dei omnipotentis nomine, et novem ordinibus angelorum, et omnium electorum Christi preceptum ponimus, ut nullus umquam regum vel principum, aut alicujus personis homo magnis sive modicis, in aliquo tempore hanc prescriptam libertatis gratiam infringere ausus sit; sed semper stabilis et indiscussa firmiterque firmata ille congregatione on Breodune, coram Deo et hominibus jugiter permaneat in evum.

Hæc autem cartula caraxata est anno dominicé incarnationis DCCCXLI, indictione IIIJ, in die natalis Domini, in celebre vico on Tomeworðie, his testibus consentientibus et signum crucis Christi scribentibus quorum subter nomina notata sunt.

Ego Berhtuulf, largiflua Dei munificentia rex Merciorum, hanc meam libertatis gratiam, ac omnium Merciorum, cum signo sanctæ crucis firmiter consignabo [*and others*].

[*Late* 11*th cent. copy in MS. Cott. Tiberius A* 13 (*ed. Hearne* I. 28, 453, 566).
    C.S. No. 434.]

8. *Remission of Customs dues upon one ship in the Port of London in favour of the Bishop of Rochester* (734).

✠ In nomine domini Dei salvatoris nostri Jhesu Christi.

Si ea quae quisque pro recipienda a Deo mercede hominibus verbo suo largitur et donat stabilia jugiter potuissent durare supervacaneum videretur ut litteris narrarentur ac firmarentur, sed dum ad probanda donata ad convincendumque volentem donata infringere nihil prorsus robustius esse videretur quam donationis manibus auctorum ac testium roboraté non inmerito plurimi petunt, ut quae eis conlata dinoscuntur paginaliter confirmentur quorum postulationibus tanto libentius tantoque promptius consensus prebendus est quanto et illis quae precatores sunt utilior res secundum hoc visibile seculum nunc inpertitur, et illis qui concessores existunt pro inpertito opere pietatis uberior fructus secundum invisibile postmodum tribuetur. Quam ob rem ego Ethilbaldus rex Merciorum presentibus litteris indico me dedisse pro anima mea Alduulfo episcopo ecclesiæque beati Andreæ apostoli quam gubernat unius navis sive illa proprie ipsius sive cujuslibet alterius hominis sit incessum id est vectigal, mihi et antecessoribus meis jure regio in portu Lundoniæ usque hactenus conpetentem quemammodum mansuetudinem nostram rogavit, quæ donatio ut in perpetuum firma et stabilis sit, ita ut nullus eam, regum vel optimatum vel teloniariorum vel etiam juniorum, quilibet ipsorum, in parte aut in toto [in irri]tum præsumat aut possit adducere manu proprio signum sanctæ crucis subter in hac pa[gina faciam testesque] ut subscribant petam. Quisquis igitur id quod pro anima mea donavi aut [donatu]m est inlibatum permanere permiserit habeat communionem beatam cum presente Christi ecclesia atque futura, si quis autem non permiserit, separetur a societate non solum sanctorum hominum sed etiam angelorum, manente hac donatione nostra nihilominus in sua firmitate. Actum mense Septembrio die indictionis, ij, anno regni nostri xvij.

Ego Æthilbald rex subscripsi.

Ego Danihel Episcopus scripsi.

Signum manus Oba.

Signum manus Sigibed.

Hoc etiam iterum confirmatum est a Beorhtuulfo regi Merciorum in vico regali Uuerburgewic.

Ego Berhtuulf rex Merciorum hanc meam donationem et predecessoris mei Ethilbaldi regis cum signo sanctæ crucis Christi confirmavi, his testibus consentientibus et quorum nomina hic continentur ad indulgentiam delictorum meorum atque predecessoris mei Æthelbaldi regis. Si quis autem successorum meorum regum aut principum vel thelonariorum hanc donationem nostram infringere vel minuere voluerit sciat se separatum a congregatione omnium sanctorum in tremendo die judicii, nisi prius digne emendaverit.

Ego Berhtuulf rex Merciorum [*and others*].

[*Original Charter*, Cotton Ch. XVII. I.
Textus Roffensis, f. 120.
B. M. Facs. II. *p.* I.
C.S. No. 152.]

9. *Grant of land to the Church of Rochester quit of all royal service for ever* (942—946).

In nomine Dei summi et salvatoris nostri Jhesu Christi, ipso quoque in perpetuo regnante disponenteque suaviter omnia.

Quapropter ego Eadmundus rex Anglorum, necnon et Merciorum, meo amabili episcopo, nomine Burhric, concedo aliquantulum mei telluris, ubi dicitur Meallingas, trium videlicet aratrum, pro remedio animæ meæ, in sempiternam hereditatem, ad augmentum monasterii ejus, qué est dedicata in honore sancti Andreæ apostoli, germanus Petri et socius in passione, cum omnibus rebus ad eam pertinentibus, cum campis, silvis, pratis, pascuis, necne et aucupiis; et hoc quoque cum consilio optimatum et principum meorum, quorum nomina infra scripta reperiuntur. Unde adjuro in nomine domini Dei nostri Jhesu Christi, qui est omnium justus judex, ut terra hæc sit libera ab omni regali servitio inperpetuum.

Si quis vero minuere vel fraudare presumpserit hanc donationem, sit separatus a consortio sanctorum, ita ut, vivens, benedictione Dei sit privatus, et sit damnatus in inferno inferiori, nisi satisfactione ante ejus obitum emendaverit quod inique gessit; manente tamen hac cartula nichilominus in sua firmitate. Qui vero tunc augere voluerit dona nostra, augeat illi Dominus cælestia dona et æternam vitam tribuat.

Bis syndon tha ·land gemæro [*etc.*].

Ego Eadmundus rex Anglorum signo crucis confirmavi

[*and others*].

[*Text. Roff. fo.* 143.
Ibid. (*ed. Hearne*) *p.* 108.
C.S. No. 779.]

10. *Grant of lands to Edmund the King's thegn and to his heirs, free of all secular service* (947).

In nomine Dei summi et altissimi Jhesu Christi.

Manifestum est cunctis quod omnia celestia [*etc.*].

Ideo certis adstipulacionibus [*etc.*].

Quam ob causam ego Eadredus, rex Anglorum, ceterarumque gencium in circuitu persistencium gubernator et rector, cuidam fideli meo ministro vocitato nomine Edmundo, pro ejus amabili obediencia, ejusque placabili pecunia quam michi in suæ devocionis obsequio detulit, III mansas agelluli ei libenter largiendo donavi in illo loco ubi jamdudum solicolé illius regionis nomen imposuerunt aet Hanecan Hamme; quatinus ille bene perfruatur ac perpetualiter possideat, quamdiu istius caducis seculi vitam tenere presumet, et post se cuicunque voluerit [*etc.*] liber ab omni [*etc.*] excepto [*etc.*].

Si quis autem, quod non optamus, hanc nostram diffinicionem, elacionis habitu incedens, infringere temptaverit, perpessus sit gelidis glaciarum flatibus et pennino exercitu malignorum spirituum, nisi prius inriguis penitenciæ gemitibus et pura emendacione emendaverit.

Isque terminibus [*etc.*].

Acta est hæc prefata donacio anno ab incarnacione domini nostri Jhesu Christi DCCCCXLVIJ, indictione v.

Ego Eadredus rex Anglorum prefatam donationem sub sigillo sanctæ crucis indeclinabiliter consensi, atque roboravi [*and others*].

[*Wells, Liber Albus,* II. *fol.* 288 *d.*
Ibid. (*ed. Hist. MSS. Commission,* I. p. 449).
C.S. No. 821.]

B. ANGLO-NORMAN CHARTERS (11TH AND 12TH CENTURIES)

These important instruments have been so frequently and so fully described by modern experts[1], as well as by earlier writers[2], that no general description of their character need be given here, especially since the notices of the several forms printed below include several of the most familiar diplomatic types that occur in the 12th century. A further description of these will be found in ' Studies' (Part II)[3].

(a) General Forms

11. *Anglo-Norman Charter in the Old English style.*—It has been remarked that in the period immediately following the Norman Conquest the formal 'diplomata' issued by the Crown were frequently modelled on Old English forms. In the example of this diplomatic style given here, it will be seen that there is an Invocation, resembling the style of continental charters. The Conventional Preamble and Superscription are after the Old English pattern. The Exposition is more irregular, but the Disposition though very comprehensive is correct in form. There is no Sanction nor any injunctive Final Clause, but an announcement of sealing is added to the Old English formula. The subscriptions appear to the editor of the excellent edition of this Charter in the *Transactions* of the Som. Arch. and N. H. Soc. (vol. XXII. p. 114) to have been written at random by the scribe, only those subsequently verified by a signature in the shape of a cross being recognised. It may be doubted, however, whether this was the established practice, and it seems more probable that

---

[1] e.g. Mr J. H. Round in *Ancient Charters* (Pipe Roll Society, Vol. X.) and *Calendar of Documents, France* (Rolls Series).

[2] e.g. Madox in *Formulare Anglicanum.*   [3] *See* Preface.

the crosses affixed to certain signatures were intended to distinguish between the original signatories of 1188 and those who took part in the confirmation of 1190, as is suggested by the interpolation regarding Archbishop Lanfranc.

12. *Anglo-Norman Writ-Charter.*—This instrument prevailed during the post-Conquest period and left its traces on the diplomatic forms of the 13th century (*see* Nos. 46—49). The formŭlas of this Charter are seen to resemble closely those of the Old English vernacular Writ, namely the brief style of the royal Superscription, the local Address, the personal identification of the Grant, and the injunctive Final Clause with the conventional enumeration of franchises. For the resemblance between such Charters and certain reputed Confirmations in this period, see below No. 36. As usual in Charters of this century there is no regnal or dominical date, the place only being given. It will be noticed that the Charter is attested by a number of 'Curiales,' this being one of the most obvious distinctions between a Charter and a Writ previous to the reign of Richard I.

The original Charter is in the form of a writ to which the Great Seal (now missing) was appended by a marginal strip, below which a narrow filament was cut to serve as a ligature for securing the folded writ. A scar on the edge of the bottom margin of the writ shows where this lower strip has been torn away. The handwriting of this Charter appears to be strictly contemporary. A very interesting description of the transaction with an identification of the grantee is given by Mr J. H. Round in *Geoffrey de Mandeville*, pp. 305—310.

13. *The New-Model Charter.*—In this Charter we have a royal grant of the same manor (Chalk) half a century later, and the style shows the progress made by the irregular 'writ-charter' in the direction of a conventional diploma. This 'new-model Charter' is here characterized by a formal Superscription and a ceremonious Address, which are henceforth stereotyped with appropriate changes; a Dispositive Clause expressing the legal idea of feudal tenure, and an injunctive Final Clause, which is so far conventional in that it begins with 'Quare volo' and recites the general description and conditions of the grant, but still retains the detailed description of the premises derived from earlier models, side by side with the compendious formula 'cum omnibus libertatibus et liberis consuetudinibus suis,' though without the further conventional *compendium*, 'sicut predictum est.' The final protocol has undergone no changes.

This Charter, like the great majority of the 'new-model' type, is not shaped and sealed like a writ. The parchment is cut almost to a square, of which the lower third was allowed to remain blank for the purpose of forming a 'fold' to support the weight of the seal, which was appended by a parchment label.

The writing is strictly contemporary. For the identification of the date and the motive of the grant, see the observations by Mr J. H. Round in *Ancient Charters* (Pipe Roll Soc. X. No. 40) and *Geoffrey de Mandeville* (p. 308).

14. *The Transitional Charter.*—The last specimen given here of the general form of the post-Conquest Charter shows the further development which had taken place in the last decade of the 12th century. The Superscription now invariably includes the words 'Dei gratia,' a formula which is said to have been definitely revived from the year 1173[1].

The King's style still retains the archaic 'Rex Anglorum,' but in his speech from the throne the sovereign now affects the plural number. The formula of Concession is in oblique oration and is becoming stereotyped with the addition of the word 'confirmasse,' and the condition of feudal tenure is further elaborated. The injunctive Final Clause is still in the stage of transition from an amplification of the Dispositive Clause to a mere recital thereof.

Finally the Dating Clause exhibits two important amendments in the insertion of the words 'per manum A. Cancellarii nostri' and the addition of the calendar and regnal dates.

The original Charter is square with a folded margin, the left side of which has been torn away by the attachment of the Great Seal. The writing appears to be contemporary.

(b) Special Forms

15. *Free Alms.*—The characteristic formula of the grant in Frankalmoigne is seen in the condition of the donation as described by the words 'in liberam et puram et perpetuam elemosinam.'

The Address and Notification are in the ceremonious style frequently employed in the case of ecclesiastical instruments. The exposition is here well developed in the form of a narrative.

The original Charter is somewhat elongated in shape. The writing

[1] M. L. Delisle in *Bibl. de l'École des Chartes*, T. LXVII. and LXVIII., but cf. Mr J. H. Round in *Archaeological Journal*, LXIV. p. 63 sq.

also is of the type of 'elongated minuscules.' The seal suspended from silk cords is apparently genuine.

16. *Charter of Liberties.*—This form, which is so characteristic of the constitutional growth witnessed during the 12th century, has scarcely been recognised as a special diplomatic type. The following characteristics may, however, be noticed in these public acts. The Address is brief and universal or general, and in place of the usual formula of donation, the royal Concession is effected by an Injunctive Clause, which is differentiated by means of successive paragraphs to meet existing or hypothetical cases, each of these clauses usually beginning with the words 'Et si.' It will be noticed that a general resemblance exists between these diplomatic acts and later Statutes which are occasionally found in a diplomatic form. In fact we have here initial and final Protocols (varying according to the contemporary style of the royal Chancery) which enclose a Text foreign to the conventional subjects of diplomatic instruments.

The text printed below is derived from the exhaustive edition of Professor Liebermann. For the process of issuing such charters, reference should be made to this learned writer's edition of the Coronation Charter of Henry I (*Trans. R. Hist. Soc.*, N. S. VIII. 21), and for an explanation of these 'liberties' to Stubbs, *S. C.* (1890), p. 103, and C. Bémont, *Chartes des Libertés Anglaises (Intro.).*

17. *License to assart Forest Lands.*—This document belongs to a class of 12th century instruments, which though commonly regarded as Charters (cf. *Dialogus* I. xi.—xiii.) are in fact Writs. The writ in question may be regarded as a License to 'assart' forest lands, as well as an Exemption from the hated jurisdiction of the royal foresters.

Like most instruments of the same species this writ is only preserved in the form of a later enrolment. Similar privileges are also found in monastic cartularies. This document should be compared with the more conventional form of Disafforestment used in a later period (No. 25) and also with the License to impark (No. 27).

This writ is not entered in the Tewkesbury Cartulary (Cleo. A. 7), nor is the grant of assart referred to in the *Monasticon* or in local histories.

18. *Forged Charter (Anglo-Norman).*—This purports to be a writ-charter of Henry I granting to the Church of Gloucester exemption from the forest jurisdiction in respect of a certain wood. Further information is given by an Inquisition taken in the 24th year of Henry VIII (*Cart. Mon. S. Petri Glouc.* (Rolls) II. 187), on which

occasion it is interesting to find that the original charter of Henry I was produced to the jurors who thereupon found in favour of the Abbot's claim. Presumably this charter is the one now preserved in the Record Office and printed below.

It is scarcely necessary to point out the several flaws in the diplomatic style of this production, which, however, reproduces several archaic formulas and is probably based upon a genuine writ. The Great Seal appears to be authentic and is correctly attached by a broad strip with the usual ligature, but the parchment is of the date of the script itself, namely the middle of the 13th century.

---

11. *Charter of William II granting the Abbey of Bath to Bishop John de Villula* (1088).

Pax in perpetuum deicolis omnibus tam futuris quam presentibus. Quoniam Deo omnitenente tempora seculorum ordinante et his prout placuerit finem imponente, coelum et terra et omnia qué in eis sunt suo fine transibunt, et vita nostra qué ad tempus floret, et cito tanquam flos foeni decidit, videtur esse momentanea; idcirco cunctis agendum, ut hic bonis actibus futuré beatitudinis mercemur gaudia absque omni immutatione perenniter mansura. Quo circa ego Willelmus, Willelmi regis filius, Dei dispositione monarches Britannié, pro meé meique patris remedio animé et regni prosperitate et populi, a Domino mihi collati, salute, concessi Johanni Episcopo abbatiam Sancti Petri Bathonié cum omnibus apenditiis, tam in villis quam in civitate, et in consuetudinibus illis, videlicet quibus saisita erat ea die qua regnum suscepi. Dedi inquam ad Summersetensis episcopatus augmentationem, eotenus presertim ut inibi instituat presuleam sedem. Anno dominicé incarnationis millesimo XC, regni vero mei iiii, indictione xiii, vi Kalendas Februarii, luna iii, pepigi id in eorum optimatum meorum presentia, quorum nomina subtus sunt annexa, et, ut per posteritates succedentes apud quosque homines veritatis amatores perseveret ratum, meé regié auctoritatis annecto sigillum, sed et propria manu mea depingo crucis dominicé signum[1].

[Lanfranco archipresule machinante, Wintonié factum est donum hujus beneficii, millesimo lxxxviii anno ab incarnatione Domini, secundo vero anno regni regis Willelmi, filii prioris Willelmi. Confirmatio autem hujus charté facta est apud Doveram eo tempore quod superius determinatum est[2].]

Ego Thomas, archiepiscopus Eboracensis, laudavi.

Ego Mauricius, Lundoniensis episcopus, corroboravi.

[1] An elaborate 'chrismon' is prefixed to the Invocation and crosses are prefixed to the subscriptions of the king, the archbishop, 3 bishops, 2 abbots, 3 earls, the chancellor, 7 chaplains and 4 *curiales*.

[2] Interpolated in MS.

Ego Walchelinus, Wintoniensis episcopus, aptavi.
Ego Osmundus, Sarisberiensis episcopus, consolidavi.
Ego Osbernus, Exoniensis episcopus, confirmavi.
Ego Remigius, Lincoliensis episcopus, astruxi.
Ego Rotbertus, Herefordensis episcopus, audivi.
Ego Rotbertus, Cestrensis episcopus, conspexi.
Ego Gunnulfus, Rovercestrensis episcopus, annui.
Ego Wolestannus, Wigrecestrensis episcopus, concessi.
Ego Radulfus, Cicestriensis episcopus, vidi.
Ego Herbertus, Tetfordensis episcopus, audivi.
Ego Goisfridus, Constantiensis episcopus, hoc exquisivi.
Ego Hoellus, Cenomannensis episcopus, interfui.
Ego Wido, abbas Sancti Augustini, Cantuarié [*and twelve other abbots*].
Ego Rogerus comes [*and seven other earls*].
Ego Rotbertus cancellarius.
Ego Philippus capellanus [*and ten other chaplains*].
Ego Eudo dapifer [*and four other dapiferi*].
Ego Rotbertus dispensator [*and others*].

[*Original Charter amongst the muniments of the Dean and Chapter of Wells* (*Orig. Deeds No.* 3) (*ed. Som. Arch. and N. H. Soc.* XXII. 114).
Liber Albus, ibid. fo. 14 *d.*
Liber Ruber, ibid. fo. 341.
(*Ed. Hist. MSS. Comm. Liber Albus* (*Wells*) I. 12, 13.)
MS. Corp. Camb. CXI. (*Bath Cartulary*) (*ed. Somerset Record Soc.* VII. 40).]

---

12. *Grant to Roger nepos Huberti of the land of Chalk which Fulk the Chamberlain held at farm* (1115—20).

Henricus Rex Anglorum, Radulfo Cantuariensi archiepiscopo, et Ernulfo Rofensi episcopo, et vicecomiti, et omnibus baronibus et fidelibus suis, Francis et Anglis, de Chent, salutem. Sciatis me dedisse et concessisse Rogero nepoti Huberti terram de Chelca, quam Fulco Camerarius habuit et tenuit ad firmam, sibi et heredi suo, in feodo et hereditate, pro servicio suo. Et volo et precipio, firmiter, ut bene et in pace, et quiete et honorifice teneat, cum saca et soca, et toll et team et infanguenetheof, et omnibus con-suetudinibus, sicut ego ipse tenebam dum esset in meo dominio. Testibus [*etc.*]. [*Names of witnesses follow.*] Apud Pen'.

[*Original Charter, Duchy of Lancaster, Royal Charters,* 3.]

---

13. *Grant to Gervase de Cornhulla of the land of Chalk which Roger Nepos Huberti held* (1164—65).

Henricus, Rex Anglorum et Dux Normannorum et Aquitannorum et Comes Andegavorum, archiepiscopis, episcopis, abbatibus, comitibus, baronibus, justiciis, vicecomitibus et omnibus ministris et fidelibus suis, Salutem.

Sciatis me dedisse et concessisse Gervasio de Cornhulla terram de Chalcha quam Rogerus nepos Huberti tenuit; tenendam sibi et heredibus suis, de me et heredibus meis, cum omnibus qué ad terram illam pertinent. Quare volo et firmiter precipio quod idem Gervasius et heredes sui post eum habeant et teneant eandem terram, cum omnibus pertinentiis suis, bene et in pace, libere et quiete, plenarie, integre, et honorifice; cum socha et sacha, et thol et theam, et infangenthef, et cum omnibus libertatibus et liberis consuetudinibus suis. Testibus [*etc.*]. Apud Westmonasterium.

[*Original Charter*, *D. of L., R. C.*, 26 (*A. C. No.* 40).]

---

14. *Grant to Henry filius Comitis of certain manors in Devon and Cornwall* (24 *April*, 5 *Richard I*).

Ricardus, Dei gratia Rex Anglorum, Dux Normannorum, Aquitannorum, Comes Andegavorum, archiepiscopis, episcopis, abbatibus, comitibus, baronibus, justiciis, vicecomitibus, senescallis, prepositis et omnibus ministris et fidelibus suis, Salutem.

Sciatis nos dedisse et concessisse et presenti carta confirmasse dilecto et fideli nostro, Henrico, filio comitis, manerium de Carsuilla et manerium de Depeforda, qué sunt in Devonia, et manerium de Liscaret in Cornubia, cum pertinentiis, tenenda de nobis et heredibus nostris, ipsi et heredibus suis per servicium feodi unius militis pro omni servicio. Quare volumus et firmiter precipimus quod idem Henricus et heredes sui post eum predictas terras habeant et teneant de nobis et heredibus nostris bene et in pace, libere et quiete, integre, plenarie, et honorifice; in bosco et plano, in pratis et pascuis, in vivariis et stagnis, in aquis et molendinis, in viis et semitis, et in omnibus locis et omnibus rebus ad predicta maneria pertinentibus, cum omnibus libertatibus et liberis consuetudinibus suis. Testibus [*etc.*]. Data per manum Willelmi, Eliensis episcopi, Cancellarii nostri, xxiiii die Aprillis. Apud Portesmues [anno quinto] regni nostri.

[*Original Charter*, *D. of L., R. C.*, 46 (*A. C. No.* 62).]

15. *Grant of lands in Farndon to the Abbey of Stanley in Free Alms* (1186—88).

Henricus, *etc.* [*as in No.* 13], abbati et universo capitulo Cisterciensi, et omnibus ad quos presens carta pervenerit, Salutem.

Noverit universitas vestra quod cum, Deo largiente, adeptus fuerim regnum Anglié, repperi quod tempore regis Stephani, ablatoris mei, multa dispersa fuerant, et a dominiis regni alienata, tum in feodis militum, tum in elemosinis ecclesiarum. Inter quas abbatia de Tame membrum quoddam manerii mei Ferendoné, quod vocatur Worda, tenebat ex dono inimicorum meorum, quod in integrum mihi resignavit. Sed quia fuerat religiosé domui quoquomodo collatum, ad petitionem Imperatricis, dominé et matris meé, et Gilleberti, tunc tempore abbatis Cisterciensis, et coabbatum suorum petitione et assensu, dedi predictum membrum manerii mei Feredoné, Worda vocatum, modo predeterminato ex toto mihi resignatum, abbatié de Stanleia, qué est de fundatione prefaté Inperatricis, dominé et matris meé et mea, et monachis ibidem Deo servientibus, cum omnibus rebus et libertatibus et liberis consuetudinibus ad illud pertinentibus, in liberam et puram et perpetuam elemosinam possidendum. Quare volo et firmiter precipio quod eadem abbatia de Stanlea et monachi in ea Deo servientes predictum membrum manerii mei Ferendoné, Worda nomine, habeant et teneant bene et in pace, libere et quiete, plenarie et integre et honorifice, sicut meam dominicam elemosinam, in bosco et in plano, in pratis et pascuis, in aquis et molendinis, in stagnis et vivariis, et piscariis, in viis et semitis, et in omnibus locis et rebus, cum omnibus libertatibus, et liberis consuetudinibus, ad illud pertinentibus. Testibus [*etc.*]. Apud Wudestocham.

[*Original Charter, Ancient Deeds A.* 1685 (*A. C. No.* 52).]

---

16. *Charter of Henry I restoring the local courts to their former position* (1100)[1].

Henricus, Dei gratia Rex Anglorum, Samsoni episcopo et Ursoni de Abetot et omnibus fidelibus suis, Francis et Anglis, de Wirecestrescira, Salutem.

Sciatis quod concedo et precipio, ut amodo comitatus mei et hundreta in illis locis et eisdem terminis sedeant, sicut sederunt in tempore regis Eadwardi, et non aliter.

Et nolo ut vicecomes meus, propter aliquod necessarium suum, quod sibi pertineat, faciat ea sedere aliter. Ego enim, quando

[1] This is an eclectic text based on the exhaustive edition of Professor Liebermann (*Gesetze*, I. 524). The most intelligible readings are given as the document is only presented for the sake of displaying the characteristic formulas.

voluero, faciam ea satis submoneri, pro mea dominica necessitate, secundum voluntatem meam.

Et si amodo exurgat placitum de divisione terrarum vel de pre-occupatione, si est inter dominicos barones meos, tractetur placitum in curia mea. Et si est inter vavasores alicujus baronis mei honoris, tractetur placitum in curia domini eorum. Et si est inter vavasores duorum dominorum, tractetur in comitatu. Et hoc duello fiat, nisi in eis remanserit.

Et volo et precipio ut omnes de comitatu eant ad comitatus et hundreta, sicut fecerunt in tempore regis Eadwardi; et non remaneant propter aliquam pacem meam vel quietudinem quin sequantur placita mea et judicia mea, sicut tunc temporis fecissent.

Teste [etc.]. Apud Rading[iam].

[*Die Gesetze der Angelsachsen* (*ed. F. Liebermann*, 1899 *etc.*), I. 524.]

---

17. *License to the Monks of Tewkesbury to assart certain forest lands* (*Temp. Hen. I*).

Henricus, Rex Anglorum, Waltero de Gloecestria et Gilleberto de Umfravilla et baronibus et forestariis de Gloecestria, Salutem.

Sciatis me concessisse monachis de Theokesbiria ut prorsus es-sartent Walesgravam et Broces qui sunt inter haias eorum de Suinlea. Et faciant inde voluntates suas. Et non implacitentur ab aliquibus meis placitatoribus in aliquo tempore. Testibus Rannulfo Cancellario et Johanne de Baiocis. Apud Theokesbiriam.

[*Cartæ Antiquæ*, *T.* 32.]

---

18. *Grant of the wood of Sundrugge* (*in co. Glouc.*) *to the Monastery of St Peter's, Gloucester, free from forest jurisdictions* (*tested and sealed as temp. Henry I, but in a hand and style of Henry III*).

Henricus, Rex Anglié et Dux Normannié et Aquitanié et Comes Andegavié, Justiciariis, vicecomitibus et omnibus ballivis suis de Gloucestresira, Salutem. Notum sit omnibus me dedisse, concessisse et ista carta mea firmiter confirmasse Deo et Sancto Petro et monachis meis Gloucestrié totum nemus suum de Sudrugg' quod pertinet ad manerium suum de Rudele; ut habeant et teneant in bona pace et quiete et libere absque omni servicio vel demanda; et ut liceat eis de predicto nemore capere quantum voluerint et wastare, et omnino facere unde quicquid eis sederit et melius viderit expedire in usum et commodum ecclesié sué. Et fortiter prohibeo, sub foris-factura decem librarum, ne quis de ministris vel forestariis meis ibidem aliquam habeat dominationem vel preceptum, nisi tantum de venatione capienda, si forsan illuc devenerint. Et sit dictum nemus extra regardum et defensum ; nullusque super ista libertate a me dictis monachis concessa molestiam vel gravamen inferre, presumat quin per vicecomitem Gloucestresiré statim corrigatur. Et pro ista mea concessione volo habere unum cereum jugiter ardentem ante majus altare beati Petri Gloucestrié. Teste Henrico Wintoniensi Episcopo, apud Wintoniam.

Endorsed in a 13*th century hand,* '*Carta Henrici senioris de Sudrugge bosco s[cilicet] sacristé Gloucestrié'*; *and in a* 16*th century hand,* '*Woodrudge, Registratur.'*

[*Original Charter, Anct. Deeds A. S.* 308.]

C. THE CONVENTIONAL CHARTER (1200—1516)

(*a*) *General Forms*

With the closing years of the 12th century, further changes in the normal construction of the Royal Charter are witnessed. Of these the most familiar instances will be the change of style from 'Rex Anglorum,' etc. to 'Rex Anglié,' etc. accompanied by the ceremonious use of the plural number in the usual words of Notification and Donation. These changes of style, however, occur in every species of diplomatic instrument and a most distinctive innovation in the case of Charters is seen in the development of the Final Protocol by the insertion of a regnal date and the indication of the method of execution.

But more important than any of these changes is the fact that the Royal Charter begins from this date to assume an invariable form[1] which it preserves for another two centuries without material alteration.

The gradual process of devolution by which the Royal Charter was assimilated to the Letters Patent which finally took its place early in the 16th century cannot be described here and it is perhaps enough to call attention to the fact. The amplifications of the Final Clause which will be noticed in the later forms (No. 20) cannot therefore be considered apart from the like expansions which occur in Letters Patent (No. 51).

---

[1] For a description of this see Bémont, *Rôles Gascons,* Suppl. T. I. p. xiii.

19. *Conventional Charter* (13*th cent.*).—It is well known that the practice of the Chancery in respect of Royal Charters was somewhat disorganized during the minority of Henry III. A little later, however, we find a conventional form of charter in regular use, the features of which may be described as follows. (1) The initial Protocol is invariably formal. (2) The Exposition or Movent Clause varies but is usually sententious and rarely narrative. (3) The words of concession are now stereotyped as 'concessisse et hac carta nostra confirmasse[1].' The 'Habendum et Tenendum' clause, which appeared in the reign of John, marks the division of the Dispositive Clause into two well-defined parts. The first of these states the nature of the concession, and the second defines its conditions. Following the Dispositive Clause, we find the old injunctive Final Clause beginning with the same words ('Quare volumus') but now systematically reciting the whole of the Dispositive Clause and concluding with a general reference ('sicut predictum est').

Then follows the final Protocol, as before; but within a few years we shall see the formula 'per manum cancellarii' altered to 'per manum nostram,' which thenceforth obtains.

20. *The Conventional Charter* (15*th century*).—The changes which had taken place in the general character of the Conventional Charter of the 13th century before its final discontinuance in the year 1516, will be seen from the abstract of a charter of the year 1499 printed below. The points to be chiefly noticed are the formula 'de gratia nostra speciali—quantum in nobis est' which occurs briefly as early as the reign of Edward II, but was not generally used in this amplified form before the reign of Edward IV. It has been asserted that its use was to prevent the legality of the grant from being lightly called in question.

The final Protocol is preceded by another characteristic clause 'Eo quod...non obstante,' announcing the execution, in which we see a compliance with certain statutory obligations (1 .Hen. IV, c. 6) in suing for a grant of a Charter or Letters Patent (see No. 51). There is also a clause of reservation ('salvis semper nobis,' etc.) but the earlier 'Habendum et Tenendum' and 'Quare volumus' clauses are wanting. Attention should also be called to the repeated clauses ('Et ulterius' and 'Insuper,' etc.) which were formerly a suspicious indication, but are now conventional.

---

[1] Rarely still *dedisse, concessisse,* etc. as in the present instance.

(*b*) Special Forms

The political purpose and diplomatic character of these instruments are briefly indicated in the descriptive notes appended to the specimens printed below which, however, by no means exhaust the resources of the mediaeval Chancery in this direction. The imitative character of many of these types is especially noticeable.

21. *Charter of Incorporation.*—We have seen (No. 16) that in the 12th century, the grant of privileges to towns took the general form of a charter of liberties. In its simplest form, however, the grant in question might take the conventional shape of the 13th century Charter as we may see from the specimen printed here. In addition to the essential attributes of civic liberty, it will be noted that, as usual, the grant is modelled upon an earlier type[1]. The ' Habendum et Tenendum ' clause is of course dispensed with, but the Final Clause recites the Disposition as indicated above (No. 19).

For the later Confirmations and Bibliography of this Charter see below (No. 61).

22. *Creation of an Earl.*—This instrument, though generally regarded as a formal charter of creation, is nominally concerned with the grant of 20 librates of yearly rent out of the royal revenues of the county of Louth in virtue of the title and dignity of Earl of Louth. The Letters Patent of the same date by which this creation is usually supposed to have been effected (Pat. 12 Edw. II, pt. 2, m. 12) are concerned with still further provision for the support of the dignity, and several other instruments were issued for this purpose[2].

The narrative Exposition is interesting, and with this is coupled a Movent Clause referring to the consent of the ' optimates ' in the old way.

23. *Grant of a Market.*—From the middle of the 13th century to the beginning of the 16th, the Charter Rolls would probably be found to contain more grants of markets, fairs and warrens than any other type of privilege. It will be noticed, however, that the grant is of a hereditament in perpetuity and not merely a license. The proviso safeguarding local interests was presumably accomplished by means of an Inquisition ' Ad quod Damnum[3],' confirmed by a royal license

---

[1] For this model (Aberconway, etc.) see *Calendar of Charter Rolls*, Vol. II. p. 276 sq.

[2] Cf. Lodge, *Peerage of Ireland* (Archdall), III. 33.

[3] None are preserved before the 28th year of Henry III.

in the shape of Letters Patent. The Charter is square, with the Great Seal attached by cords plaited on to the parchment fold in the usual lozenge-shaped pattern.

24. *Grant of a Fair.*—The above remarks regarding grants of Markets apply equally to Fairs. It will be noticed, however, that the Ashford Charter recites the proviso respecting other interests in the Final Clause, whereas the Laycock Charter omits this conventional detail.

In the original Charter the Initial letters of the royal style are elongated. The Charter is in the form of a long strip with a broad fold and the Great Seal is suspended by red and green cords braided alternately. On the margin of the seal are four prominent scars showing the contact of the matrix.

25. *Charter of Disafforestation.*—Although this title is usually applied to General Charters or Letters Patent in the nature of a Charter of Liberties (No. 16) relinquishing such assertions of the royal prerogative in respect of Forest lands as were considered to be encroachments upon public or private rights[1], the diplomatic procedure was much the same in cases where exemption from the jurisdiction of the forest courts and officers was conceded as an individual privilege. In the present instance the royal jurisdiction is replaced by a private franchise, but the supreme jurisdiction of the chief justice of the Forests is retained. It will be noticed that the Movent Clause mentions the patron by whom the Charter was procured.

The text of this Charter has been derived from a contemporary draft, which does not appear to have been sealed and it has been collated with the enrolment on the Charter Roll.

26. *Grant of Free Warren.*—The characteristic feature of these grants is the Proviso appended to the several Dispositive clauses, (1) excepting the area of the royal forest from the scope of this liberty, (2) imposing a fixed penalty for trespassing in pursuit of game without license. The deterrent effect of this exclusive license was much the same as that of the later game license, since trespassers who had been roughly handled by the grantee's servants dared not seek a remedy for fear of standing self-convicted in a statutory penalty which could be sued for in the king's courts. The Movent Clause of this Charter is in a form which had become largely conventional in the 14th century.

[1] Cf. *Select Pleas of the Forests* (Selden Soc.), p. 93 sq.

27. *License to impark.*—The technical term 'imparcare' must not be confused with the manorial franchise of impounding waifs and strays which it was also used to express. The importance attached to these concessions may be gathered from the number of Licenses issued in the form of Letters Patent during the Edwardian period and by the inclusion of trespasses against such property in the 'Chapters of the Eyre.' The issue of a Charter for this purpose, instead of Letters Patent (p. 59), may be regarded as an archaic procedure, and this is further indicated by the omission of the 'Quare volumus' clause. In fact the construction of this instrument bears a considerable resemblance to that of the ancient Assart license of the 12th century (No. 17).

This Charter is not enrolled in the Charter Roll which, however, is apparently imperfect. The King was at Southwick at this date.

28. *Grant of Office (with provision for a Deputy).*—This Charter is of considerable interest as supplying evidence of the rapid elaboration of Grants of Office in comparison with actual Feoffments during the 13th century. It is of further interest as indicating the official procedure in connection with the assignment or deputation of an Office. This was, like many others of the same kind, a 'fee,' though not a 'heritable jurisdiction,' and such a grant should properly be made by Royal Charter.

29. *Composite Charter (granting divers privileges).*—This is a not uncommon diplomatic variety which occurs as early as the 11th century (cf. No. 42). It was especially used for repeated grants of cognate liberties such as Markets, Fairs and Warrens, generally granted by separate Charters.

The specimen printed below is a tripartite Charter comprising (1) Grant of Exemption from certain forest tolls, (2) Free Warren, and (3) a Market; each grant being couched in an abbreviated but appropriate diplomatic form[1]. The Final Clause contains the usual recital of each grant.

A large fragment of the Great Seal, in green wax with a brown varnish, is appended by red cords with yellow borders, braided on the fold in the usual lozenge-shaped pattern.

30. *Grant in the nature of a Demise in Fee-farm.*—Although the conventional words 'ad feodi firmam' do not occur in this Charter it

---

[1] See other Charters relating to this grant in *Monasticon* VI. 502—3.

is shown by the terms of payment to be a demise in Fee-farm and it is so termed in a later Charter (Charter Roll, 3 Ed. I, m. 4).

An original Confirmation of this Charter, dated 2 July, 18 Henry III, in the same words, is still preserved (No. 39), and as the original of the Charter of 1204 does not appear to exist, the enrolment is confirmed by this later version which equally supports the authenticity of the later original. For notices of the premises and franchises hereby granted, see the Bath Cartulary (Somerset Record Society), pp. 88 and 215.

31. *Commutation of money rent for rent in kind.*—This Grant is perhaps to be regarded as a type of the improvident grants made by certain kings, rather than as a typical commutation of a money payment for payment in kind which, in an earlier age, had been commonly recognised at the Exchequer as value received (*Dialogus De Scaccario*, I. vii.).

The special conditions of the present grant justify the use of a narrative Movent Clause. Possibly the recognition of hawks in the forest laws will explain the inclusion of 'Foresters' in the Address.

32. *Grant with Reservation of reversion to the English Crown.*— The interest of this Charter lies in the Final or Reservative Clause declaring the premises to be inalienable from the English Crown. The effect of this instrument is to confirm an Exchange of lands between the King's uncle and eldest son, and to settle the proceeds upon the latter with the above Reservation. Charters granting the premises assigned to the King's uncle will be found on the Charter Roll (*Calendar* II. 42, 45).

33. *Grant by the Crown with Special Reservations and Warranty.*— In this Charter we have a long narrative Exposition which informs us (1) That the premises formed part of the forfeited estates of Robert de Crevequor, an adherent of Simon de Montfort[1]. (2) That these (with others) were placed at the King's disposal (with certain exceptions) by common counsel and consent. (3) That the present grant is part assignment of lands which Prince Edward is bound to assign to this grantee. In view of the exceptions referred to, the Dispositive formula is carefully worded with regard to the feudal rights of the chief lords. These precautions are strengthened by Provisos contained in two Final Clauses which are recited with the rest of the

---

[1] Cf. Hunter, *Rot. Select.* p. 137.

Disposition in the usual way. Finally there is an ulterior precept barring the claims of the former tenant's heirs, and there is a simple but interesting clause of royal Warranty. It is possible, that we have here an instance of that legal chicanery which is so intimately associated with the *régime* of Edward I.

34. *Grant of an Assignment for value received.*—This Charter refers to one of those complex financial transactions in which the King's 'Jews' were concerned as financiers of the Crown. Transactions of this sort were usually effected by Letters Patent. In the next reign we shall find many similar instruments preserved as semi-official deeds in the Books of Remembrance (cf. p. 129). The terms of this arrangement will be seen from a grant made in the following year to William de Valence (*Calendar of Charter Rolls* I. p. 455).

The diplomatic interest of this Charter lies in the fact that in the place of a narrative Exposition, the Depositive and Final Clauses contain a recital of the previous transactions.

The Charter Roll is missing for this year, but this Charter was evidently used as the model of the later grant above referred to.

---

19 *Grant of the manor of Martley to Geoffrey Dispensarius* (12 *March*, 18 *Henry III*).

Henricus, Dei gratia Rex Anglié, Dominus Hibernié, Dux Normannié, Aquitannié et Comes Andegavié, archiepiscopis, episcopis, abbatibus, prioribus, comitibus, baronibus, justiciariis, forestariis, vicecomitibus, prepositis, ministris et omnibus ballivis et fidelibus suis, Salutem. Sciatis nos dedisse, concessisse et hac carta nostra confirmasse dilecto et fideli nostro Galfrido Dispensario, pro homagio et servicio suo, manerium de Martelega cum advocatione ecclesié ejusdem manerii et omnibus aliis pertinentiis suis. Habendum et tenendum de nobis et heredibus nostris, sibi et heredibus suis, in feodo et hereditate; libere, quiete et integre; in dominicis, vilenagiis et serviciis liberorum hominum; in aquis, molendinis, pratis, pascuis, boscis; in viis et semitis, stagnis et vivariis, et omnibus locis et rebus et libertatibus et liberis consuetudinibus ad idem manerium pertinentibus, infra villam et extra, sine aliquo retenemento; faciendo inde nobis et heredibus nostris, ipse et heredes sui, servicium quarté partis feodi unius militis pro omni servicio, consuetudine et demanda. Quare volumus et firmiter precipimus, pro nobis et heredibus nostris, quod predictus

Galfridus et heredes sui habeant et teneant de nobis et heredibus nostris predictum manerium de Martelega, cum omnibus pertinentiis suis, libere [*etc.*], per predictum servicium quarté partis feodi unius militis, sicut predictum est. Hiis testibus [*etc.*]. Data per manum venerabilis patris Radulphi Cycestriensis episcopi, cancellarii nostri, apud Wudestoke, xij die Martii, anno regni nostri decimo octavo.

[*Original Charter, Anct. Deeds A.* 14889.]

20. *Charter for the City of Bristol* (17 *Dec.* 15 *Henry VII*).

Henricus, Dei gratia rex Anglié et Francié et dominus Hibernié, universis et singulis archiepiscopis, episcopis, abbatibus, prioribus, ducibus, comitibus, baronibus, justiciariis, vicecomitibus, majoribus, prepositis, ministris et omnibus ballivis et fidelibus suis, Salutem. Sciatis quod nos, ob singularem affectionem et dilectionem quas penes nunc majorem et communitatem villé nostré Bristollié gerimus et habemus, ac pro conservacione pacis nostré ac salvo regimine, et pro bono reipublicé villé et communitatis illius, de gratia nostra speciali ac ex certa scientia et mero motu nostris concessimus, ac per presentes concedimus, pro nobis, heredibus et successoribus nostris, quantum in nobis est, prefatis nunc majori [*etc.*].

Et ulterius concedimus pro nobis, heredibus et successoribus nostris [*etc.*].

Volumus etiam, et per presentes concedimus, prefatis [*etc.*]. Et ulterius volumus et concedimus, per presentes, prefatis [*etc.*]. Concessimus insuper et per presentes concedimus prefatis [*etc.*]. Volumus etiam et per presentes concedimus [*etc.*]. Et volumus et insuper concedimus quod [*etc.*]. Concessimus etiam et per presentes concedimus [*etc.*]. Ulterius concessimus [*etc.*]. Et quod [*etc.*]. Et quod [*etc.*]. Et ulterius volumus [*etc.*]. Et quod [*etc.*]. Cumque etiam nos, per alias literas nostras patentes, datas apud Westmonasterium xxiiij^to die Septembris, anno regni nostri primo, dederimus et concesserimus [*etc.*]. Insuper concessimus [*etc.*]. Et quod [*etc.*]. Eo quod expressa mentio de vero valore annuo [*etc.*]. Hiis testibus [*etc.*]. Data per manum nostram apud Knolle, decimo septimo die Decembris, anno regni nostri quindecimo.

[*Charter Roll,* 15 *Hen. VII.*
(*S. Seyer, ' Charters and Letters Patent of Bristol,' pp.* 123—163.)]

21. *Grant of Liberties and Free Customs to the Men of Caerwys as the same are enjoyed by certain other towns in Wales* (25 *October,* 18 *Edward I*).

Rex, archiepiscopis, etc. Salutem. Sciatis nos concessisse et hac carta nostra confirmasse hominibus villé nostré de Keyros in Wallia quod villa illa de cetero liber burgus sit, et quod homines eundem burgum inhabitantes liberi sint burgenses, et quod habeant gildam mercatoriam, cum hansa et omnibus libertatibus et liberis consuetudinibus ad liberum burgum pertinentibus, quales, videlicet, habent liberi burgenses nostri de Aberconewey et Rothelan' in burgis suis, vel alii burgenses nostri in Wallia. Quare volumus et firmiter precipimus, pro nobis et heredibus nostris, quod villa predicta de cetero liber burgus sit, et quod homines eundem burgum inhabitantes liberi sint burgenses, et quod habeant gildam mercatoriam cum hansa et omnibus libertatibus et liberis consuetudinibus ad liberum burgum pertinentibus, quales videlicet habent liberi burgenses nostri de Aberconewey et Rothelane in burgis suis, vel alii burgenses nostri in Wallia sicut predictum est. Hiis testibus [*etc.*]. Datum apud Kingisclipstone, xxv die Octobris. [18 Edward I.]

[*Charter Roll,* 18 *Edward I, No.* 6.
(*Calendar,* I. 372.)]

---

22. *Grant to John de Bermyngeham of £20 rent in Co. Louth* (*Ireland*) *as Earl of Louth* (12 *May,* 12 *Edward II*).

Edwardus, Dei gratia Rex Anglié, Dominus Hibernié, et Dux Aquitanié, archiepiscopis, episcopis, abbatibus, prioribus, comitibus, baronibus, justiciariis, vicecomitibus, prepositis, ministris et omnibus ballivis et fidelibus suis, Salutem. Sciatis quod pro bono et laudabili servicio quod dilectus et fidelis noster Johannes de Bermyngeham nobis nuper in partibus Hibernié impendit in quodam conflictu inter ipsum Johannem et quosdam fideles nostros partium illarum, de quibus idem Johannes capitaneus fuit, et Edwardum de Brus, inimicum et rebellem nostrum qui se Regem Hibernié, in nostri exheredationem, fecerat coronari, et complices et fautores suos, inito. In quo quidem conflictu dictus Edwardus et plures de complicibus suis, prout Domino placuit, ceciderunt. Necnon et pro bono servicio quod idem Johannes nobis et heredibus nostris impendet in futurum; in presenti parliamento nostro apud Eboracum convocato, de assensu prelatorum, comitum, baronum et aliorum procerum regni nostri in eodem parliamento existencium, dedimus, concessimus, et hac carta nostra confirmavimus prefato Johanni viginti libras annui redditus de exitibus comitatus nostri de Loueth', in terra predicta, sub nomine et honore comitis de Loueth', ad festa Pasché et Sancti Michaelis per equales porciones percipiendas, ipsumque Johannem in comitem dicti comitatus de Loueth' prefecimus. Habendum et tenendum eidem Johanni et heredibus suis masculis de corpore suo legitime procreatis, sub nomine et honore comitis comitatus predicti, de nobis et heredibus nostris, per servicium quarté partis feodi unius militis imperpetuum. Et si idem Johannes obierit sine herede masculo de corpore suo legitime procreato, tunc viginti libré annui redditus predicté ad nos et heredes nostros integre revertantur, sicut predictum est. Hiis testibus [*etc.*]. Data per manum nostram apud Eboracum, duodecimo die Maii, anno regni nostri duodecimo.

Per ipsum Regem. Dupplicatur.
Sumery.

[*Original Charter, O. L. P.* 1: *Charter Roll,* 12 *Edw. II, No.* 11.]

---

23. *Grant of a Market to the Nuns of Lacock (co. Wilts.) (6 May, 26 Henry III).*

Henricus, Dei gratia Rex Anglié, Dominus Hybernié, Dux Normannié, Aquitanié et Comes Andegavié, archiepiscopis, *etc.* [*as in No.* 22], Salutem. Sciatis nos concessisse et hac carta nostra confirmasse, pro nobis et heredibus nostris, dilectis nobis in Christo Elé Abbatissé de Lacoke et monialibus ibidem Deo servientibus quod ipsé et successores earum in perpetuum habeant quoddam mercatum apud manerium suum de Laycoke, singulis septimanis per diem Martis, nisi mercatum illud sit ad nocumentum vicinorum mercatorum. Quare volumus et firmiter precipimus, pro nobis et heredibus nostris, quod predicta Ela, Abbatissa et moniales ibidem Deo servientes et successores earum in perpetuum habeant et teneant predictum mercatum apud manerium predictum de Lacoke bene et in pace, libere et quiete, cum omnibus libertatibus et liberis consuetudinibus ad huiusmodi mercatum pertinentibus, sicut predictum est. Hiis testibus [*etc.*]. Data per manum nostram apud Portesmuam, vj die Maii, anno regni nostri vicesimo sexto.

[*Original Charter, O. L. P.* 2: *Charter Roll,* 26 *Hen. III, M.* 2 (*Cal. Vol.* I. *p.* 274).]

---

24. *Grant of a Fair at Ashford (co. Kent) to William, Earl of Huntingdon (7 April, 22 Edward III).*

Edwardus, Dei gratia Rex Anglié et Francié et Dominus Hibernié, archiepiscopis, *etc.* [*as in No.* 22], Salutem. Sciatis nos, de gratia nostra speciali, concessisse et hac carta nostra confirmasse dilecto et fideli nostro Willelmo de Clyntona, comiti Huntyngdonié, et Juliané, uxori ejus, quod ipsi et heredes ipsius Juliané imperpetuum habeant unam feriam singulis annis apud manerium suum de Essheteford, per tres dies duraturam, videlicet, in vigilia, in die et in crastino Sancté Anné, nisi feria illa sit ad nocumentum vicinarum feriarum. Quare volumus et firmiter precipimus, pro nobis et heredibus nostris, quod predicti comes et Juliana, et heredes ipsius Juliané, imperpetuum habeant dictam feriam apud manerium suum predictum, cum omnibus libertatibus et liberis consuetudinibus ad hujusmodi feriam pertinentibus, nisi feria illa sit ad nocumentum vicinarùm feriarum, sicut predictum est. Hiis testibus [*etc.*]. Data per manum nostram, apud Westmonasterium, septimo die Aprilis, anno regni nostri Anglié vicesimo secundo, regni vero nostri Francié nono.

Per breve de privato sigillo.
Searle.

[*Original Charter in P. R. O. Museum, Case B, No.* 32 : *Charter Roll,* 22 *Edward III, No.* 26.]

---

25. *Grant to the Canons of Studley* (*co. Worc.*) *of exemption from forest jurisdictions* (26 *December,* 26 *Henry III*).

Henricus, *etc.* [*as in No.* 23], archiepiscopis, *etc.* [*as in No.* 22], Salutem. Sciatis nos intuitu Dei et pro salute animé nostré et pro animabus antecessorum et heredum nostrorum et ad instanciam dilecti et fidelis nostri Willelmi de Cantilupo concessisse et hac carta nostra confirmasse, pro nobis et heredibus nostris, priori de Stodlega et canonicis ibidem Deo servientibus et imperpetuum servituris quod bosci sui quos habent infra forestam nostram de Feckenham imperpetuum sint quieti de regardo et visu forestariorum et viridariorum et omnium ballivorum et ministrorum suorum : et quod boscos illos custodiri faciant per forestarios suos proprios. Ita quod de boscis illis in nullo sint respondentes alicui forestario vel viridario nostro, aut eorum baillivis et ministris, nisi solummodo capitali justiciario nostro de foresta et heredum nostrorum : et quod nullus forestarius aut ballivus vel minister ejusdem foresté de cetero, occasione predicté foresté, veniant ad domum suam predictam vel aliquas terras suas ad hospitandum ibidem vel mendicandum, nisi de bona voluntate predictorum prioris et canonicorum ; nec ecciam ballivi hundredorum, quotiens contingit eos domum suam predictam aut terras suas intrare ad ea exequenda qué ad officium suum pertinent. Quare volumus et firmiter precipimus, pro nobis et heredibus nostris, quod predicti prior et canonici et successores sui imperpetuum habeant boscos suos predictos quietos de regardo et visu forestariorum [*etc.*] [*reciting the whole of the above Dispositive clause*], sicut predictum est. Hiis testibus [*etc.*]. Data per manum nostram, apud Westmonasterium, vicesimo sexto die Decembris, anno regni nostri vicesimo sexto.

[*Contemporary apograph, O. L. P.* 2 : *Charter Roll,* 26 *Hen. III, M.* 8 (*Cal.* I. 264).]

26. *Grant of Free-Warren to Henry de Haddone in Caundle and Lydlinch (5 April, 34 Edward I).*

Edwardus, Dei gratia Rex Anglié, Dominus Hibernié et Dux Aquitanié, archiepiscopis, *etc.* [*as in No.* 22], Salutem. Sciatis nos, ad instanciam dilecti et fidelis nostri Mathei de Forneaus, et pro bono servicio quod Henricus de Haddone nobis faciet in futurum, concessisse et hac carta nostra confirmasse eidem Henrico quod ipse et heredes sui imperpetuum habeant liberam warennam in omnibus dominicis terris suis de Caundel et Lydelinche in comitatu Dorsete: dum tamen terré illé non sint infra metas foresté nostré. Ita quod nullus intret terras illas ad fugandum in eis, vel ad aliquid capiendum quod ad warennam pertineat, sine licencia et voluntate ipsius Henrici vel heredum suorum, super forisfacturam nostram decem librarum. Quare volumus et firmiter precipimus, pro nobis et heredibus nostris, quod predictus Henricus et heredes sui inperpetuum habeant liberam warennam in omnibus dominicis terris suis predictis. Dum tamen [*etc.*]. Ita quod [*etc.*], sicut predictum est. Hiis testibus [*etc.*]. Data per manum nostram, apud Wyntoniam, quinto die Aprilis, anno regni nostri tricesimo quarto.

Per breve de privato sigillo.

[*Original Charter, O. L. P.* 1 : *Charter Roll,* 34 *Edw. I, No.* 30.]

---

27. *License for Fulk Basset, bishop of London, to impark a wood in the forest of Bradene (1 July, 37 Henry III).*

Henricus, *etc.* [*as in No.* 23], archiepiscopis, episcopis, abbatibus, prioribus, comitibus, baronibus, justiciariis, forestariis, vicecomitibus, prepositis, ministris et omnibus ballivis et fidelibus suis, Salutem. Sciatis quod concessimus, pro nobis et heredibus nostris, venerabili patri Fulconi Londoniensi episcopo quod de dominico bosco suo de Derfaude, et in circuitu infra forestam nostram de Bradene, includere possit fossato et haya sexties viginti acras et parcum inde facere ad voluntatem suam ; et boscum illum clausum et parcum teneat inperpetuum, sine impedimento et contradictione nostri et heredum nostrorum et omnium ballivorum nostrorum, sicut predictum est. Hiis testibus [*etc.*] Data per manum nostram apud Suwike, primo die Julii, anno regni nostri tricesimo septimo.

[*Original Charter, O. L. P.* 2. (*The Charter Roll is apparently mutilated for this date.*)]

---

28. *Grant to Peter de Rivallis of the Office of Keeper of the Wardrobe Chamber and Treasury of the King's House* (11 *June,* 16 *Henry III*).

[Pro] Petro de Rivallis, de Custodia Garderobé et Thesaurarié Regis.

Henricus, Dei gratia Rex Anglié, etc., archiepiscopis, episcopis, etc., Salutem. Sciatis nos concessisse et hac carta nostra confirmasse, pro nobis et heredibus nostris, dilecto et fideli nostro Petro de Rivallis, capicerio Pictavensi, pro homagio et servicio suo, custodiam garderobé, cameré et thesaurarié domus nostré. Ita quod toto tempore vité sué sit custos garderobé nostré et camerarius et thesaurarius, cum omnibus ad predictam garderobam, cameram et thesaurariam domus nostré pertinentibus. Concessimus etiam ei, et hac carta nostra confirmavimus, pro nobis et heredibus nostris, quod si forte contingat quod idem Petrus statum suum mutaverit per vocationem ad ecclesiasticam dignitatem vel ad honorem secularem laicalem, nichilominus sit custos predicté garderobé nostré et camerarius et thesaurarius domus nostré per assignatum suum, ad hoc nobis presentatum, sufficientem et idoneum. Ita quod ille quem idem Petrus assignaverit loco suo ad custodiam predictorum garderobé, cameré et thesaurarié domus nostré, in receptione earumdem faciet nobis fidelitatem quod predictas garderobam, cameram et thesaurariam loco suo fideliter custodiet tota vita ipsius Petri, in hiis qué ad predicta officia pertinent, quamdiu ipsi Petro placuerit. Concessimus etiam, pro nobis et heredibus nostris, quod omnes servientes et ministri de officiis predictis subsint eidem Petro et ei sint intendentes et respondentes de officiis predictis, et quod eos possit amovere et alios substituere cum voluerit. Quare volumus et firmiter precipimus, pro nobis et heredibus nostris, quod idem Petrus capicerius Pictavensis, toto tempore vité sué sit custos [*etc.*]. Et si forte contingat eundem Petrum statum suum mutare per vocationem [*etc.*]. Et quod omnes servientes [*etc.*]. Et quod eos possit amovere [*etc.*], sicut predictum est. Hiis testibus [*etc.*]. Data per manum venerabilis patris Radulfi Cicestriensis episcopi, Cancellarii nostri, apud Otintone, xj die Junii.

[*Charter Roll*, 16 *Hen. III, M.* 9 (*Cal. Vol.* I. *p.* 156).]

---

29. *Grant of quittance from Cheminage, grant of Free-Warren, and grant of a Market to the Nuns of Lacock* (1 *October,* 44 *Henry III*).

Henricus, etc. [*as in No.* 26], archiepiscopis, *etc.* [*as in No.* 22], Salutem. Sciatis nos, ad instanciam dilecté consanguineé nostré Elé comitissé Warwyki, et pro salute animé nostré et animarum antecessorum et heredum nostrorum, concessisse et hac carta nostra confirmasse Abbatissé et monialibus de Lacocke quod ipsé et earum successores imperpetuum sint quieté de cheminagio per omnes forestas nostras in comitatibus Wyltesciré et Gloucestresiré. Et quod habeant imperpetuum liberam warennam in omnibus dominicis terris suis quas in presenti habent in Anglia extra metas foresté nostré. Ita quod nullus intret terras illas ad fugandum in eis, vel ad aliquid capiendum quod ad warennam pertineat, sine licencia et voluntate predictarum abbatissé et monialium vel successorum suorum, super forisfacturam nostram decem librarum. Et quod habeant imperpetuum unum mercatum, singulis septimanis per diem Veneris, apud manerium suum de Lacocke, in comitatu Wyltesiré, nisi mercatum illud sit ad nocumentum vicinorum mercatorum. Quare volumus et firmiter precipimus, pro nobis et heredibus nostris, quod predicté Abbatissa et moniales et earum successores imperpetuum sint quieté de cheminagio in omnibus forestis nostris predictis ; et quod habeant liberam warennam in omnibus dominicis terris suis predictis, et quod habeant predictum mercatum apud manerium suum predictum, cum omnibus libertatibus et liberis consuetudinibus ad hujusmodi mercatum pertinentibus ; nisi mercatum illud sit ad nocumentum vicinorum mercatorum, sicut predictum est. Hiis testibus [*etc.*]. Data per manum nostram, apud Wyndesores, primo die Octobris, anno regni nostri quadragesimo quarto.

[*Original Charter, O. L. P.* 2 : *Charter Roll,* 44 *Hen. III, M.* 3 (*Cal. Vol.* II. *p.* 29).]

---

30. *Grant of lands and franchise to the Priory of Bath to be held by a Fee-farm rent* (30 *January,* 5 *John*).

rta mo-
chorum
thonié.

Johannes, Dei gratia, etc. Sciatis nos, intuitu Dei. et pro salute animé nostré et animarum antecessorum et successorum nostrorum, concessisse et presenti carta nostra confirmasse Deo et ecclesié Apostolorum Petri et Pauli et monachis in ea Deo servientibus bertonam nostram extra civitatem Bathonié cum toto hundredo forinseco ad predictam bertonam pertinente et omnibus aliis pertinenciis suis : habenda et tenenda in perpetuam elemosinam ; reddendo inde annuatim ad Scaccarium nostrum Londonié viginti libras ad duo Scaccaria ; scilicet, ad Scaccarium Pasché decem libras ; ad Scaccarium Sancti Michaelis decem libras. Quare volumus et firmiter precipimus quod predicti prior et monachi predictam bertonam cum predicto hundredo forinseco ad predictam bertonam pertinente et omnibus aliis pertinenciis suis habeant et teneant bene et in pace, libere et quiete, integre, plenarie et honorifice ; in bosco et plano, in pratis et pascuis, in viis et semitis, in aquis et molendinis, et in omnibus aliis locis cum omnibus libertatibus et liberis consuetudinibus ad ea pertinentibus, per predictas viginti libras pro omni servicio, sicut supradictum est. Hiis testibus [*etc.*]. Data per manum S[imonis] prepositi Beverlaci et archidiaconi Wellensis, apud Turrim Londonié, xxx die Januarii, anno regni nostri v^{to}.

[*Charter Roll,* 5 *John, M.* 13 (*Rot. Chart. p.* 119).]

---

31. *Grant to Gilbert Basset of a Fee-farm rent, he rendering yearly, in lieu thereof, a mewed sparrow-hawk* (30 *September*, 15 *Henry III*).

Henricus, *etc.* [*as in No.* 23], archiepiscopis, episcopis, abbatibus, prioribus, comitibus, baronibus, justiciariis, forestariis, vicecomitibus, prepositis, ministris et omnibus baillivis et fidelibus suis, Salutem. Sciatis nos dedisse concessisse et hac carta nostra confirmasse dilecto et fideli nostro Gilberto Basset, pro homagio et servicio suo, illas quindecim libratas redditus, cum pertinentiis, quas dilectus et fidelis noster Alanus Basset, pater ipsius Gilberti, consuevit·reddere singulis annis ad Scaccarium nostrum pro manerio de Berewico, quod fuit Adé de Port qui, appellatus de morte Henrici Regis, avi nostri, abjudicatus fuit de tota hereditate sua ; et quod idem Alanus habuit de dono domini Johannis Regis patris nostri ; habendas et tenendas de nobis et heredibus nostris eidem Gilleberto et heredibus suis, imperpetuum ; reddendo inde nobis et heredibus nostris, singulis annis, ad festum Sancti Michaelis, unum espervarium mutarium pro omni servicio, consuetudine et demanda. Quare volumus et firmiter precipimus, pro nobis et heredibus nostris, quod idem Gilbertus et heredes sui imperpetuum habeant et teneant predictas quindecim libratas redditus, cum pertinentiis, bene et in pace, libere et quiete; reddendo inde nobis et ·heredibus nostris, singulis annis, unum espervarium mutarium sicut predictum est. Hiis testibus [*etc.*]. Data per manum venerabilis patris Ricardi Cicestriensis episcopi, cancellarii nostri, apud Herefordiam, tricesimo die Septembris, anno regni nostri quinto decimo.

[*Charter Roll*, 15 *Hen. III*, M. 3 (*Cal. Vol.* I. *p.* 140).]

---

32. *Grant to Edward, the King's eldest son, of manors exchanged with Peter of Savoy the King's uncle, with Reservation of the reversion to the Crown* (8 *July*, 46 *Henry III*).

Henricus, *etc.* [*as in No.* 26], archiepiscopis, *etc.* [*as in No.* 22], Salutem. Sciatis quod dilectus avunculus noster, Petrus de Sabaudia, in nostra presencia constitutus, reddidit in manus nostras et quietum clamavit de se et heredibus suis, ad opus Edwardi primogeniti nostri dilecti, manerium de Radenhale in comitatu Norfolkié et maneria de Wissete, Kettelberge, Nettlested et Wike subtus Gippeswicum, cum feodis militum, advocationibus ecclesiarum, et omnibus aliis ad maneria predicta pertinentibus, et quatuor libras et tresdecim solidos redditus, cum pertinentiis, quos idem Petrus annuatim percipit in Gippeswico in comitatu Suffolkié, qué sunt de honore Richemundié. Et nos eidem filio nostro maneria predicta dedimus, concessimus et hac presenti carta nostra confirmavimus pro honore, castro, et rapo

de Hastinges in comitatu Sussexié, et pro terris qué fuerunt Walteri
de Scoteny, cum feodis militum, advocationibus ecclesiarum et pre-
bendarum et aliis omnibus ad honorem, castrum et rapum in predicto
comitatu Sussexié spectantibus, et cum servicio feodi unius militis in
Tuiroke in comitatu Essexié, quod Bartholomeus de Brientun tenet
de honore de Hastinges, qué idem Edwardus in manus nostras reddidit et quietum clamavit ad opus prefati Petri ; habenda et tenenda
eidem Edwardo et heredibus suis, de corpore suo legitime procreatis,
imperpetuum. Ita tamen quod maneria predicta numquam separentur
a corona Anglié, et quod nullus alius, preter predictum Edwardum et
heredes suos, reges Anglié, racione istius donacionis eidem Edwardo
facté, aliquid juris vel clamium aliquo tempore sibi vendicare possit
in maneriis predictis ; set integre remaneant regibus Anglié imperpetuum. Hiis testibus [*etc.*]. Data per manum nostram, apud
Cantuariam, octavo die Julii, anno regni nostri quadragesimo sexto.

[*Original Charter, O. L. P.* 2 : *Charter Roll,* 46 *Henry III, M.* 2
(*Cal.* II. 44).]

---

33. *Grant of the forfeited lands of Robert de Crevquor to Roger de
Leyburne, with special Reservations and Warranty* (50 *Henry III*).

Henricus, *etc.* [*as in No.* 26], archiepiscopis, *etc.* [*as in No.* 22],
Salutem. Sciatis nos dedisse, concessisse et hac carta nostra confirmasse dilecto et fideli nostro Rogero de Leyburne, pro fideli servicio
suo, in partem assignacionis terrarum et tenementorum qué karissimus
Edwardus primogenitus noster ei assignare tenetur, omnes terras et
tenementa, cum suis pertinentiis, in Anglia qué fuerunt Roberti de
Crevquor, inimici et rebellis nostri, qui Symoni de Monteforti, quondam comiti Leycestrié, inimico et feloni nostro, et imprisis suis
adhesit tempore guerre qué nuper in regno nostro mota fuit per
ipsum Symonem et dictos imprisos suos, ad exheredationem nostram
et destrucionem coroné nostré, usque ad bellum inter nos et dictos
inimicos et rebellos nostros commissum, et quorum inimicorum et
rebellium terré et tenementa per forisfactum eorum, de communi con-
sessu et consilio magnatum ac fidelium regni nostri, ad nostram
ordinacionem et dispositionem hac vice pertinent, salvis capitalibus
dominis homagiis et servitiis suis ; habenda et tenenda eidem Rogero
et heredibus suis de capitalibus dominis feodi illius seu nobis vel aliis
imperpetuum, cum feodis militum, advocationibus ecclesiarum, dotibus,
cum acciderint, escaetis, et omnibus aliis ad predictas terras et tenementa spectantibus, dum tamen terré et tenementa predicta non sint
de dominico coroné nostré ; faciendo omnia servicia inde debita et
consueta ; ita quod occasione hujus donationis nostré nichil capitalibus dominis predictis, in wardis, releviis, aut rebus aliis ad eos
pertinentibus, depereat imperpetuum. Salvis nobis et heredibus
nostris hiis qué ad nos, secundum regni nostri consuetudinem, per-

tinent ratione terrarum et tenementorum qué de nobis in capite tenentur. Quare volumus et firmiter precipimus, pro nobis et heredibus nostris, quod predictus Rogerus et heredes sui predictas terras et tenementa, cum pertinenciis, habeant et teneant de capitalibus dominis [*etc.*], sicut predictum est.

Et volumus et precipimus, pro nobis et heredibus nostris, quod nullus, ratione juris quod sibi per predictum Robertum hereditar[ie] competere posset, actionem vel clamium ullis temporibus habeat de cetero in terris et tenementis predictis, sed ab omni jure, actione et clamio penitus excludatur imperpetuum. Et nos et heredes nostri hanc nostram donacionem defendere et conservare tenemur, sicut nos et antecessores nostri alias donationes nostras et feoffamenta conservare et defendere consuevimus, et sicut ea conservare et defendere tenemur. Hiis testibus [*etc.*]. Data per manum nostram, apud Westmonasterium, tricesimo die[1]   anno regni nostri quinquagesimo.

[*Original Charter, O. L. P.* 2.]

---

34. *Grant to Guy de Luzignan, the King's brother-in-law, of 50 marcs of yearly rent hitherto paid to Aaron the Jew and surrendered by him to the King; the said rent to be henceforth paid to the present grantee by the heir of the Jew's debtor* (1 *August*, 40 *Henry III*).

Henricus, *etc.* [*as in No.* 23], archiepiscopis, *etc.* [*as in No.* 22], Salutem. Sciatis nos dedisse et concessisse dilecto fratri et fideli nostro Guidoni de Lezignun et heredibus vel assignatis suis quinquaginta marcas annui redditus in quibus Petrus filius Mathei pro se et heredibus suis tenebatur Aaroni filio Abraham Judeo Londonié et heredibus suis, usque ad finem seculi, per cyrographum inter eos inde confectum. Quas quidem quinquaginta marcas annuas idem Aaron nobis reddidit et concessit, pro se et heredibus suis, pro debitis qué eidem Aaroni concessimus et assignavimus. Quas etiam quinquaginta marcas annuas prius dedimus dilecto militi nostro Petro Everard, qui eas nobis postea remisit et quietas clamavit, de se et heredibus suis, inperpetuum. Volentes et concedentes, pro nobis et heredibus nostris, quod predictus Guido et heredes vel assignati sui recipiant predictas quinquaginta marcas annuas de cetero de Johanne filio Mathei, fratre et herede predicti Petri filii Mathei, et heredibus suis inperpetuum, ad eosdem terminos ad quos idem Aaron illas percipere debebat, secundum tenorem carté sué quam habuit de predicto Petro filio Mathei, videlicet, ad festum Sancti Michaelis, viginti et quinque marcas, et ad Pascha, viginti et quinque marcas. Hiis testibus [*etc.*]. Data per manum nostram, apud Herefordiam, primo die Augusti, anno regni nostri quadragesimo.

[*Original Charter, O. L. P.* 2 (*cf. Charter Roll,* 41 *Henry III, M.* 12).]

---

[1] The omission of the date cannot be supplied from the Charter Roll, which is imperfect.

II. CONFIRMATIONS

The position of these instruments in the classification of Diplomatic Documents will be apparent from the arrangement of the specimens printed below. Their general character will be sufficiently explained in the several headings which immediately follow. From these it will be seen that a distinction between the Charter of donation and its Confirmation was essential. The issue of the latter in the form of Letters Patent was an alternative practice which is described elsewhere (Nos. 60—63)[1].

(a) *General Forms*

35. *Old English ' Confirmation.'*—The official practice of confirming earlier charters, both royal and private, though not necessarily improbable, cannot be exemplified by original charters. In the existing forms which occur in various cartularies we have either an alleged re-issue of the original charter, fortified by additional subscriptions, or a grant *de novo*, referring to the former grant, somewhat in the style of the later Anglo-Norman confirmations. The essential words in the specimen printed below are 'eadem '—'qua.' The question of the authenticity of this charter which is from a cartulary of the highest repute need not be discussed here.

36—38. *Royal Charters of Confirmation (Anglo-Norman period).*— Three forms of confirmation or renewal of a Charter were in general use during the 12th century. In one of these (No. 36) a grant is made in the usual form but omitting the word 'dedisse,' with a Final Clause, also in the usual form, but including some conventional condition ('ita bene,'—'sicut melius,' etc., 'tenuit aliquo tempore'). It is, however, by no means clear that these reputed confirmations of earlier grants to an 'individual' predecessor, are not in fact fresh donations, the 'sicut' clause without reference to a previous charter being merely a *compendium* to obviate a description of the premises, a device consistent with the personal and graphic style of this diplomatic era.

The second form (No. 37) is more specific and refers to a condition

---

[1] For the subject generally reference should be made to the Introduction to the *Rotuli Chartarum* (Record Commission).

recorded by former Charters ('sicut A. dedit et carta sua confirmavit': or, 'sicut carta quam inde habet rationabiliter testatur'). Here again we have no clear indication of a Confirmation in the official sense. In other cases, however, private Charters granted by various donors are recited and confirmed (cf. Nos. 41 and 42) and the actual donation is sometimes recited (No. 38). These Charters are naturally of a formal and imposing character and the Great Seal is usually suspended by silk cords.

In the case of the Charter last mentioned the cord is braided on the lower margin by three holes only, and the seal itself is of the brownish green wax so commonly found from this period onwards.

39. *Conventional Confirmation* (*13th Century*).—As in the case of the Royal Charter of donation, the form of simple Confirmation became stereotyped at an early period of the 13th century. Here as a rule the existing Charter was renewed in the same words with modern protocols. In other cases the opportunity was taken to make additional grants which are contained in 'insuper' clauses, and the question may arise whether such instruments are Confirmations or fresh grants. Indeed from one point of view, as we have seen (Nos. 36, 37), it is open to doubt whether such renewals are really Confirmations at all. It would seem, however, that the term is used in a general and a limited sense, and in the latter sense an actual recital of the former charter is supposed. This requirement is fulfilled in certain cases, especially in those of private grants, and it is finally supplied by the 'Inspeximus' which practically supersedes all other forms from the middle of the 13th century onwards.

The Great Seal of green wax with a brown varnish, is suspended by cords, which are braided on the centre of the fold in the usual way. The Charter Roll is missing for this year. For further references see No. 30 (p. 29).

40. *Confirmation of a private Donation.*—This is a simple Confirmation, in general terms, of a single private donation, and should be compared with the like Confirmation by way of 'Inspeximus' (No. 41) and with two other instruments (Nos. 38 and 42). The Final Clause of Reservation is in harmony with the legal atmosphere of the Chancery under the influence of the first Edward.

The Great Seal (mutilated) of green wax is attached in an unusual way by two parchment labels passed through two slits in the lower folded margin in the same line, the ends being brought together in the matrix of the Seal.

(b) Special Forms

41. *Charters of Confirmation by* 'Inspeximus.'—Although a royal 'Inspeximus' should properly be in the form of a Charter, a decided preference was shown for Letters Patent for this purpose from the middle of the 13th century. In both types the same general construction may be observed, but the distinctive formula of Notification and the actual statement of confirmation in the Final Protocol will enable the 'Inspeximus' to be distinguished at a glance.

It may be noted that whereas the original Charter is dated 5 November, the enrolment is dated on the 4th of that month.

42. *Composite Confirmation of divers private grants.*—Confirmations of this kind were common from an early period and might include Royal as well as private Charters[1]. The object of this form of confirmation was presumably to save the cost and labour of reciting the full texts.

43. *Innovation of an earlier Charter under a new Great Seal.*— This Confirmation under the second seal of Richard I of a Charter issued under the first seal of that King, which was lost at sea, gives us a well-defined formula, the significance of which has been well explained by Mr J. H. Round (*Archaeological Review*, No. 2. Cf. M. L. Delisle in *Bibl. de l'École des Chartes*, LXVIII. 306).

44. *Confirmation of a Provisional Charter.*—The interest of this Charter lies in the announcement of authentication under the Great Seal for the purpose of confirming a Charter granted five months earlier under the small seal which the King 'uses in Gascony.' The more important instruments issued under this local seal seem to have been confirmed under the Great Seal in England as a matter of course. For the procedure in point and instances of such confirmations see *Rôles Gascons* (ed. C. Bémont), Supplt. T. I. p. xix. For the Reservation expressed in the Charter here confirmed see No. 32.

A fragment of the Great Seal (green wax) is attached to the Charter by blue and red silk cords. The Charter Roll is missing for this year.

45. *Charter innovating a mutilated Charter by means of an* 'Innotescimus.'—The usual form of such instruments was that of

---

[1] Cf. *Historical MSS. Comm. Various Collections*, Vol. I. p. 367, Confirmation to the Church of Salisbury, temp. Henry II, edited by Dr R. L. Poole.

Letters Patent (No. 62), though that of a Charter would be used for a simple re-issue. In a later period an 'Innotescimus' was frequently used for the purpose of a Diploma or Certificate, an instrument which is better known through the muniments of private corporations.

The whole procedure here described is of interest, and it will be noticed that the mutilated seal of Henry V is stated to have been 'in cedula,' denoting apparently a label cut from the lower margin. A fragment of the Great Seal is suspended by silk cords from a broad fold, and was protected by a pouch of embroidered silk, thickly quilted with yellow baize and canvas.

It may be noted that the enrolment on the Charter Roll is dated 14th February.

---

35. *Confirmation by King Offa of lands given to the Church of Worcester by King Æthelbald* (A.D. 778—9).

✠ In nomine domini nostri Jhesu Christi, qui cuncta sæcula jugiter pio moderamine regit. Constat, ergo, et incunctanter verum esse patet, omnia quæ hic humanis cernuntur visibus vana a[c] caduca, transitoriaque fieri, atque ea quæ hominum oculis velantur, semper mansura et sine fine stabiliter perdurare in sæcula. Unde et certissime notum est, ex auctoritate testimoniorum sacrorum voluminum, quod cum istis fugitivis mundanis rebus sempiterna mercare possint cælestia regna. Quapropter ego Offa, gratia gratuita Dei patris concedente Merciorum rex, majorum meorum imitans exemplum, cogitavi ergo in corde meo quatenus ex his, sceptris regalibus mundanis regni perceptis a conditore ac largitore omnium bonorum, aliquid, quamvis minus dignum, pro remedio animæ meæ et pro adipiscenda præmia polorum, in usus monasticæ liberalitatis æcclesiis donarem. Ideoque ego et Aldredus sub-regulus Huicciorum in commune, pro Domino omnipotenti, et in æterna salute animæ nostræ, terram bis quinas mansiones habentem, id est vicum qui nominatur aet Gete, ad monasterium quod proprie nuncupatur aet Wigorna ceastre, et ad æcclesiam beatæ Mariæ matris Domini quæ ibi fundata est, libenter in æcclesiasticam possessionem donantes, concedimus eadem per omnia libertatis dicione in ejusdem æcclesiæ jure permanendam qua eandem æcclesiam Æðelbaldus rex avo meo Eanulfo conscripsit. Id est, ut in omnibus causis, magnis et modicis, libera et inconcussa permaneat usque in sæculum, tamdiu fides Christiana apud Anglos in Brittannia maneat: soluta sit ab omni vi regum et principum et subditorum ipsorum, in summo Dei nomine præcipimus. Ut hæc munificentia nostra pro Christo concessa eo firmiore stabilimento perpetualiter permaneat, testium et consentientium episcoporum, abbatuum ac principum nostrorum signa et nomina in hac cartula testimonii, infra perscriptas adnotare curavimus.

Ego Offa domino concedente rex Merciorum huic donationi nostræ pro majore firmitate vexillum crucis Christi propria manu inpressi.

Ego Aldredus Dei dono subregulus Huuicciorum hanc donationem nostram muniens signum salutiferæ crucis cunctis gentibus impono.

Ego Eadberhtus Christo domino concedente episcopus, his dictis consensi et subscripsi [*and six other Churchmen*].

Signum manus Brordani principis [*and four other* 'principes'].

Signum manus Brordani præfecti.

[*MS. Cott. Tib. A.* XIII. *f.* 54 *b.*
C. S. 231.
Heming (ed. *Hearne*), *Vol.* I. *p.* 114.]

---

36. *Confirmation by Henry II to Eustace Cade of land in Navenby* (1163—6).

Henricus, *etc.* [*as in No.* 13], archiepiscopis, episcopis, comitibus, baronibus, justiciariis, vicecomitibus, ministris et omnibus fidelibus suis Francis et Anglis totius Anglié, Salutem. Sciatis me concessisse et presenti carta confirmasse Eustachio Cade, filio Willelmi Cade, decem libras terré in Navenebi, de feodo Rogeri Pictavensis, qué sunt de honore de Lancastre, ipsi et heredibus suis, tenendas de me et de heredibus meis, unde ipse fecit mihi homagium. Quare volo et firmiter precipio quod predictus Eustachius et heredes sui post eum illas decem libras terré habeant et teneant, cum omnibus pertinentiis suis [*etc.*]; ita bene [*etc.*], sicut predictus Willelmus pater ejus, eas melius [*etc.*] tenuit aliquo tempore. Testibus [*etc.*], apud Westmonasterium.

[*Original Charter, D. of L., R. C.* 28 (*A. C. No.* 39).]

---

37. *Confirmation to Milo of Gloucester of the lands of Eadric son of Chetel* (1136).

Stephanus, Rex Anglorum, Samsoni episcopo Wirecestrié, et justiciariis et vicecomitibus et baronibus Gloucestresciré, Salutem. Sciatis me reddidisse et dedisse Miloni Gloecestrié totam terram et teneuram qué fuit Edrici filii Chetelli, quicunque eam teneat, ita plenarie sicut rex Henricus eam dedit Waltero patri ejusdem Milonis et carta sua confirmavit. Quare volo et firmiter precipio quod bene et in pace et honorifice et libere et quiete teneat, cum omnibus consuetudinibus et libertatibus cum quibus Edricus vel Chetellus, pater suus, melius tenuerunt. Et omnes ejusdem teneuré tenentes intendant Miloni sicut domino suo. Testibus [*etc.*], ·apud Ferham.

[*Original Charter, D. of L., R. C.* 12 (*A. C. No.* 20).]

---

38. *Confirmation of a Convention made in the presence of the King's father between the heirs of William de Say, which is herein recited* (15 *June*, 9 *Richard I*).

Ricardus, Dei gratia Rex Anglorum, dux Normannorum, Aquitanorum, Comes Andegavorum, archiepiscopis, episcopis, abbatibus, comitibus, baronibus, justiciariis, vicecomitibus et omnibus ballivis et fidelibus suis, Salutem. Sciatis nos concessisse et presenti carta nostra confirmasse subscriptam conventionem, assensu et voluntate domini Henrici Regis patris nostri, factam in presentia sua inter Beatricem de Say et Matildem sororem ejus, filias Willelmi de Say, de partitione totius hereditatis ipsarum, sicut cyrographum inde inter eos factum testatur. Scilicet quod [*etc.*] [*the deed recited*].

Quare volumus et firmiter precipimus quod supradicta conventio firmiter et inconcusse teneatur. Sicut [*etc.*] [*Proviso for this binding the parties after marriage*] secundum quod in cyrographo inter eos facto continetur, et sicut carta Domini Henrici Regis patris nostri testatur.

Testibus [*etc.*].

Data per manum E[ustachii] Elyensis Episcopi, cancellarii nostri, apud bellum castrum de Rupe Andeliaci, xv die Junii, anno regni nostri nono.

[*Original Charter in P. R. O. Museum, Case A, No.* 11 (*A. C. No.* 66).]

---

39. *Confirmation to the Priory of Bath of lands and franchises as contained in a former Charter herein recited* (2 *July*, 18 *Henry III*).

Henricus, Dei gratia Rex Anglié, dominus Hibernié, dux Normannié et Aquitanié et Comes Andegavié, archiepiscopis, *etc.* [*as in No.* 22], Salutem. Sciatis nos intuitu Dei [*repeating the text of the charter of* 5 *John* (*No.* 30) *verbatim to the words* 'sicut supradictum est']. Sicut Carta domini Johannis regis, patris nostri, quam inde habent, testatur. Hiis testibus [*etc.*]. Apud Westmonasterium, secundo die Julii, anno regni nostri decimo octavo.

[*Original Charter, O. L. P.* 2. (*The Charter Roll for this year is missing.*)]

---

40. *Royal Confirmation of a private donation to the Nuns of Catesby (co. Northants.) (6 November, 51 Henry III).*

Henricus, etc. [*as in No.* 26], archiepiscopis, etc. [*as in No.* 22], Salutem. Donacionem et concessionem quas Thomas Thulusié fecit Felicié Priorissé de Katesby et ejusdem loci conventui de sex virgatis terré cum dotibus, cum acciderint, et omnibus aliis pertinenciis suis, qué fuerunt Willelmi de Esseby in Katesby et quas idem Thomas habuit de dono nostro, ratas habentes et gratas, eas pro nobis et heredibus nostris prefatis Priorissé et conventui et successoribus suis concedimus et confirmamus, sicut carta ejusdem Thomé quam predicté Priorissa et conventus inde habent rationabiliter testatur. Salvis nobis et heredibus nostris regalibus et aliis dominiis qué de tenemento predicto ad nos pertinent. Hiis testibus [etc.]. Data per manum nostram, apud Kenilleworthe, sexto die Novembris, anno regni nostri quinquagesimo primo.

[*Original Charter, O. L. P.* 2 : *Charter Roll*, 51 *Hen. III, M.* 11 (*Cal. Vol.* II. *p.* 61).]

41. *Royal Confirmation, by* Inspeximus, *of a private Charter granted to the Church of Waltham* (5 *November*, 9 *Edward I*).

Edwardus, etc. [*as in No.* 26], archiepiscopis, etc. [*as in No.* 22], Salutem. Inspeximus cartam quam venerabilis pater Robertus Bathoniensis et Wellensis Episcopus fecit Abbati et conventui ecclesié Sancté Crucis de Waltham in hec verba :—[*Charter recited*]. Nos autem predictas donacionem et concessionem ratas habentes et gratas, eas pro nobis et heredibus nostris, quantum in nobis est, concedimus et confirmamus, sicut carta predicta rationabiliter testatur. Hiis testibus [etc.]. Data per manum nostram, apud Westmonasterium, quinto die Novembris, anno regni nostri nono.

[*Original Charter in P. R. O. Museum, Case B, No.* 31 : *Charter Roll*, 9 *Edw. I, M.* 4 (*Calendar, Vol.* II. *p.* 256).]

42. *Royal Charter of Confirmation reciting the tenor of divers private grants to Henry de Aldithelegha* (2 *May*, 11 *Henry III*).

Henricus, Dei gratia Rex Anglié, Dominus Hibernié, Dux Normannié et Aquitanié, Comes Andegavié, archiepiscopis, etc. [*as in No.* 22], Salutem. Sciatis nos concessisse et hac carta nostra confirmasse dilecto et fideli nostro Henrico de Aldithelegha omnes

terras et tenementa subscripta : videlicet, ex dono [*etc.*] totam terram
de [*etc.*] qué fuit [*etc.*] cum omnibus pertinenciis suis [*etc.*]. [*A long
list of similar donations follows.*]

Quare volumus et firmiter precipimus quod predictus Henricus et
heredes sui habeant et teneant predictas terras et tenementa predicta
bene et in pace, libere, quiete et integre, cum omnibus libertatibus et
liberis consuetudinibus ad easdem terras et tenementa predicta pertinentibus, sicut carté predictorum donatorum, quas inde habet,
rationabiliter testantur. Hiis testibus [*etc.*]. Data per manum venerabilis patris Radulfi Cicestriensis Episcopi, Cancellarii nostri, apud
Mortelake, secundo die Maii, anno regni nostri undecimo.

[*Original Charter, O. L. P.* 2: *Charter Roll,* 11 *Hen. III, Pt.* 1, *M.* 6
(*Cal. Vol.* 1. *p.* 36).]

---

43. *License under the King's first Seal to Alan Basset and his
heirs to hunt vermin throughout the kingdom, dated 7 January,* 9
Richard I, renewed (under the new Seal) 22 August, 9 Richard I.

Ricardus, Dei gratia Rex Anglorum, Dux Normannorum, Aquitanorum, Comes Andegavorum, archiepiscopis, episcopis, abbatibus,
comitibus, justiciariis, vicecomitibus, forestariis, ballivis, ministris et
omnibus fidelibus, totius terré sué, Salutem. Noverit universitas
vestra nos concessisse, dedisse et hac presenti carta nostra confirmasse
dilecto et fideli nostro Alano Basset et heredibus suis quod ipse et
heredes sui post eum habeant canes suos per totam terram nostram
ad capiendum vulpes, lepores et catos, bene et in pace, libere et
hereditarie et honorifice et in perpetuum absque ulla vexatione,
causatione, molestia, gravamine et inpedimento. Quod ut firmum et
stabile permaneat inperpetuum, presentis paginé inscriptione et sigilli
nostri appositione confirmavimus. Testibus [*etc.*]. Data per manum
magistri Eustachii, Elyensis Electi, vices Cancellarii tunc agentis,
apud Vallem Rodolii, septima die Januarii, anno regni nostri nono.

Is erat tenor carté nostré in primo sigillo nostro. Quod quia
aliquando perditum fuit et dum capti essemus in Alemania in aliena
potestate constitutum, mutatum est. Hujus autem innovationis testes
sunt hii [*etc.*]. Data per manum E[ustachii] Elyensis episcopi, cancellarii nostri, apud Rupem Aureé Vallis, xxii die Augusti, anno regni
nostri nono.

[*Original Charter, Anc. Deeds A.* 5924 (*A. C.* 68).]

44. *Confirmation under the Great Seal of a former grant of divers lordships, etc., made to Edward the King's son under the Small Seal used by the King in Gascony* (11 *October*, 38 *Henry III*).

Henricus, *etc.* [*as in No.* 23], archiepiscopis, *etc.* [*as in No.* 22], Salutem. Sciatis nos dedisse, concessisse et hac carta nostra confirmasse Edwardo, filio nostro primogenito et heredi, totam Hyberniam [*etc.*]. [*The Parcels follow.*] Salvis nobis [*etc.*]. Habenda et tenenda eidem Edwardo et heredibus suis de corpore suo legitime procreatis, inperpetuum. Ita tamen quod predicté terré et castra omnia numquam separentur a corona Anglié, et quod nullus, ratione istius donationis eidem Edwardo facté, aliquid juris vel clamii aliquo tempore sibi vendicare possit in terris aut castris predictis, set integre remaneant regibus Anglié inperpetuum. Preterea presenti carta innovamus donacionem quam prius dicto Edwardo fecimus de tota terra Vasconié et insulé Oleronis, cum omnibus pertinenciis suis ; ita quod inperpetuum remaneant dominio coroné Anglié, sicut in predicta carta plenius continetur. Hiis testibus [*etc.*]. Data per manum nostram apud Vasatum, quarto decimo die Februarii, anno regni nostri tricesimo octavo.

Istam autem donacionem et concessionem quam fecimus per Parvum Sigillum nostrum, quo utimur in Vasconia, iterato facimus, innovamus, concedimus, et irrevocabiliter quantumcumque possumus ratificamus per Magnum Sigillum nostrum. In cujus rei testimonium dictum Magnum Sigillum nostrum presenti carté apponi fecimus, presentibus testibus [*etc.*]. Data per manum nostram, apud Burdegaliam, undecimo die Octobris, anno regni nostri tricesimo octavo.

[*Original Charter, O. L. P.* 2 (*cf. Calendar of Charter Rolls,* I. 389, *and* Rôles Gascons, *No.* 3826 *and* passim).]

---

45. *Notification that whereas a Charter of Henry I produced at the Exchequer by the Prior of Levesham was found to have lost the Great Seal, the same* (*as now recited*) *is hereby restored to its former authority* (16 *February,* 13 *Henry III*).

Henricus, *etc.* [*as in No.* 23], archiepiscopis, *etc.* [*as in No.* 22], Salutem. Ad omnium vestrum Noticiam volumus pervenire quod cum Arnulphus, Prior de Leveseham, cartam Henrici Regis, avi Henrici Regis avi nostri, factam abbati et monachis Sancti Petri de Gaunt ad Scaccarium nostrum proferret et baronibus nostris de Scaccario inspiciendam exhiberet pro quibusdam consuetudinibus qué ab eis exigebantur contra tenorem carté predicté, per infortunium et ex incuria tractantium cartam illam coram eisdem baronibus, sigillum carté illius contigit a cedula fuisse avulsum. Et quia per venerabilem patrem W[alterum] Karleolensem episcopum, tunc Thesaurarium nostrum, et per alios barones nostros de Scaccario nostro, qui cartam illam integram et illesam inspexerant coram nobis, est protestatum sigillum carté illius in eorum presentia ita fuisse avulsum, nos nolentes quod dictum infortunium dictis Abbati et monachis cederet in dispendium vel aliquid detrimentum, volumus et concedimus, pro nobis et heredibus nostris, quod carta ista ipsis abbati et monachis et successoribus suis tantum valeat inperpetuum quantum predicta carta Henrici Regis, avi Henrici Regis avi nostri, valeret si integra remansisset. Tenor autem carté illius talis est. [*Charter recited.*]

Ut igitur carta ista predictis abbati et monachis et successoribus suis valeat inperpetuum quantum predicta carta Henrici Regis, avi Henrici Regis avi nostri, valeret si integra remansisset, sicut predictum est, ipsam sigilli nostri munimine duximus roborandam. Hiis testibus [*etc.*]. Data per manum venerabilis patris Radulfi Cycestriensis episcopi, Cancellarii nostri, apud Westmonasterium, sexto decimo die Februarii, anno regni nostri tercio decimo.

[*Original Charter, O. L. P.* 2: *Charter Roll,* 13 *Hen. III, Pt.* I, *M.* 12 (*Cal. Vol.* I. *p.* 91).]

III. WRITS UNDER THE GREAT SEAL

A. GENERAL WRITS

46. *General Writ (Old English).*—This is a specimen of the Old English writs of the pre-Conquest period which it may be suggested served as the model of the post-Conquest writ, which was in one direction developed as a charter of feoffment and in another as a general writ used both for ministerial and legal purposes.

47. *Bilingual Writ (Anglo-Norman).*—An eccentric type of the early post-Conquest 'diplomata,' the interest of which lies in the contrast between the archaic Old English instrument and the formal Latin version which has as yet no conventional diplomatic character.

48. *General Writ (Anglo-Norman).*—The post-Conquest writ was at first employed for the same general purposes as the two preceding (Nos. 46 and 47); but from the reign of Henry I it assumes a conventional form which prevailed for many centuries, and to which the terms 'original' and 'judicial' are usually applied. The form in question may be described as follows. The language is Latin; the royal Superscription is curtailed; the Address is to individuals; the writ is executed in the presence of one or few witnesses and is dated, as usual, at the place of execution. The Text itself consists usually of a simple Injunction of an administrative or judicial character.

49. *General Writ (Missive).*—This is a transitional form between the general administrative writ of the 12th century (No. 48) and the well-known Letters Patent and Close which began with the 13th century. It differs from the former in respect of the Superscription and Address (which are full, like those of the Writ-Charter) and the Attestation, by the King himself. It differs again from Letters Patent and Close in respect of the Address and Execution whilst the Seal is pendant from a mere tag like that of the early writ.

It is well known that no Letters Patent or Close exist before the 3rd and 6th years of the reign of John respectively, and it is during this period that such transitional writs may be chiefly found on the Charter Rolls.

---

46. *Writ notifying a gift of land to St Peter's, Westminster, with the King's consent* (1057—65).

Eadward kyngc gret wel Wulfwi biscop and Leofwine eorl and ealle mine theignes on Heortfortscire freondlice; and ic kythe eow thaet Leofsi Dudde sunu hafath gegiven Criste and Sancte Petre into Westmynstre thridde healve hide landes aet Wurmelea, be minre geleafan and be minre unnan. God eow gehealde.

[*Original Writ, MS. Cotton, Aug.* II. 81 (*B. M. Facs.* IV. 41).]

47. *Writ of William I in English and Latin enjoining the payment of Peter's Pence* (c. 1068).

Willelm kyng, Willelme de Curcello gret frendliche. And ic bidde the thaet thu do thaet this Romfeoh forth cume of minan mann[um], and sythan oelchen thegene and hire mannum aet thisse Michaelis massen bifullan vite, and tou cythe this to Munt Acuht and to Bristoue, thaet mann the hit undon habben, the hit don and thaer hit forth ne cumeth, sethe se b[isco]p and thu thar after; and aec ic beode thaet namman ne sy suo thearf the nyme aenige name in Gyse b[iscopes] lande aer hyt to foran hym syfe cume, ne thu ne nan thiurre manna. God the gehealde.

Willelmus rex Willelmo de Curcello salutem. Mando tibi quatinus intromittas ut denarii Romani solvantur ad instans festum Sancti Michaelis, de hominibus meis et preter de liberis et servis. Et hoc notum facias apud Montem Acutum et Bristolliam, ut qui nondum solverunt, solvant. Et de hiis qui non solverunt, fiat inquisitio per dictum Episcopum et preterea per te. Prohibeo etiam ut nullus sit ita temerarius quod capiat namium super terram G[isonis] episcopi antequam veniat coram eo, nec tu nec aliquis tuorum. Valete.

['*Liber Albus*' (*Wells*), *fo.* 18 (*Historical MSS. Commission, Calendar of MSS. of the Dean and Chapter of Wells, Vol.* I. *p.* 17).]

48. *Writ of William II confirming an exchange of lands between two barons* (1095—1100).

Willelmus, Rex Anglorum, Rotberto episcopo Lincolié, Osberto Vicecomiti Lincolié, et baronibus suis et fidelibus, Francis et Anglis, Salutem. Sciatis quod concedo escambium quod fecerunt Urso de Abetot et Rotbertus de Laceio de Ingoluesmera et de Witchona. Testibus Rotberto, episcopo Lincolié et Rotberto, filio Haimonis, apud Brichestocham.

[*Original Writ, D. of L., R. C. No.* 1 (*A. C. No.* 1).]

49. *Writ (Precept) for Robert Earl of Leicester to have full and peaceful possession of all his inheritance* (21 *July* [1199]).

Johannes, *etc.* [*as in No.* 42], justiciis, vicecomitibus et omnibus baillivis et fidelibus suis, Salutem.

Sciatis quod volumus et precipimus quod Robertus, Comes Leigrecestrié, teneat omnes terras suas et feuda sua, bene et in pace, et honorifice, libere et quiete de Siris et Hundredis et placitis et omnibus querelis aliis, cum omnibus libertatibus et liberis consuetudinibus suis, sicut Robertus, Comes Mellenti, proavus suus, melius aut liberius tenuit tempore Henrici Regis proavi nostri.

Teste me ipso, apud Aurivallem, xxi die Julii.

[*Original Charter, D. of L., R. C. No.* 50 (*A. C. No.* 69): *Charter Roll,* 1 *John, M.* 30 (*ed. Record Commission, p.* 5).]

B. LETTERS PATENT

(a) General Forms

It will be evident from the mere number of the specimens printed in this section that these instruments play an important part in the history of English Diplomatic. It is well-known that Letters Patent are distinguished from other instruments under the Great Seal by the special formulas employed in the Address and clause announcing Execution, the former being of a general nature ('omnibus ad quos presentes litteré pervenerint'), and the latter containing the announcement, 'In cujus rei testimonium, has litteras nostras fieri fecimus patentes.'

The connection of this writ with the Old English and Anglo-Norman ministerial writ (Nos. 46—49) for general purposes has been previously suggested, whilst its evolution at the expense of the old Royal Charter will be noted in the General Forms printed below (Nos. 50, 51).

50. *Letters Patent (Early Form).*—Although Letters Patent had been freely used since the year 1201, the conventional formulas that are so familiar to us in the 13th and 14th centuries were not firmly established until the close of the minority of Henry III. The primitive form of the clause announcing Execution is seen here as

elsewhere until the 8th year of the reign. The common form in use from that date may be seen in many of the instruments printed below.

51. *Letters Patent (Later Form).*—The later form of Letters Patent, which is fully developed from the reign of Edward IV, resembles, as we have seen (No. 20), that of the contemporary Royal Charters : that is to say, a special Movent Clause occurs, together with several statutory Final Clauses.

The reference in the Departmental minute at the foot of this instrument ('de dato predicto,' etc.) is to the well-known statute of 18 Henry VI (cf. p. 102).

A fragment of the Great Seal is affixed to a strip of the bottom margin on which is inscribed the official memoranda 'Examinatur per B. Traherne' and 'Irrotulatur.'

(b)   *Special Forms*[1]

52. *Grant in the nature of a Feoffment.*—It has been previously observed (p. 24) that formal grants were from the middle of the 13th century frequently made in the form of Letters Patent. These 'substituted charters' have at first sight the appearance of orthodox Charters, the Great Seal being pendant from silken cords, but the diplomatic formulas used are those of Letters Patent and not of Charters.

In the present instance the reversion only is granted, though in the usual terms of a feoffment.

The cords and seal are missing.

53. *Grant of Office.*—Although Offices, even when not hereditary, were originally granted by conventional Charters, in a subsequent period they formed a more appropriate subject for a grant by Letters Patent, especially when the enjoyment of the office was not granted in perpetuity. The distinction between such a Grant of Office and an Appointment (No. 58) is perhaps a slight one, but the word 'constituimus' has a certain significance.

In the later Grants of Office, which occupy such a prominent position in the Patent Rolls of the 18th century, a different form was used. These begin with a recital of the Patent made to the Grantee's

---

[1] For drafts of the following and other forms cf. Nos. 105—132 and see Nos. 109 and 112.

predecessor in office and repeat the same concession. They are valuable therefore for the purpose of tracing the successive holders of particular offices.

In the Grant printed here, there is a clause of 'Assistance' at the end, such as would be serviceable in the execution of the search duties which have always been connected with this office.

54. *Grant of Liberties.*—Just as we have seen the Letter Patent fulfilling the functions of a formal Charter in respect of Grants of Lands and Offices, so it was utilized for constitutional purposes. In the specimen printed below we have an instrument of a somewhat composite diplomatic construction, the Address being particular, as in a Departmental writ, whilst the general tenor is that of a Charter of Liberties[1]. The clause of execution, however, is that of Letters Patent. This document has an individual interest as being apparently the original of the famous writ entered as a Precedent in the Red Book of the Exchequer (Rolls ed. pp. xciv, cccvii, and 822).

The parchment is cut in the form of a writ but no trace of the method of sealing has survived.

55. *Creation.*—This document should be compared with the Charter of Creation (No. 22). In ceremonious instruments of this kind, especially during a still later period, we notice a remarkable development of the Movent Clause which is usually preceded by a distinct Preamble which is here linked to this Exposition by an introit (' Hinc est '), which reminds us of the Old English 'Quam ob rem.' Another feature of these grants is the prolixity of the Dispositive formula. The Grant of a suitable maintenance is contained in an ' Insuper' clause.

56. *Commission (singular).*—Amongst the most numerous and important of the administrative instruments of the Middle Ages may be reckoned the Commission by which individual officers or groups of officers received their powers and instructions for military, political or judicial purposes.

Of the two instruments printed below the first is the Commission of a governor or castellan, who is, however, a civilian especially charged with the duty of accounting for the issues of his custody. The clause of Assistance is the usual one in such cases and corresponds to the individual Address. This writ, being of a fiscal

---

[1] Similar departmental privileges were enjoyed by the officers of the Royal Mint and Ordnance (cf. *Report on the Royal Mint*, 1849).

nature, is attested by the Treasurer and not by the King himself, and it is not enrolled on the Patent Roll, but probably in the Exchequer Memoranda Rolls, for departmental reasons.

A fragment of the (? Exchequer) Seal is affixed to a strip.

57. *Commission (plural).*—The second commission printed below relates to the appointment of four commissioners (of whom two are to form a 'quorum') for the purpose of an enquiry into the circumstances of a serious outbreak at Bristol, the history of which is related in an interesting narrative Exposition (cf. Hall, *History of the Customs Revenue*, Vol. II. p. 12 sq.). The clause of Assistance is addressed to all bailiffs and liegemen regardless of local jurisdictions.

The Great Seal (fragment) is affixed to a strip.

58. *Appointment.*—This instrument closely resembles an Office in its general character, and it may also be used for the purposes of a Commission. The distinctive features are here the personal Address and the words 'Nos assignavimus vos ad,' whilst the temporary nature of an Appointment is generally indicated. For the use of the Coket as a Departmental Seal see No. 134.

59. *Commission of Array.*—This Commission is to be compared with those issued in the form of Letters Close (No. 75) and under the smaller Seals (No. 103) for similar emergencies. The formal Address is noticeable, but the chief interest lies in the interchange of departmental methods of expedition for ministerial circulars of this nature.,

60. *Confirmation.*—Although this instrument purports to be a Confirmation by Letters Patent of a private donation, making use of the typical formulas of the Royal Charter of Confirmation, it also serves as a License for a Grant in Mortmain (No. 69), the consideration for this confirmation being alluded to in the Movent Clause, and specified in a departmental minute which is familiar in connection with fines paid in the Hanaper.

The formulas 'quantum in nobis est' and 'non obstante' may henceforth be regarded as conventional.

The Great Seal, which was attached by a cord in this instance, is now missing.

61. *Inspeximus.*—From the middle of the 13th century onwards the official and perfunctory 'Inspection' of earlier Royal Charters was chiefly made by way of Letters Patent. The general form of these instruments is very similar to that of Confirmations by 'Inspeximus'

in the style of Royal Charters (No. 41), with exception of the Address and Clause announcing Execution.

In the specimen printed below, we have an 'Inspeximus' by Henry IV of an 'Inspeximus' by Richard II confirming a Charter of the Black Prince (30 Ed. III), amplifying the original Charter of incorporation granted to the town of Caerwys in Wales by Edward I (No. 21).

For the subject of this Charter see *The Place of Caerwys in Welsh History* by E. Owen (Arch. Camb.) (5 Ser.) VIII. 166 ; *The First Report on Municipal Corporations* (1835) IV. 2610, and *English Local Government* by S. and B. Webb, Book III. p. 237.

62. *Innotescimus.*—This form of certification should be compared with the Charter form printed above (No. 45). The characteristic formula is contained in a Final Clause replacing the usual Injunction, whilst the Address and Notification are also adapted for the purpose in view.

63. *Exemplification.*—As the production of an original Charter or other instrument in the nature of a title or authority had been required in connection with official or legal procedure from the earliest times, and as this requirement could not always be fulfilled, relief was eagerly sought in the shape of the admission in evidence of a certified copy of the original Charter or Record. The importance attached in later times to the concession in this direction obtained by the Commons in 1372 (*Rot. Parl.* II. 314) is well-known, and it is possible that the praedial revolt of the next reign may have been aggravated by the rejection of Exemplifications of Domesday Book (*Rot. Parl.* III. 21, Stat. 1 Ric. II, c. 6). In any case the evidences which they were no longer permitted to adduce were the object of the vindictive fury of the villeins, and the Exemplification of 'diplomata' obtained in default of the original a legal recognition (*Rot. Parl.* III. 138, Stat. 6 Ric. II, c. 4). The scope of this enactment was widened by the Acts of 3 and 4 Edward VI, c. 4, and 13 Elizabeth, c. 6; but the distinction between a document exhibited 'pro evidentia' and pleaded 'pro Recordo' was preserved till the modern 'Office Copy' was finally admitted as evidence under the Record Act (1 and 2 Vic. c. 94).

The specimen printed below gives us a somewhat unusual motive for an Exemplification. For the case of William Rickhill in connection with the murder of the Duke of Gloucester at Calais in 1398, see Prof. Tait in *Owens Coll. Historical Essays*, p. 193.

Another instrument usually associated with the Exemplification and 'Innotescimus' is the 'Constat,' which is regarded as an analogous process confined to the certification of Records (cf. Hardy, *Rot. Chart.* p. xi). This description, however, is somewhat misleading. The form was, in fact, used for several official purposes such as a mere recital of the tenor of a Record[1] or to obtain an abstract of a grant by Letters Patent for convenience of production in accordance with the Acts of Edward VI and Elizabeth[2].

64. *Royal Bond.*—The personal indebtedness of the sovereign was often expressed in the terms of Letters Patent. 'Noveritis' is frequently substituted for 'Sciatis' in the Notification. Here the Exposition sets forth the nature of the transaction and the Dispositive Clause contains the promise to pay. This appears from the Patent Roll to have been one of a batch of similar bonds to London merchants, the present grantee being also a Florentine. Royal obligations were recorded in the form of private contracts in the Books of Remembrance and elsewhere (cf. p. 129) and the literature of the subject is extensive[3].

65 and 66. *Protections.*—The writ of Protection was one of the most ancient, as it was also one of the most highly valued of all royal missives. Besides the simple and indefinite Protection first used (No. 65), several variants can be found which have been distinguished by the insertion of a clause for a particular purpose. Of these those furnished with the clauses known as 'Volumus' (No. 66), 'Nolumus,' 'Profecturus' and 'Quia moratur' are well-known, their object being to afford protection to persons engaged in the King's service (cf. No. 54) for certain periods and in varying degrees with regard to exemption (cf. Stat. 13 Ric. II (1) c. 16) from legal process. Similar protection might be given to hermits and other holy men as Licenses to beg, whilst they were largely used as Passes or Safe Conducts in time of war (cf. *Rot. Scotiæ* passim).

The Privy Seals or Signet Bills authorizing these Letters Patent form one of the largest classes of Warrants for Issue under the smaller seals (see No. 123). In the 17th and 18th centuries Protections under the titles of Passes or Passports were issued under the

---

[1] Cf. No. 84. This was usually the result of an official scrutiny (*scrutatis rotulis*).

[2] Cf. *D. of L. Drafts of Patents*, No. 53.

[3] Cf. E. A. Bond in *Archæologia*, XXVIII.; H. R. Luard, *Relations of England and Rome* (1877); C. Johnson in *S. Alban's Arch. Soc. Trans.* (N.S.) I. 320; R. J. Whitwell in *Trans. R. Hist. Soc.* (N.S.) XVII.

Sign Manual only or even by secretarial or consular authority (Nos. 173, 174, 188, 189). It will be noticed that there is a strong resemblance between these Protections and the License for Letters of Exchange (No. 83) which were also known as Passes (cf. Nos. 50 and 127).

These instruments are cut and sealed in the form of Writs.

67. *Royal Pardon.*—The Pardon, like the Protection, was one of the commonest instruments that passed the Great Seal and, as in the case of others in perennial use, its issue was effected in later times by means of a Sign Manual Warrant.

The formulas of the Pardon are somewhat distinctive and were preserved in substance for many centuries. The instrument printed here is of the type known as 'General Pardon.'

68. *Exemption.*—The royal Protection might be carried a step further by exempting a subject not only from ordinary taxation, but also from filling honourable though onerous posts.

Similar dispensations were often sought for both in earlier and later times, and the term 'libertates' applied to them in the specimen printed below has a special significance.

There are no signs of the attachment of the Seal to the instrument printed here, which is possibly a draft.

69. *License to alienate in Mortmain.*—Amongst the royal Licenses that were so commonly issued in the shape of Letters Patent none are more familiar to us than the dispensation from the penalties of Mortmain. The procedure in this case was very formal, an Inquisition 'Ad quod damnum' being first taken. These premises involve the use of a long narrative Exposition or Movent Clause in the License itself.

The nature of the concession is indicated in an appropriate formula, but the most important part of the instrument consists in the Final Clause barring the operation of the Statute of Mortmain with a further clause of protection. The instrument is duplicated because it contains an equal authority to the donor and donee.

Licenses in the form of Letters Patent were also frequently granted to 'crenellate' or fortify a mansion-house, to impark, to hunt or hawk, and in later times to use 'artillery' in the shape of a hand-gun ; but the best known types of more modern Licenses are connected with Denization and Inventions. For a License to issue Letters of Exchange see Nos. 82 and 83.

70. *Proclamation.*—This is one of a somewhat miscellaneous group of instruments which before long received a special form and a distinct system of enrolment.

From the 16th century Proclamations may be regarded as Secretarial rather than Chancery instruments, and in addition to being printed they are sometimes proclaimed in the King's Courts and enrolled in the Records thereof. In later times Proclamations are frequently found on the Patent Rolls but their post-mediaeval form is not that of Letters Patent (No. 172).

Although this famous ' Proclamation ' is usually supposed to have been issued in a trilingual form (Stubbs, *S. C.* 378, citing ' Annals of Burton ' (Rolls), p. 453), only the French and English texts now exist. There appears, however, to have been a gap in the enrolment (ed. New Pal. Soc. Pt. 3, Pl. 73). The diplomatic interest of this instrument is of course found in the existence of a bilingual version and the credible statement that a trilingual version existed at that time. It will be noted, however, that although the Freneh and English versions agree closely in respect of the royal style, there are important and possibly significant omissions in the list of witnesses in the latter version, whilst there is also no indication in the former of the address to a particular county. It is probable therefore that the French version represents the official draft prepared by the Council and adapted for general circulation in a vernacular form, whilst a Latin version of the French would probably have been used by the historiographers of the period.

---

50. *Letters Patent (Safe Conduct) for Saher, Earl of Winchester, to pass the seas* (20 *January*, 3 *Henry III*).

De conductu.   Rex omnibus baillivis et fidelibus suis ad quos Litteré presentes pervenerint, Salutem. Sciatis nos recepisse in Salvum Conductum nostrum, usque ad festum Nativitatis Beati Johannis Baptisté anno regni nostri tercio, navem quam dilectus et fidelis noster Saherus, comes Wintonié, sibi parari fecit in partibus Galweié, ad eundem in partes Bristollié pro victualibus et armis et aliis sibi necessariis ad iter peregrinacionis sué quod facere disponit in terram Jerosol[imitanam]. Et ideo vobis mandamus quod navi illi, sive ducentibus eam, nullam faciatis, vel fieri permittatis, molestiam vel gravamen in eundo, redeundo, morando, usque ad terminum predictum. Et in hujus rei testimonium, has Litteras nostras Patentes

ei fieri fecimus. Teste comite [Willelmo Marescallo], apud Westmonasterium, xx die Januarii, anno regni nostri tercio.

Per eundem et Petrum Wintoniensem et Justiciarium, anno eodem.

[*Patent Roll*, 3 *Hen. III*, *M.* 5 (*Calendar, p.* 185).]

---

51. *Letters Patent granting an Annuity to Sir Anthony Denny*
(27 *March*, 36 *Henry VIII*).

Henricus Octavus, Dei gratia Anglié, Francié et Hibernié Rex,
Fidei Defensor et in terra Ecclesié Anglicané et Hibernicé Supremum
Caput, omnibus ad quos presentes Litteré pervenerint, Salutem.

Sciatis quod nos, de gratia nostra speciali, ac ex certa sciencia et
mero motu nostris, dedimus et concessimus, ac per presentes damus et
concedimus, dilecto et fideli servienti nostro Anthonio Denny militi,
uni Generosorum Privaté Cameré nostré quandam annuitatem [*etc.*].
Et si contingat [*etc.*] tunc, de uberiori gratia nostra, damus et concedimus [*etc.*]. Et hoc absque compoto [*etc.*]. Et ulterius, de uberiori
gratia nostra, dedimus et concessimus, ac per presentes damus et
concedimus [*etc.*]. Et hoc absque compoto seu aliquo alio nobis,
heredibus vel successoribus nostris, proinde reddendum, solvendum,
seu faciendum. Eo quod expressa mencio de vero valore annuo, aut
de certitudine premissorum, sive eorum alicujus, aut de aliis donis
sive concessionibus per nos prefato Anthonio Denny ante hec tempora factis, in presentibus minime facta existit ; aut aliquo statuto,
actu, ordinacione, provisione sive restrictione incontrarium inde
habito, facto, ordinato sive proviso ; aut aliqua alia re, causa vel
materia quacumque in aliquo non obstante. In cujus rei testimonium,
has Litteras nostras fieri fecimus Patentes. Teste me ipso, apud
Westmonasterium, vicesimo septimo die Marcij, anno regni nostri
tricesimo sexto.

*Per breve de Privato Sigillo et de dato predicto, auctoritate Parlia-
menti.*

Southwell.

[*Original Letters Patent, O. L. P.* 9.
Patent Roll, 36 *Henry VIII, Pt.* 13, *M.* 15.]

---

52. *Letters Patent granting the reversion of the manor of Soham
to Hugh le Despencer* (22 *March*, 7 *Edward II*).

Edwardus, *etc.* [*as in No.* 26], omnibus, *etc.* [*as in No.* 51], Salutem.
Sciatis quod, pro bono et laudabili servicio quod dilectus et fidelis

noster Hugo le Despencer senior nobis hactenus impendit, concessimus ei, pro nobis et heredibus nostris, quod manerium de Saham cum pertinentiis in comitatu Cantebrigié, quod Margareta Regina Anglié, mater nostra carissima, tenet ad terminum vité sué ex concessione domini Edwardi, quondam Regis Anglié, patris nostri, et quod, post mortem ipsius Margareté, ad nos et heredes nostros reverti deberet, post decessum ejusdem Margareté remaneat prefato Hugoni et heredibus suis ; tenendum de nobis et heredibus nostris cum stagnis, vivariis, piscariis, lacubus, marris, mariscis, et turbariis ; una cum feodis militum, advocationibus ecclesiarum, libertatibus, liberis consuetudinibus et omnibus aliis ad predictum manerium qualitercunque spectantibus, per servicium unius feodi militis, imperpetuum. In cuius, *etc.* [*as in No.* 51]. Teste, *etc.* [*as in No.* 51], vicesimo secundo die Marcij, anno regni nostri septimo. *Per ipsum Regem.*
Marchumleye.

[*Original Letters Patent, O. L. P.* 1 : *Patent Roll, 7 Edw. II, Pt.* 2, *M.* 19 (*Calendar, p.* 95).]

53. *Letters Patent granting to Adam de Rokesleye the Office of the King's Butler, etc.* (15 *April,* 27 *Edward I*).

Edwardus, *etc.* [*as in No.* 26], omnibus, *etc.* [*as in No.* 50], Salutem. Sciatis quod constituimus dilectum nobis Adam de Rokesleye, civem Londonié, Pincernam nostrum necnon et Captorem vinorum de Recta Prisa nostra ac eciam Emptorem vinorum ad expensas nostras, per totum regnum nostrum, quamdiu bene et fideliter se habuerit in officio illo exequendo. Ita quod nobis inde respondeat ad Scaccarium nostrum et inde percipiat sicut alii Pincerné nostri inde prius percipere consueverunt. Et ideo vobis mandamus quod eidem Adé et illis quos sub ipso ad hoc deputare voluerit in premissis intendentes sitis, respondentes, consulentes et auxiliantes, in forma predicta. In cuius, *etc.* [*as in No.* 51], quamdiu nobis placuerit duraturas. Teste, *etc.* [*as in No.* 51], xv die Aprilis, anno regni nostri vicesimo septimo.

[*Original Letters Patent, O. L. P.* 1 : *Patent Roll,* 27 *Edw. I, M.* 30 (*Calendar, p.* 408).]

54. *Letters Patent granting to the Barons of the Exchequer all their former liberties and privileges* (20 *January,* 39 *Henry III*).

Henricus, *etc.* [*as in No.* 23], baronibus suis de Scaccario, Salutem. Attendentes utilitatem fidelis obsequii quod nobis impenditis, volumus, et vobis ac aliis qui ex mandato nostro vobiscum assident in prefato Scaccario nostro et ibidem compotis ballivorum nostrorum audiendis intendunt, concedimus, quod habeatis omnes antiquas libertates et liberas consuetudines quas Barones de eodem Scaccario habuerunt temporibus predecessorum nostrorum, Regum Anglié, et eciam quas vos tempore nostro habuistis, tam in placitis motis et movendis, exactionibus factis et faciendis, de terris, redditibus, tenementis, feodis, possessionibus et rebus vestris, quam in transgressionibus et injuriis vobis et hominibus vestris factis et faciendis. Et quod predictis libertatibus et liberis consuetudinibus, a tempore quo inceperitis sedere in dicto Scaccario et compotis predictis intendere, libere possitis uti, sicut aliqui Barones de eodem Scaccario, temporibus predecessorum nostrorum Regum Anglié, melius et liberius usi fuerunt, et vos nostro tempore usi estis. In cuius, *etc.* [*as in No.* 51]. Teste me ipso, apud Mertonam, xx die Januarii, anno regni nostri xxxix[1].

[*Original Letters Patent, O. L. P.* I: *Patent Roll, 39 Hen. III, M.* 16: *Red Book of the Exchequer, p.* 822.]

---

55. *Creation of Sir John Nevyll de Montague as Earl of Northumberland* (27 *May,* 4 *Edward IV*).

Pro Johanne Nevyll de Montague milite in prefeccionem Comitis Northumbrié.

Rex omnibus ad quos, etc., Salutem. Sciatis quod cum viros illustros clara virtutis premia dignum sit assequi quos generis alta nobilitas toti nostro reddit orbi conspicuos ; quam maximo dignos honore tales censebimus qui sedulam operam nequaquam desistunt impendere, quoadusque maximis suis pro meritis et abs se rebus optime gestis, cum favorem et amorem publicum, tum eciam regalia quelibet munera non immerito provocarunt. Hinc est quod in carissimo ·consanguineo nostro Johanne Nevylle de Montague, milite, qui, preter sanguinis claram propinquitatem qua nobis carus, amandus et honorandus redditur, propter suam nichilominus in armis et re militari singularem industriam, multo clarior illustrior et regno denique nostro notior efficitur, clarissimam eam nobilitatis originem simul et armorum ac militié strenuitatem plurimum famatam merito contemplantes, eundem carissimum consanguineum nostrum plurimum nobis cordi est sublunioribus honorum insignis decorare, ipsum propterea, de gratia nostra speciali, suis exigentibus meritis, in comitem Northumbrié preficere, erigere, et creare disposuimus, ipsumque per cincturam gladii comitem Northumbrié preficimus, erigimus et creamus : eique nomen, statum, dignitatem, honorem, preeminenciam et stilum comitis Northumbrié damus et imponimus. Habendum, tenendum et gerendum nomen, statum, dignitatem, honorem, preeminenciam et stilum predicta sibi et heredibus suis, de corpore suo legitime procreatis, imperpetuum. Et insuper de uberiori gratia nostra, et ut prefatus consanguineus et heredes sui predicti hujusmodi statum suum comitis honorificencius manutenere, sustinere et sup-

---

[1] The reading has been restored in parts from the Patent Roll.

portare valeant, dedimus et concessimus, ac per presentes damus et concedimus eidem consanguineo nostro et heredibus suis predictis, viginti libras percipiendas annuatim de exitibus, proficuis et revencionibus de comitatu Northumbrié provenientibus per manus vicecomitis ejusdem comitatus pro tempore existentibus, ad terminos Sancti Michaelis et Pasché, per equales portiones.   In cujus rei, etc. Teste Rege, apud Eboracum, xxvii die Maij.

Per ipsum Regem oretenus.

[*Patent Roll,* 4 *Edw. IV, Pt.* 1, *M.* 10 (*Calendar, p.* 332).]

---

56. *Letters Patent* (*Commission*) *to Thomas de Westone as warden of the Castle of Cockermouth* (10 *June,* 23 *Edward I*).

Edwardus, *etc.* [*as in No.* 26], militibus libere tenentibus et omnibus aliis de castro de Cokermue et terris et tenementis ad idem castrum pertinentibus in comitatu Cumbria, Salutem.   Sciatis quod commissimus dilecto clerico nostro Thomé de Westone castrum et terras et tenementa predicta, cum omnibus pertinentiis suis, custodienda quamdiu nobis placuerit : ita quod de exitibus inde provenientibus nobis respondeat ad Scaccarium nostrum.   Et ideo vobis mandamus quod eidem Thomé, tamquam custodi nostri castri et terrarum predictarum, in omnibus qué ad custodiam illam pertinent sitis intendentes et respondentes, in forma predicta.   In cuius, *etc.* [*as in No.* 51].   Teste venerabili patre W[illelmo] Bathoniensi et Wellensi Episcopo, thesaurario nostro, apud Westmonasterium, x die Junij, anno regni nostri xxiij.

[*Original Charter, O. L. P.* 2 : *K. R. Mem. Roll Trin.* 23 *Ed. I.*]

---

57. *Letters Patent* (*Commission*) *notifying the despatch of the Earl of Pembroke and two other Commissioners to inquire into the circumstances of the insurrection at Bristol* (20 *June,* 9 *Edward II*).

Edwardus, *etc.* [*as in No.* 26], omnibus ballivis et fidelibus suis, tam infra libertates quam extra, ad quos presentes Litteré pervenerint, Salutem.   Sciatis quod cum nuper per brevem nostrum de judicio, sub testimonio dilecti et fidelis nostri Rogeri le Brabanzon tunc capitalis Justiciarii nostri ad placita coram nobis tenenda, precepissemus vicecomiti nostro Gloucestrié quod ipse propter libertatem villé Bristollié non omitteret quin Johannem le Taverner [*etc.*], ad sectam nostram pro morte Alexandri de Villers in dicta villa Bristollié felonice interfecti utlagatos, ubicumque eos inveniri contingeret, sive infra dictam libertatem sive extra in comitatu predicto, caperet et in prisona nostra custodiri faceret : ita quod haberet corpora eorum coram nobis a die Sancti Martini proximo preterito in xv dies, ubicumque tunc essemus in Anglia, ad faciendum et recipiendum quod curia nostra consideraret in hac parte : ad quem diem dictus vicecomes nobis retornavit quod accessit ad dictam villam Bristollié ad capiendum predictos, *etc.* [*A long narrative of the Bristol rebellion follows here.*] Nos admirantes quod tam intollerabiles contemptus et inobediencié ab aliquibus subditis nostris alicubi nobis fierent quoquo modo, et licet contra Communitatem predictam ex causis premissis possemus procedere et ipsam quam plurimum pregravare, volentes tamen super premissis informacionem pleniorem habere et dictam Communitatem, etiam si contra nos taliter deliquisset, ad obedienciam debitam cum mansuetudine revocare, dilectum consanguineum et fidelem nostrum Adomarum de Valencia, Comitem Pembrochié, et dilectos et fideles nostros Willelmum Inge, Johannem de Insula et Johannem de Mutford conjunctim et divisim, una cum predicto consanguineo nostro, ad dictam villam Bristollié duximus destinandos ad informandum se plenius de premissis, et ad inducendum Communitatem predictam ut nobis obediat ut debebit ; et si forsitan Communitas illa in rebellione voluerit remanere, tunc ad ordinandum, vice, auctoritate et nomine nostro, vias et modos quibus Communitas predicta castigari valeat et puniri. Et ideo vobis mandamus, in fide et dilectione quibus nobis tenemini firmiter injungentes, quod prefatis Comiti, Willelmo, Johanni et Johanni, tribus et duobus eorum, quorum prefatum Comitem unum esse volumus, in premissis et ea tangentibus sitis intendentes, respondentes, consulentes et cum toto posse vestro auxiliantes, prout ipsi, tres vel duo eorum, quorum prefatum Comitem unum esse volumus, vobis scire faciant ex parte nostra. Et hoc sicut nos et honorem nostrum diligitis modis omnibus faciatis. In cuius, *etc.* [*as in No.* 51]. Teste, *etc.* [*as in No.* 51], xx die Junij, anno regni nostri nono.   *Per ipsum Regem et Consilium.*

[*Original Letters Patent, O. L. P.* 1 : *Patent Roll,* 9 *Edw. II, Pt.* 2, *M.* 3 (*Cal. p.* 489).]

---

58. *Letters Patent* (*Appointment*) *for Adam de Glidde and William le Mareschal to collect the Great Customs in the port of Melcombe answering for the same at the Exchequer* (8 *May,* 10 *Edward I*).

Edwardus, *etc.* [*as in No.* 26], dilectis sibi Adé de Glidde et Willelmo le Mareschal, Salutem. Sciatis, quod assignavimus vos ad colligendum et recipiendum, ad opus nostrum, in portu de Melcombe, subscriptam custumam de lanis, coriis et pellibus lanutis extra portum predictum vehendis, videlicet, de quolibet sacco lané, dimidiam marcam ; de quolibet lasto coriorum, unam marcam, et de quibuslibet trescentis pellibus lanutis, dimidiam marcam ; et ad alteram partem sigilli nostri quod dicitur Coket custodiendam, quamdiu nobis placuerit ; ita quod de exitibus inde provenientibus nobis respondeatis ad Scaccarium nostrum. Et ideo vobis mandamus quod premissa omnia et singula faciatis et exequamini in forma predicta. In cuius, *etc.* [*as in No.* 51]. Teste me ipso, apud Wyndesore, octavo die Maij, anno regni nostri decimo.   *Per Consilium.*

[*Original Letters Patent, O. L. P.* 2. (*This writ is not entered in the Patent Roll.*)]

---

59. *Letters Patent (Appointment) for the Commissioners of Array in the County of Chester* (24 *January,* 19 *Edward II*).

De arraia-cione facienda in Comitatu Cestrié.

Rex archiepiscopis, episcopis, abbatibus, prioribus, comitibus, baronibus, militibus, liberis hominibus, et omnibus aliis ballivis, ministris et fidelibus suis in comitatu Cestrié, tam infra libertates quam extra, ad quos [*etc.*], Salutem. [Sciatis quod cum, de communi consilio regni nostri [*etc.*] ordinatum sit et concessum quod, in singulis comitatibus regni nostri, tam pro conservatione pacis nostré [*etc.*], quam eciam pro securiori defensione ejusdem regni et populi nostri contra hostiles agressus [*etc.*] assignarentur certi fideles nostri [*etc.*] cum sufficienti potestate ad arraiandum omnes homines comitatus ejusdem secundum formam Statuti dudum apud Wyntoniam editi ; Nos premissa volentes [*etc.*] effectui mancipari et][1] de fidelitate et circumspectione dilectorum et fidelium nostrorum Ricardi Damary [*etc.*] fiduciam gerentes pleniorem, assignavimus prefatos Ricardum [*etc.*], conjunctim et divisim, ad dictum statutum [*etc.*] in dicto comitatu Cestrié [*etc.*] observari faciendum, et ad omnia alia et singula premissa facienda [*etc.*] in forma predicta : necnon ad ducendum omnes hujusmodi homines sic arraiatos [*etc.*] quando et quociens opus fuerit, ad resistendum, insequendum et expugnandum omnes illos qui regnum nostrum hostiliter ingredi presumpserint, et ad omnes illos quos eis contrariantes seu rebelles invenerint, per capcionem et arestacionem corporum [*etc.*] suorum, et omnibus aliis viis et modis quibus fore viderint faciendum, tanquam rebelles et inimicos nostros et regni nostri puniendum. Et ideo vobis omnibus et singulis mandamus, firmiter injungentes, quod eisdem Ricardo [*etc.*], duobus vel uni eorum in premissis sitis intendentes [*etc.*]. In cujus [*etc.*]. Teste Rege apud Norwycum, xxiiij die Januarii.   *Per ipsum Regem.*

[*Patent Roll,* 19 *Edw. II, M.* 3 (*Cal. p.* 221, *Parl. Writs, Vol.* II. *p.* 738).]

---

[1] Formula supplied from exemplar on M. 4 of this Roll.

60. *Letters Patent confirming a private donation to the Monks of Bordesley (co. Worc.) with License to hold the same in Mortmain (6 June, 34 Edward I).*

Edwardus, *etc.* [*as in No.* 26], omnibus, *etc.* [*as in No.* 51], Salutem. Donacionem, concessionem, et confirmacionem quas dilectus et fidelis noster Guido de Bello Campo, Comes Warrewyki, per scriptum suum cirographatum fecit dilectis nobis in Christo Abbati de Bordesleye et monachis ejusdem loci et successoribus suis de medietate unius acré terré, cum pertinenciis, in manerio suo de Wickewane, et advocacione ecclesié ejusdem villé, ratas habentes et gratas, eas per finem quem idem Abbas fecit nobiscum ad Scaccarium nostrum, pro nobis et heredibus nostris, quantum in nobis est, concedimus et confirmamus, sicut scriptum predictum racionabiliter testatur; statuto nostro de terris et tenementis ad manum mortuam non ponendis edito, non obstante. Et per eundem finem concessimus et licenciam dedimus, pro nobis et heredibus nostris, quantum in nobis est, prefatis Abbati et monachis quod ipsi ecclesiam predictam sibi et successoribus suis in proprios usus perpetuo possidendam appropriare, et eam sic appropriatam tenere possint sibi et successoribus suis predictis, imperpetuum; sine occasione vel impedimento nostri vel heredum nostrorum, Justiciarum, Escaetorum, vicecomitum aut aliorum ballivorum seu ministrorum nostrorum quorumcumque. In cuius, *etc.* [*as in No.* 51]. Teste, *etc.* [*as in No.* 51], sexto die Junij, anno regni nostri tricesimo quarto. *Per finem xx marcarum nunciante J. de Kirkeby.*

Ayremynne.

[*Original Letters Patent, O. L. P.* 1: *Patent Roll,* 34 *Edward I, M.* 21 (*Cal. p.* 439).]

---

61. *Letters Patent* (Inspeximus) *confirming former Charters of the town of Caerwys* (1 *September,* 9 *Henry IV*).

e Confir-
atione,
ayrus.

Rex omnibus ad quos, etc., Salutem. Inspeximus quasdam Litteras Patentes domini Ricardi nuper Regis Anglié, secundi post conquestum, factas in hec verba: Ricardus, Dei gratia Rex Anglié et Francié et dominus Hibernié, omnibus ad quos presentes litteré pervenerint, Salutem. Inspeximus cartam quam dominus Edwardus, nuper princeps Wallié, dux Cornubié et comes Cestrié, pater noster, fieri fecit in hec verba: Edwardus illustris regis Anglié filius, princeps Wallié, dux Cornubié et comes Cestrié, episcopis, abbatibus, prioribus, comitibus, baronibus, militibus, justiciariis, vicecomitibus et omnibus ballivis et fidelibus suis, Salutem. Inspeximus cartam quam celebris memorié dominus Edwardus quondam Rex Anglié, proavus noster, fecit burgensibus villé nostré de Cayrus, in hec verba: Edwardus, Dei gratia, Rex Anglié, dominus Hibernié et dux Aquitanié, archiepiscopis, episcopis, abbatibus, prioribus, comitibus, baronibus, justiciariis, vicecomitibus, prepositis, ministris et omnibus ballivis et fidelibus suis, Salutem. Sciatis nos concessisse et hac presenti carta nostra confirmasse hominibus villé nostré de Cayrus in Wallia quod [*etc.*] [*reciting the Charter of* 18 *Edw. I* (*No.* 21)]. Et quia in Carta predicta prefatis burgensibus concessa, aliqué certé meté [*etc.*] concessimus, pro nobis et heredibus nostris, eisdem burgensibus quod [*etc.*]. Et quia nolumus abreviare vel minuere in aliquo proficua nobis pertinencia [*etc.*] volumus quod [*etc.*]. In cujus, etc. [*as in No.* 51]. Hiis testibus [*etc.*]. Data apud Cestriam sub sigillo Scaccarii nostri ibidem, vicesimo die Augusti, anno regni domini Edwardi regis patris nostri, tricesimo.

Nos autem concessiones et voluntatem predictas ratas habentes et gratas, eas, pro nobis et heredibus nostris, quantum in nobis est, dilectis nobis nunc burgensibus burgi predicti et eorum heredibus et successoribus burgensibus burgi illius concedimus et confirmamus, sicut Carta predicta rationabiliter testatur, et prout iidem burgenses et eorum predecessores burgum predictum hactenus tenuerunt et libertatibus et acquietanciis predictis rationabiliter usi sunt et gavisi. In cujus, etc. [*as in No.* 51]. Teste me ipso apud Westmonasterium, tercio die Junii, anno regni nostri secundo.

Nos autem concessiones, voluntatem et Confirmationem predictas ratas habentes et gratas, eas pro nobis et heredibus nostris quantum in nobis est, dilectis nobis nunc burgensibus burgi predicti et eorum heredibus et successoribus burgensibus burgi illius, concedimus et confirmamus, sicut Carta et Litteré predicté rationabiliter testantur, et prout iidem burgenses et eorum predecessores burgum predictum hactenus tenuerunt et libertatibus et quietanciis predictis rationabiliter usi sunt et gavisi. In cujus rei, etc. Teste Rege, apud Westmonasterium, primo die Septembris. *Per* XL*s. solutos in Hanaperio.*

[*Patent Roll*, 9 *Henry IV*, *Pt.* 2, *M.* 5 (*Cal. p.* 466).]

---

62. *Letters Patent* (Innotescimus) *notifying that Ralph de Albiniaco, a minor, is the son and lawful heir of Elias de Albiniaco* (2 *July*, 16 *Edward II*).

Pro Radulfo de Albiniaco. Rex nobili viro domino Johanni Duci Britannié, consanguineo suo carissimo, ac venerabili patri eadem gratia Episcopo Dolon[ensi] et omnibus aliis ad quos, etc., Salutem. Universitati vestré fieri volumus manifestum quod Radulfus de Albiniaco, filius Elié de Albiniaco defuncti, qui de nobis tenuit in capite, est heres ejusdem Elié legitimus, et quod terré et tenementa qué fuerunt ipsius Elié, ratione minoris etatis predicti Radulfi, in manu nostra existunt. Et hoc vobis et omnibus aliis quorum interest vel interesse poterit in futuro, innotescimus per presentes. In cuius, etc. Teste Rege, apud Eboracum, secundo die Julij. *Per ipsum Regem.*

[*Patent Roll,* 16 *Edw. II, Pt.* 2, *M.* 2 (*Cal. p.* 304).]

---

63. *Letters Patent exemplifying certain State Papers on behalf of William Rickhill* (18 *September,* 21 *Richard II*).

De Exemplificatione.

Rex omnibus ad quos, etc., Salutem. Inspeximus quasdam Litteras nostras Patentes dilecto et fideli nostro Willelmo Rikhille directas, in hec verba. Ricardus, Dei gratia Rex Anglié et Francié et dominus Hibernié, dilecto et fideli suo Willelmo Rikhille, Salutem. Sciatis quod, quibusdam certis de causis, assignavimus vos ad vos versus villam nostram Calesié divertendum, et colloquium cum Thoma duce Gloucestrié, ibidem existente, habendum, ipsumque de omnibus et singulis qué vobis dicere sive exponere voluerit audiendum, et nobis inde ac de toto facto vestro in hac parte in propria persona nostra, ubicumque nos fore contigerit, sub sigillo vestro distincte et aperte certificandum, una cum hoc brevi. Et ideo vobis mandamus quod circa premissa diligenter intendatis, et ea faciatis exequi in forma predicta. Damus autem capitaneo nostro villé predicté, necnon universis et singulis fidelibus et subditis nostris, tenore presencium, firmiter in mandatis quod vobis, in executione premissorum, intendentes sint, prout decet. In cuius rei testimonium, has Litteras nostras fieri fecimus Patentes. Teste me ipso, apud Wodestoke, xvij die Augusti, anno regni nostri vicesimo primo.

Inspeximus eciam quandam confessionem sive recognicionem per Thomam ducem Gloucestrié, per nomen Thomé de Wodestoke, coram prefato Willelmo, pretextu Litterarum nostrarum predictarum, factam et nobis per ipsum Willelmum sub sigillo suo liberatam in hec verba....

Inspeximus insuper Certificationem responsionis predicti Willelmi, nobis inde sub sigillo eiusdem Willelmi similiter liberatam, in hec verba...

Nos autem tenores Litterarum, Confessionis, Recognicionis, et Certificationis predictarum tenore presencium duximus exemplificandos. In cuius rei, etc. Teste Rege apud Westmonasterium, xviij die Septembris. *Per ipsum Regem.*

[*Patent Roll,* 21 *Ric. II, Pt.* 1, *M.* 3 (*Cal. p.* 222), *cf. Rot. Parl.* III. 378 *and* 430 *b.*]

64. *Letters Patent acknowledging that the King is bound to a citizen of London in a certain sum of money and promising the repayment of the same* (12 *February*, 31 *Edward I*).

Edwardus, *etc.* [*as in No.* 26], omnibus, *etc.* [*as in No.* 51], Salutem. Sciatis nos teneri Roberto le Convers, civi nostro Londonié, in viginti et septem libris, quinque solidis, et octo denariis, pro jocalibus ab eodem Roberto ad opus carissimé consortis nostré, Margareté Reginé Anglié, anno regni nostri tricesimo emptis ; quam quidem pecunié summam prefato Roberto in festo Sancti Michaelis proxime futuro nos promittimus soluturos.   In cuius, *etc.* [*as in No.* 51].   Teste me ipso, apud Langeleye, xij die Februarij, anno regni nostri tricesimo primo.   *Per ipsum Regem nunciante J. de Sandale.*

[*Original Letters Patent, O. L. P.* 1.
Patent Roll, 31 *Edw. I, M.* 36 (*Cal. p.* 115).]

---

65. *Letters Patent announcing that the King has taken into his Protection the Nuns of Stamford* (6 *November*, 17 *Henry III*).

Henricus, *etc.* [*as in No.* 42], omnibus ballivis et fidelibus suis ad quos presentes Litteré pervenerint, Salutem.   Sciatis quod suscepimus in protectionem et defensionem nostram Priorissam et Sanctimoniales Sancti Michaelis de Stanforde, homines, terras, res, redditus, et omnes possessiones suas : et ideo vobis mandamus quod predictas Priorissam et Sanctimoniales, homines, terras, res, redditus, et omnes possessiones suas manuteneatis, protegatis, et defendatis ; non inferentes eis vel inferri permittentes, injuriam, molestiam, dampnum aut gravamen. Et si quid eis forisfactum fuerit, id eis sine dilacione faciatis emendari. In cuius, *etc.* [*as in No.* 51].   Teste me ipso, apud Lameh[ethe], vj die Novembris, anno regni nostri xvij°.

[*Original Letters Patent, O. L. P.* 1.
Patent Roll, 17 *Hen. III, M.* 9 (*Cal. p.* 1).]

---

66. *Letters Patent notifying that the King has taken into his protection Hugh de Plessetis till Easter, with the clause* Volumus *exempting him from certain legal process* (24 *January*, 26 *Edward I*).

Edwardus, Dei gratia, *etc.* [*as in No.* 26], omnibus ballivis, fidelibus suis ad quos [*etc.*].   Sciatis quod suscepimus [*etc.*] fidelem nostrum Hugonem de Plessetis qui cum dilecto et fideli nostro Johanne de Segrave in obsequium nostrum per preceptum nostrum profecturus est ad partes Scocié, homines [*etc.*] ipsius Hugonis : et ideo vobis mandamus [*etc.*]

non inferentes [*etc.*]. In cujus, *etc.* [*as in No.* 51] usque ad festum Pasché proximo duraturas. Volumus eciam quod idem Hugo interim sit quietus de omnibus placitis et querelis, exceptis placitis de [*etc.*]: presentibus minime valituris si contingat ipsum Hugonem iter illud non arripere vel postquam, citra terminum illum, in Angliam redierit a partibus supradictis. Teste Edwardo, filio nostro, apud West-monasterium, xxiiij die Januarii, anno regni nostri vicesimo sexto.

Per testimonium Johannis de Segrave.

Intratur in Banco in primo rotulo de protectionibus de termino Sancti Hillarii anno regni Regis Edwardi xxvi.

[*Original Letters Patent, O. L. P.* 1.]

---

67. *Letters Patent pardoning Archibald Ridley, of Langley, all manner of offences etc. committed by him from the beginning of the reign to May* 20*th last* (1 *June,* 4 *Edward IV*).

De Perdo-
nacione. Rex omnibus ballivis et fidelibus suis ad quos, etc., Salutem. Sciatis quod, de gratia nostra speciali, ac ex mero motu et certa scientia nostris, perdonavimus, remisimus et relaxavimus Archibaldo Ridley de Langeleye, gentilman, omnimoda offensas, mesprisiones, contemptus, felonias, murdra, insurrecciones, rebelliones, interfectiones, roberias, et omnimoda forisfacturas per ipsum, contra majestatem nostram regiam et leges hujus regni nostri Anglié, a primo die regni nostri usque vicesimum diem Maij ultimo preteritum, qualitercumque facta sive perpetrata. In cujus, etc. Teste Rege apud Eboracum, primo die Junij. *Per ipsum Regem et de data predicta, etc.*

[*Patent Roll,* 4 *Edw. IV, Pt.* 1, *M.* 3 (*Cal. p.* 343).]

---

68. *Letters Patent granting to Bernard Haryng' exemption from all royal taxes as well as from the performance of certain civic offices and duties* (20 *March,* 10 *Edward II*).

Edwardus, *etc.* [*as in No.* 26], omnibus ballivis et fidelibus suis ad quos presentes Litteré pervenerint, Salutem. Sciatis quod, de gratia nostra speciali, concessimus, pro nobis et heredibus nostris, dilecto nobis Bernardo Har[yn]gi, civi civitatis nostré Londonié, quod ipse, toto tempore vité sué, has habeat libertates ; videlicet, quod sit quietus de omnibus tallagiis, auxiliis, vigiliis, et contributionibus quibuscum-que qué ab ipso, racione terré seu tenementi vel reddituum suorum aut aliarum rerum seu mercandisarum suarum, infra eandem civi-tatem, per nos aut heredes nostros, ballivos seu ministros nostros,

quoscumque exigi poterunt in futuris, salvis nobis prisis nostris debitis et consuetis ; et quod in eadem civitate non ponatur in assisis,
juratis, aut recognicionibus aliquibus ; et quod non fiat major, vicecomes, escaetor, prepositus, coronator, aldermannus, seu alius minister
ibidem contra voluntatem suam. Et ideo vobis mandamus quod
eundem Bernardum contra hanc concessionem nostram non vexetis,
molestetis in aliquo, seu gravetis. In cuius, *etc.* [*as in No.* 51]. Teste
me ipso, apud Claryndon', vicesimo die Martij, anno regni nostri
decimo.   *Per ipsum Regem.*   *Examinatur.*

[*Original Letters Patent, O. L. P.* 1.
Patent Roll, 10 *Edw. II, Pt.* 2, *M.* 23 (*Cal. p.* 631).]

---

69. *Letters Patent giving license to John la Ware to assign certain
lands to Dore Abbey, notwithstanding the Statute of Mortmain
(*12 *February,* 1 *Edward III*).*

Edwardus, *etc.* [*as in No.* 26], omnibus, *etc.* [*as in No.* 51]. Quia
accepimus per inquisitionem per dilectum nobis Johannem de
Hamptone, nuper escaetorem domini Edwardi, nuper Regis Anglié,
patris nostri, in comitatibus Gloucestresiré, Herefordesiré, Salopesiré,
Staffordesiré et Wygornesiré, de mandato ejusdem patris nostri
factam et in Cancellaria sua retornatam, quod non est ad dampnum
vel prejudicium nostrum aut aliorum si concedamus Johanni la Ware,
quod ipse unam acram terré cum pertinenciis in Albrightone et
advocacionem ecclesié ejusdem villé, qué de nobis tenentur in capite,
dare possit et assignare dilectis nobis in Christo Abbati et Conventui
de Dore ; habenda et tenenda sibi et successoribus suis ad inveniendum tres monachos capellanos divina pro anima ipsius Johannis et
animabus antecessorum suorum et omnium fidelium defunctorum in
ecclesia Beaté Marié Abbathié de Dore singulis diebus celebraturos,
imperpetuum. Nos volentes eisdem Abbati et Conventui gratiam in
hac parte facere specialem, concessimus et licenciam dedimus, pro
nobis et heredibus nostris, quantum in nobis est, prefato Johanni quod
ipse terram predictam cum pertinenciis et advocacionem illam dare
possit et assignare prefatis Abbati et Conventui, habenda et tenenda
sibi et successoribus suis de nobis et heredibus nostris per servicia
inde debita et consueta, imperpetuum ; ad inveniendum tres monachos
capellanos divina pro animabus predictis in ecclesia predicta singulis
diebus celebraturos imperpetuum. Et eisdem Abbati et conventui
quod ipsi terram predictam cum pertinenciis et advocacionem illam
a prefato Johanne recipere, et ecclesiam illam appropriare, et eam
appropriatam in proprios usus tenere possint sibi et successoribus
suis imperpetuum tenore presencium similiter licenciam dedimus
specialem ; statuto de terris et tenementis ad manum mortuam non

ponendis edito, non obstante. Nolentes quod predictus Johannes vel heredes sui aut prefati Abbas et Conventus seu successores sui ratione premissorum per nos vel heredes nostros, justiciarios, escaetores, vice-comites aut alios ballivos seu ministros nostros quoscumque occa-sionentur, molestentur in aliquo, seu graventur. In cujus, *etc.* [*as in No.* 51]. Teste, *etc.* [*as in No.* 51], duodecimo die Februarij, anno regni nostri primo.   *Dupplicatur.*

[*Original Letters Patent, O. L. P.* 1. (*Cal., p.* 58.)]

---

70 a. *Notification of the King's intention that certain Ordinances* (*Provisions of Oxford,* 1258), *lately made by the Council and the repre-sentatives of the Commonalty should be strictly observed and maintained* (18 *October,* 42 *Henry III*).

Henri, par la grace de Deu Rey de Engleterre, Sire de Irlande, Duc de Normandie, de Aqui[t]en et Cunte de Angou, a tuz ses feaus clers et lays, Saluz. Sachez ke nus volons et otrions ke ce ke nostre Cunseil u la greignure partie de eus, ki est escluz par nus et par le commun de nostre Reaume, a fet u fera al honur de Deu et nostre fei et pur le profit de nostre Reaume, sicum il ordenera, seit ferm et estable en tuttes choses a tuz jurz. Et comandons et enjoinons a tuz nos feaus et leaus en la fei kil nus devient, kil fermement teignent et jurgent a tenir et a maintenir les establissemenz ke sunt fet u sunt a fere par l'avantdit Cunseil u la greignure partie de eus en la maniere kil est dit desuz; et kil s'entreeident a ce fere par meismes tel serment cuntre tutte genz dreit fesant et parnant; et ke nul ne preigne de terre ne de moeble par quei ceste purveance puisse estre desturbee u empiree en nule manere; et se nul u nus veignent encuntre ceste chose, nus volons et comandons ke tuz nos feaus et leaus le teignent a enemi mortel; et pur ce ke nus volons ke ceste chose seit ferme et estable, nos enveons nos Lettres Overtes seelees de nostre seel en chescun Cunte a demorer la en tresor. Tesmoin Meimeismes, a Londres, le disutime jur de Octobre, l'an de nostre regne quaraunte secund. Et ceste chose fu fete devant Boniface, Arceeveske de Cantrebure [*etc.*].

[*Patent Roll,* 42 *Henry III, M.* 1.
New Palæographical Soc. Publ. Part 3, *Pl.* 73.
Fœdera 1. (1) 378.]

---

70 b. *Version of the above in the vernacular.*

Henry, thurʒ Godes fultume, King on Engleneloande, Lhoauerd on Yrloande, Duk on Norm[andy], on Aquitaine and eorl on Anjow, send igretinge to alle hise holde, ilaerde and ileawede, on Hunten-doneschire. Thaet witen ye wel alle thaet we willen and unnen thaet

thaet ure raedesmen alle, other the moare dael of heom thaet beoth ichosen thurʒ us and thurʒ thaet loandes folk on ure kuneriche, habbeth idon and schullen don in the worthnesse of Gode and on ure treowthe, for the freme of the loande, thurʒ the besiʒte of than toforeniseide redesmen, beo stedefaest and ilestinde in alle thinge abuten aende.   And we hoaten alle ure treowe in the treowthe thaet heo us oʒen, thaet heo stedefaestliche healden and swerien to healden and to werien tho isetnesses thaet beon imakede and beon to makien thurʒ than toforeniseide raedesmen other thurʒ the moare dael of heom alswo alse hit is biforen iseid.   And thaet aehc other helpe thaet for to dóne bi than ilche othe aʒenes alle men, riʒt for to done and to foangen.   And noan ne nime of loande ne of eʒte, wherthurʒ this besiʒte muʒe beon ilet other iwersed on onie wise.   And ʒif oni other onie cumen her onʒenes, we willen and hoaten thaet alle ure treowe heom healden deadliche ifoan.   And for thaet we willen thaet this beo stedefaest and lestinde, we senden ʒew this writ open, iseined with ure seel, to halden a manges ʒew ine hord.   Witnesse us seluen, aet Lunden, thane eʒtetenthe day on the Monthe of Octobre in the two and foweriʒthe yeare of ure cruninge.   And this wes idon aetforen ure isworene redesmen, Boneface Archebischop on Kanterbure [*etc.*].

And al on tho ilche worden is isend in to aevrihce othre shcire ouer al thaere kuneriche on Engleneloande, and ek in tel Irelonde.

[*Patent Roll,* 43 *Henry III, M.* 15.
(*Facsimile and texts as above.*)]

C.   LETTERS CLOSE

Letters Close form the second of the two great series of Writs under the Great Seal, the enrolments being even more numerous than those of the Letters Patent, though comparatively few originals have survived.   In distinction to Letters Patent these are 'closed' letters, though the Great Seal was not necessarily affixed as an endorsement (as in the case of Warrants under the smaller Seals) but was pendant from the lower margin as in the case of instruments of a public nature.

In keeping with this external indication it is well known that Letters Close were chiefly used for the transaction of private or departmental business; but the royal summons to attend Parliament or to perform military service was usually issued in this form, since the matter in hand concerned only the individual addressed. At the same time many statutes and ordinances were entered on the dorse of the Close Rolls as well as on the Patent Rolls. In later times the Rolls are almost entirely made up of entries of private or semi-official deeds, for the official correspondence formerly enrolled here is now to be found amongst the State Papers or on the Files of the Royal Warrants.

Some notice of these semi-official instruments will be found below (p. 129 sq.).

Besides the above distinctions, the formulas of Letters Close differ from those of Letters Patent, in the absence of a universal Address and a clause announcing Execution.

The specimens of Letters Close printed here may be considered as representing General and Special Forms of diplomatic composition.

(a)   General Forms

General Form used for a variety of subjects and differing in point of composition according to the nature of the business in hand. Thus we may recognize such styles as the Declaratory (No. 71), Narrative (No. 72), Injunctive (No. 73), Notificatory (No. 74), and possibly Conditional, if such a fanciful nomenclature may be permitted.

(b)   Special Forms

Special Forms which may be instanced are those recurring writs which relate to such matters as summons to Parliament (No. 76) and for military service (No. 75), although these instruments do not differ in point of construction from the General Forms.

---

71. *Letters Close (Precept) for delivery of certain perquisites of timber in the forest of Dene to the forester there* (19 *September*, 18 *Henry III*).

Pro Ricardo de Stantone.   Rex constabulario suo de Sancto Briavello, Salutem. Quia intelleximus quod escaeté de quercubus per nos datis ad maeremium faciendum in foresta nostra de Dene pertinent ad forestarios nostros de feodo, tibi precipimus quod Ricardo de Stauntone, forestario nostro de feodo de predicta foresta, facias habere escaetas de quinquaginta quercubus quas dedimus in eadem foresta venerabili patri J[ocelino], Bathoniensi episcopo, et ibi sunt prostraté; salvo hoc, ipsi episcopo, quod inde ad maeremium accidere poterit. Facias etiam habere eidem Ricardo escaetas de decem quercubus quas eidem episcopo dedimus in eadem foresta, preter predictas L quercus. Teste Rege, apud Radinges, xix die Septembris, anno regni xviij.

[*Close Roll*, 18 *Henry III, M.* 5 (*Cal. p.* 528).]

72. *Letters Close* (*Mandate*) *for the restitution of certain stolen jewels to the owner thereof on his giving a specified security to answer for the same* (27 *November*, 18 *Henry III*).

Pro Johanne de Novo Mercato.

Rex officiali archidiaconi Cantuariensis, Salutem. Monstravit nobis dilectus et fidelis noster Johannes de Novo Mercato quod, cum esset in itinere peregrinationis sué versus Sanctum Jacobum, in quo ítinere quidam capellanus assistebat ei comes, idem capellanus jocalia sua furatus est; quem quidem capellanum, ut idem Johannes dicit, tenetis in prisona, occasione pecunié et predictorum jocalium qué cum eo sunt inventa. Et ideo vobis mandamus quod, si idem capellanus advocare noluerit dicta jocalia sua esse, tunc ea eidem Johanni reddi faciatis, quia idem Johannes fecit nos securos, per Henricum de Longo Campo et Nicholaum de Dameneville, quod ea prompta habebit ad respondendum inde ad mandatum nostrum et ad voluntatem nostram, quando voluerimus. Teste [me ipso apud Herefordiam, xxvij die Novembris].

[*Close Roll*, 18 *Henry III, M.* 34 (*Cal. p.* 344)]

73. *Letters Close* (*Precept*) *for taking up ships in Dorset and Somerset for the King's passage to England* (16 *September*, 14 *Henry III*).

Rex vicecomiti Dorseté et Sumerseté [Salutem]. Precipimus tibi, firmiter injungendo, quod in fide qua nobis teneris et sicut te ipsum diligis, visis litteris istis, sub omni qua poteris festinatione venire facias omnes bonas naves que xx equos et amplius ferre possunt in portubus baillié tué, usque Sanctum Gildasium, ad transfretandum cum corpore nostro in Anglia. Et talem securitatem capias a singulis magistris navium inventarum in baillia tua quod erunt, quamcito poterunt, in occursum nostrum ad predictum portum, quod pro defectu tuo non retardetur transfretatio nostra, propter quod ad te nos graviter capere debeamus. Teste Rege, apud Nonetas, xvj die Septembris.

[*Close Roll*, 14 *Henry III, Pt.* 2, *M.* 4*d* (*Cal. p.* 447).]

---

74. *Letters Close* (*Precept*) *for delivery of Seisin of certain lands to a royal grantee* (10 *May*, 12 *Henry III*).

De custodia terré et heredis Elyé de Bello Campo.

Rex vicecomiti Buk[ingehamsiré], Salutem. Scias quod concessimus Johanni de Offintone, servienti dilecti et fidelis nostri Huberti de Burgo, comitis Kancié, justiciarii Anglié, custodiam terré et heredis Elyé de Bello Campo cum maritagio ejusdem heredis. Et ideo tibi precipimus quod de tota terra qué fuit ipsius Elyé in balliva tua, eidem Johanni sine dilatione plenam saisinam habere facias. Teste [me ipso apud Lamhethe, x die Maij, anno regni nostri xij].

[*Close Roll*, 12 *Henry III, M.* 8 (*Cal. p.* 47).]

---

75. *Letters Close* (*Mandate*) *to an Earl to repair to the parts of Scotland with all his forces* (18 *October*, 1 *Edward II*).

De accedendo ad partes Scocié.

Rex dilecto et fideli suo Humfrido de Bohun, Comiti Herefordié et Essexé, Salutem. Quia quidam inimici rebelles et proditores nostri de terra nostra Scocié, sué fidelitatis immemores, contra nos hostiliter insurrexerunt, dictam terram nostram vastando incendiis, homicidia et alia facinora innumera perpetrando, nos eorum maliciis obviare volentes, vobis mandamus, in fide et dilectione quibus nobis tenemini firmiter injungentes, quod, ad dictorum proditorum rebellionem viriliter reprimendam, ad partes dicté terré Scocié, cum equis et armis ac toto posse vestro, statim postquam corpus claré memorié Domini patris nostri traditum fuerit sepulturé, pro defensione et tuicione terrarum vestrarum ac eciam assecuracione partium earundem, proficisci nullatenus omittatis. Teste Rege apud Northamptonam, xviij die Octobris. [1 Edward II.]

[*Close Roll*, 1 *Edw. II, M.* 17*d* (*Parl. Writs, Vol.* II. *p.* 370, *No.* 14; *Cal. p.* 43).]

76. *Letters Close (Mandate) for the attendance of the Clergy at an adjourned meeting of Parliament (4 January, 11 Edward II).*

De pro-rogacione parlia-menti.

Rex venerabili in Christo patri W[altero] Archiepiscopo Cantuariensi, tocius Anglié Primati, Salutem. Licet nuper super diversis et arduis negociis, nos et statum regni nostri specialiter tangentibus, parliamentum nostrum apud Lincolniam in quindena Sancti Hillarii proximo futura tenere, et vobiscum ac cum ceteris prelatis, magnatibus et proceribus dicti regni habere proposuerimus colloquium et tractatum, et vobis mandaverimus quod dictis die et loco, omnibus aliis pretermissis, personaliter interessetis, ibidem nobiscum et cum ceteris prelatis, magnatibus et proceribus supradictis, super dictis negociis tractaturi vestrumque consilium impensuri; Parliamentum tamen predictum apud locum predictum tenendum, usque ad primam Dominicam Quadragesimé proximo futuram, ad requisicionem prelatorum dicti regni, duximus prorogandum. Et ideo vobis mandamus, in fide et dileccione quibus nobis tenemini firmiter injungentes, quod ad dictum locum, in dicta Dominica, omnibus aliis pretermissis, personaliter intersitis, nobiscum et cum ceteris prelatis, magnatibus et proceribus supradictis super dictis negociis tractaturi vestrumque consilium impensuri. Premunientes Priorem et Capitulum ecclesié vestré Cantuariensis, Archidiaconos, totumque clerum vestré diocesis quod iidem Prior et Archidiaconi in propriis personis suis et dictum Capitulum per unum, idemque clerus per duos procuratores idoneos, plenam et sufficientem potestatem ab ipsis Capitulo et clero habentes, una vobiscum intersint modis omnibus tunc ibidem, ad faciendum et consentiendum hiis qué tunc ibidem de communi consilio, favente Domino, ordinari contigerit super negociis antedictis. Et hoc nullatenus omittatis. Teste Rege apud Westmonasterium, quarto die Januarii. *Per ipsum Regem.*

[*Close Roll*, 11 *Edw. II*, *M.* 12d (*Parl. Writs, Vol.* II. *p.* 175, *No.* 11; *Cal. p.* 590).]

D. SERIAL WRITS

This designation has been adopted to include a class of Writs under the Great Seal which are distinguished either by separate enrolment or else are linked together in a sequence of constitutional forms. Under the former head specimens are printed here of the series of Liberate, Exchange, Passage, Scutage, Redisseisin and Statute Rolls (Nos. 77—86).

Other series, which belong to this class, are the Staple, Parliament, Coronation and Surrender Rolls. No specimens of occasional or short-lived series, such as the Protection Rolls and Pardon Rolls, have been included here, since these forms occur normally on the Patent or Close Rolls. The great series of Treaty or Foreign Rolls have not been included here as being distinctive only in a geographical sense. Again there are a few series, like the Extract and Fine Rolls, which are of departmental interest only and useless for the purpose of diplomatic study.

(a) 77—81. *Writs of* Liberate, Allocate, Computate, Perdonavimus, *and the* Contrabreve.—These form probably the most ancient class of ministerial writs and they were composed in the same style from the reign of Henry II to that of William IV. The earliest enrolment of these writs dates from the second year of King John. At first these enrolments seem to anticipate the series of Close Rolls. Then the writs are merged in the entries on the Close Rolls from the 6th year of this reign to the 10th year of Henry III, when a distinct series of Liberate Rolls again appears and is continued till the reign of Henry VI. Parallel with this series, from 10 Henry III to 34 Edward I, is another series of Exchequer enrolments, but writs 'de exitu Thesauri' are also found on reputed Gascon and Norman Rolls. Many of these writs are entered in the Exchequer Memoranda Rolls, whilst the substance of them is also found in the Issue Rolls. A small *residuum* of the original Writs filed in the Exchequer are fortunately still preserved amongst the subsidiary 'Proceedings' of that Court, and from these files several of the specimens printed here have been derived, the enrolments being considerably abbreviated.

It will be noticed that the form of the writ 'Perdonavimus' differs from that given in the *Dialogus* (I. vi.). After a certain date the writ of 'Liberate' is replaced by that of 'Solvatis,' but this is generally regarded as an identical instrument (cf. Hardy, *Rot. de Liberate, etc.*, Preface, *Pipe Roll Soc. Publ.* III. 57 and X. 96 ; *Rôles Gascons*, T. I. and Supplément).

The 'Contrabrevia' were the writs addressed in the first place to royal officers or accountants authorising a certain expenditure with an assurance of repayment ('et computabitur tibi') which was the equivalent of a writ of 'Computate.'

82, 83. *Licenses for Letters of Exchange.*—Letters of Exchange were permitted to be sent abroad by foreign merchants under a royal license (Letters Close) under the Great Seal, dispensing with the rigorous provisions of the Statute 5 Ric. II (i) c. 2. These are entered on a series of Exchange Rolls down to the reign of Henry VI. Earlier still, Passes, or licenses to cross the sea, were issued and enrolled on Passage Rolls of which two only have survived. They were subsequently entered on the Exchange Rolls (No. 83). The issue of these Licenses was further regulated by the Statute 3 Hen.VII, c. 6, and specimens of such Licenses still exist (Exch. K. R. Misc. 393). At this date Letters of Exchange were issued by the King's Exchanger by virtue of his office.

84. *Writs of Scutage.*—Writs of Scutage were instruments (Letters Close) of a departmental nature enrolled on the Scutage Rolls. As to their nature, see the exhaustive account given of these and the Marshalsea Rolls by Mr S. R. Scargill-Bird in the *Genealogist* (N. S.), Vol. I. p. 65 sq.

85. *Writs of Redisseisin.* — Writs of Redisseisin are really Original Writs of a purely legal nature (cf. Pollock and Maitland, II. 44) the object of which was to enforce the provisions of the Statutes of Merton, Marlborough and Westminster (2) against Disseisors.

The importance of these Writs as a Chancery series is due to their separate enrolment. Like the 'Liberate' writs these were also entered in an Exchequer series which is better known as the 'Originalia' Rolls. The formula of writs of Redisseisin differs materially from that of the diplomatic documents previously noticed.

86. *Statute of Parliament.*—Just as a Charter of Liberties having the force of an edict or law is found in the form of a true diploma at an early date, so some ordinances and statutes of a somewhat later date were issued in the form of Letters under the Great Seal. This fact is clearly indicated in the heading and conclusion of the Statute

of Wales (1284) printed below. The Statute Rolls, however, like the still larger series of Parliamentary Rolls contain for the most part a miscellaneous collection of instruments which are not in diplomatic form.

(*b*) A good example of a sequence of writs under the Great Seal relating to a particular subject, but not enrolled in a special series, is seen in the case of the several instruments connected with the approbation of ecclesiastical elections by the Crown. The procedure is, of course, well known, but as the notarial instruments representing the action of the ecclesiastical bodies are less easily accessible, specimens for the whole sequence have been given here (Nos. 88—93) together with a specimen of the frequent petitions for the arrest of Vagabond Monks (No. 87), for which cf. also No. 139[1].

The historical 'Congé d'élire' had been issued since the reign of John as a royal writ, and this, like the Protections and Licenses above described, was naturally continued in the 14th century as a royal missive (No. 89) in response to an ecclesiastical Petition (No. 88). The well-known ecclesiastical instruments found on the Patent Rolls are the 'Royal Assent' (No. 91) to the formal notification of the Election (No. 90) and the 'Restitution of Temporalities' (No. 93) on the signification of the canonical confirmation thereof (No. 92). In later times these royal authorizations were issued under the Sign Manual and were entered in the Secretary of State's department (cf. p. 117).

(*c*) In the case of Parliamentary proceedings a sequence of essential instruments will also be found normally recurring. As, however, the various forms in use during the 13th and 14th centuries have been exhaustively printed in Sir F. Palgrave's great work (*Parl. Writs*, I. and II.) it has not been thought desirable to reproduce them here. Instead of this, it seemed most useful to indicate the sequence above referred to and for this purpose the eventful Parliament that met at York in 1321 has been selected. Two of these forms (Nos. 11 and 15), however, are taken from another source since this Parliament was not prorogued, and a better example of a Statute in diplomatic form was already available (No. 86).

---

[1] The references to this series were kindly supplied by Mr R. C. Fowler of the Public Record Office.

Parliamentary Procedure.

1. Summons of a Peer, 15 Ed. II with 'Premunientes' clause (Palgrave, II. 234 sq. (34)).
2. Ditto.   Without do.   Ibid. (44).
3. 'Littera excusatoria.'   Ibid. (45).
4. Royal License.   Ibid. (46).
5. Proxy.   Ibid. (47).
6. Writ of Election for Knights of the Shire
    and Burgesses.   Ibid. (49).
7. Writ 'De Expensis' for same.   Ibid. (75).
8. Precept for attending Convocation.   Ibid. (39) (cf. 41).
9. Procuration for Convocation.   Ibid. (43) (cf. 9).
10. Personal Summons (Writ of Attendance). Ibid. (32).
11. Prorogation of Parliament (cf. Formula,
    No. 76, without the 'Premunientes'
    clause).
12. Certification of a Grant by Convocation. Ibid. (42) (cf. 7).
13. Petition to Parliament 15 Ed. II.   Rot. Parl. I. 394
                                                          (No. 38).
14. Ordinance of Parliament.   Rot. Parl. I. 456.
15. Statute (cf. Formula, No. 86).

(*d*) In the case of the remaining documentary sequence under notice, the several instruments connected with mediaeval diplomatic negotiations are also printed at large in the pages of Rymer or are referred to in official lists. The want of some authoritative treatise of this obscure procedure might seem to render a sequence of printed specimens a useful work[1]. On the other hand many circumstances appeared to point to the existence of a general analogy between these mediaeval instruments and the Treaty Papers and Entry Books of a much later date, specimens of which are printed in another section. Reference may, therefore, be made to that section with certain modifications which can only be indicated in general terms. That is to say, although the same sequence of the essential instru-

---

[1] A valuable account of the diplomatic procedure so profusely illustrated in the pages of the *Fœdera* is to be found in M. Maulde La Clavière's *La Diplomatie au temps de Machiavel* (1892, etc.). This, however, is concerned only with the practice of the European Courts at the end of the 15th century. An important edition of several mediaeval treatises (*De Legatis et Legationibus Tractatus varii*) on the subject by Dr W. E. Hrabar (1905) should also be referred to.

ments, the Commission, Safe-Conduct, Powers, Credentials, Instructions, Treaty (Protocols and Ratification) and Letters of Recall, can be recognized as the normal procedure from the 13th century to the 19th, these are often obscured during the mediaeval period by the number of variants and subsidiary instruments interpolated in the course of the negotiations. In addition to this redundancy of forms, the procedure varies according to the nature of the mission, whether a Treaty of Alliance or Marriage, an Arbitration, a Pacification or other negotiation, whilst many niceties of feudal and ecclesiastical law have to be reckoned with.

77. *Writ of* Liberate *addressed to the Treasurer and Chamberlains of the Exchequer* (1184—1188).

Henricus, Dei gratia Rex Anglorum et Dux Normannorum et Aquitanorum et Comes Andegavorum, R[icardo] thesaurario et Willelmo Malduit et Warino filio Giroldi, Camerariis suis, Salutem. Liberate de thesauro meo xxv marcas fratribus Cartusié de illis L marcis quas do eis annuatim per cartam meam. Teste Willelmo de Sancté Marié ecclesia, apud Westmoster.

[*Original Writ in Exch. of Rec. Warrants for Issues, Bundle* 1 (*Madox, Hist. of Exchequer,* I. 390).]

78. *Writ of* Allocate *addressed to the Barons of the Exchequer* (2 *May,* 3 *Edward I*).

Rex, Baronibus suis de Scaccario, Salutem. Allocate Roberto, filio Johannis, vicecomiti nostro Norfolkié, in exitibus ejusdem comitatus, pro custodia castri Norwici, et pro stipendiis capellani celebrantis divina in capella ejusdem castri, et pro stipendiis subconstabularii et clerici sui et janitoris ejusdem castri et custodis gaiolé nostré et unius vigilis ibidem, tantum quantum aliis vicecomitibus nostris pro custodia et stipendiis predictis allocari consueverit. Teste me ipso, apud Westmonasterium, secundo die Maii, anno regni Regis tercio.

[*Original Writ in Exch. Proc. Bundle 78, File* 5.]

79. *Writ of* Computate *addressed to the Barons of the Exchequer*
(10 *January*, 5 *John*).

Rex, etc., baronibus de Scaccario [*etc.*]. Computate vicecomiti de
Dorsete, secundum consuetudinem et legem Scaccarii, hoc quod
rationabiliter monstrare poterit per visum et legale testimonium quod
posuerit in sustentatione obsidum Amoravici, per preceptum nostrum.
Teste me ipso, apud Merlebergum, x die Januarii.

Per T[homam] de Camera.

[Liberate *Roll*, 5 *John*, *M.* 6 (*ed. Record Comm. p.* 77).]

---

80. *Counter-writ requiring the advance of certain money out
of the revenues of the See of Winchester during voidance* (12 *August*,
27 *Henry III*).

Henricus, Dei gratia Rex Angliè, dominus Hiberniè, dux
Normanniè et Aquitaniè et comes Andegaviè, custodibus episcopatus
Wintoniensis, Salutem. Precipimus vobis quod de exitibus episco-
patus Wyntoniensis faciatis habere abbati et conventui de Bono
Loco, Cysterciensis ordinis, vel eorum nuncio has litteras defe-
renti, sexaginta marcas de dono nostro. Et computabitur vobis ad
Scaccarium. Teste me ipso, apud Burdegalam, xij die Augusti, anno
regni nostri xxvij.

[*Early Chanc. Rolls, No.* 887, *M.* 8 (*Rôles Gascons, Tom.* I. *p.* 242,
No. 1872).]

---

81. *Writ of* Perdonavimus *addressed to the Barons of the Exchequer* (27 *February*, 3 *Edward I*).

Edwardus, *etc.* [*as in No.* 26] baronibus suis de Scaccario, Salutem.
Sciatis quod, ad instanciam karissimé matris nostré, Alianoré Reginé
Angliè, perdonavimus dilectis nobis in Christo Abbati et Conventui
de Messingdene quinque marcas de illis decem libris ad quas nuper
amerciati fuerunt coram nobis, apud Etone, pro disseisina. Et ideo
vobis mandamus quod prefatos Abbatem et Conventum de predictis
quinque marcis quietos esse faciatis. Teste me ipso, apud Wyndesores, xxvij die Februarii, anno regni nostri tercio.

[*Original Writ in Exch. Proc. Bundle* 78, *File* 5.]

82. *Letters Close (License) for a foreign merchant in London to draw a Letter of Exchange, with proviso against exporting bullion on pain of forfeiture* (9 *July*, 6 *Richard II*).

Ricardus, Dei gratia Rex Anglié, et Francié, et Dominus Hibernié, Nicholao Luke, mercatori de societate Guinigiorum, in civitate nostra Londonié commoranti, Salutem. Ut quandam litteram cambii sociis tuis in partibus exteris commorantibus pro quindecim libris Johanni Clerenans archidiacono Suffolkié in eisdem partibus solvendis facere valeas, licenciam tibi, tenore presencium, duximus concedendam ; dum tamen colore presentis licencié nostré aliquod aurum vel argentum versus predictas partes nullatenus transmittas seu transmitti facias quovismodo, sub pena forisfacturé ejusdem. Teste meipso, apud Westmonasterium, ix die Julii, anno regni nostri sexto.

[*Enrolment in Exchange Roll (now Supplementary Close Roll, No.* 15, *M.* 9).]

---

83. *Letters Close (Passage) for a certain chaplain proceeding to Rome by the King's License and who has given security for his loyalty, to be permitted by the* Custodes passagii *to cross the sea without impediment* (7 *October*, 6 *Richard II*).

Rex Custodibus passagii in portubus Dovorré vel Sandewici, Salutem. Quia Willelmus Otecombe, clericus, et Thomas Brokhamtone, de comitatu Somerseté, coram nobis in Cancellaria nostra personaliter constituti manuceperunt pro Willelmo Smogger, capellano, qui de licencia nostra versus curiam Romanam profecturus est, quod ipse in curia predicta aliqua nobis seu coroné nostré prejudicialia non prosequetur, seu prosequi aut attemptari faciat, videlicet, utrique predictorum Willelmi Ottecombe et Thomé sub pena viginti librarum ad opus nostrum solvendarum ; vobis mandamus quod ipsum Willelmum Smogger in altero portuum predictorum versus Curiam predictam libere et absque impedimento aliquo transire permittatis : aliquo mandato nostro vobis in contrarium directo non obstante ; dum tamen idem Willelmus Smogger aliqua nobis seu regno nostro Anglié prejudicialia secum non deferat ullo modo. Teste Rege, apud Westmonasterium, vii die Octobris.

[*Enrolment in Exchange Roll as above.*]

---

84. *Writ (Letters Close) for the executors of Gilbert de Clare 'to have his Scutage' in the counties of Surrey and Sussex, although his name is not entered in the roll of the Marshalsea* (30 *August*, 14 *Edward II*).

Rex vicecomiti Surreié et Sussexé, Salutem. Licet Gilbertus de Clare, nuper Comes Gloucestrié et Hertfordié, defunctus, non optulisset servicium suum nobis debitum in excercitu nostro Scocié anno regni nostri quarto, per quod idem servicium in rotulis Marescalcié nostré de eodem excercitu non invenitur; quia tamen constat nobis quod idem Comes fecit nobis servicium suum predictum in excercitu supradicto, tibi precipimus quod executoribus testamenti predicti Comitis habere facias scutagium de feodis militum qué de dicto Comite tunc tenebantur in balliva tua, videlicet, duas marcas de scuto pro excercitu supradicto. Teste Rege apud Croukham, xxx die Augusti.

[Enrolment in Scutage Roll, 14 *Edward II, M.* 2.]

85. *Writ of Redisseisin (Letters Close) on behalf of Rose, widow of Henry Brun of Wymundewold, in the usual form* (21 *November,* 14 *Edward I).*

Rex, vicecomes Leycestrié, Salutem. Monstravit nobis Roisia, qué fuit uxor Henrici Brun de Wymundwold, quod cum ipsa in Curia nostra coram Justiciariis nostris ultimo itinerantibus apud Leycestriam recuperasset seisinam suam versus Johannem de Nevile, Henricum de Teresant, Johannem Bastard et Simonem de Jorce de Wymundwold, de tercia parte unius messuagii et unius virgaté terré, cum pertinentiis, exceptis tribus acris terré in Wymundwold, per defaltam quam iidem Johannes, [*etc.*], versus prefatam Roisiam in eadem Curia nostra fecerunt, predicti Johannes, *etc.,* ipsam Roisiam de predicta tercia parte postea injuste disseisiverunt. Et ideo tibi precipimus quod, assumptis tecum custodibus placitorum coroné nostré et xii, tam militibus quam aliis liberis et legalibus hominibus de comitatu tuo, in propria persona tua accedas ad mesuagium illud et terram, et per eorum sacramentum diligentem inde facias inquisicionem; et si ipsam Roisiam per predictos Johannem [*etc.*] de predicta tercia parte postea disseisita inveneris, tunc ipsos Johannem [*etc.*] capias et in prisona nostra salvo custodiri facias: ita quod a prisona illa nullo modo deliberentur sine mandato nostro speciali: et ipsam Roisiam de predicta tercia parte reseisiri; et ei dampna sua in duplum, qué occasione illius postdisseissiné sustinuit, per sacramentum predictorum xii taxata, de terris et catallis predictorum Johannis [*etc.*] in balliva tua sine dilatione fieri et habere facias, juxta formam ultimi Statuti nostri Westmonasterii de hujusmodi postdisseisinis provisi; et scire facias predictis Johanni [*etc.*] quod inquisicioni illi faciendé intersint, si sibi viderint expedire. Teste Rege, apud Lyndhurst, xxi die Novembris.

[Enrolment in Redisseisin Roll, No. 1, *M.* 17, *cf. Originalia Roll,* 14 *Edw. I, Rot.* 17 *(Abbrev. Rot. Orig.* I. 52 *a).]*

86. *The Statute of Wales* (12 *Edward I*).

Edwardus, Dei gratia Rex Anglié [*etc.*] omnibus fidelibus suis de terra sua Snaudonié et de aliis terris suis in Wallia, salutem in Domino. Divina providentia, qué in sui dispositione non fallitur, inter alia dispensationis sué munera quibus nos et regnum nostrum Anglié decorare dignata est, terram Wallié cum incolis suis, prius nobis jure feodali subjectam, jam sui gratia in proprietatis nostré dominium [*etc.*]. Nos itaque nutu divino volentes [*etc.*] leges et consuetudines partium illarum [*etc.*] hactenus usitatas coram nobis [*etc.*] fecimus recitari. Quibus diligenter auditis et plenius intellectis, quasdem ipsarum de consilio [*etc.*] statuendo decrevimus [*etc.*] et eas decetero in terris nostris in partibus illis [*etc.*] teneri et observari volumus in forma subscripta.

Providimus et decernendo statuimus quod [*etc.*].

Volumus etiam et statuimus quod [*etc.*].

Et ideo vobis mandamus quod premissa decetero in omnibus firmiter observatis. Ita tamen quod quocienscumqúe et quando-cumque et ubicumque nobis placuerit, possimus predicta statuta et eorum partes singulas declarare, interpretari, addere sive diminuere, pro nostré libito voluntatis et prout [*etc.*] viderimus expedire.

In cujus rei testimonium presentibus Sigillum nostrum est appensum. Daté apud Rothelanum, die Dominica in Media Quadra-gesimé, anno regni nostri duodecimo.

[*Statutes of the Realm*, I. 55.]

---

87. *Petition of the Master of the Order of Sempringham for a vagabond canon to be attached by the secular arm* (9 *October*, 1389).

Excellentissimo principi ac domino suo ligio, domino Ricardo Dei gratia Regi Anglié et Francié ac domino Hibernié, suus semper humilis et devotus frater Willelmus, Dei misericordia magister ordinis de Semp[r]yngham, Salutem in Eo per quem reges regnant et regnorum omnium gubernacula diriguntur. Excelsé regié majestati vestré significo, per presentes, quod frater Johannes de Whiteby, canonicus et a diu professus ordinis nostri predicti, spreto obediencié jugo et observancia regulari, tam per nonnulla tempora sui ordinis obser-vanciis rebellis et inobediens, in seculo vagabundus, apostata, et fugitivus, per plures patrias dampnabiliter discurrebat, et in hujus rebellione et contumacia animo obstinato stare incorrigibiliter non formidat, professione sua et claves ecclesié contempnendo, in grave animé sué periculum, ecclesié Dei et religionis sué contemptum et scandalum plurimorum. Quare excellentissimam regié pietatis vestré dignitatem humiliter et devote require quatinus, cum idem Johannes nullo modo velit per sui ordinis regulas emendari aut per censuras ecclesiasticas coherceri, dignemini, ad honorem Dei et ecclesié sancté religionis obtentu, ad ipsius Johannis rebellionem et obstinanciam reprimendam, auxilium apponere brachii secularis. Valeat excellentissima magnificencia vestra in Domino per tempora diuturna. Scripta apud Sempryngham vii Idus Octobris, anno Domini millesimo ccc^{mo} octogesimo nono.

[*Chancery Warrants for Issues, Ser.* 2, *File* 1764, *No.* 5^1.]

---

88. *Petition of the Prioress and Convent of Barking for license to elect an Abbess in the place of one deceased* (2 *October* 1393).

Magnifico principi et domino metuendo, domino Ricardo, Dei gratia Regi Anglié et Francié et Domino Hibernié, sué humiles et devoté priorissa et conventus de Berkynge orationum suffragia devotarum cum omnimoda reverencia et honore. Vestré regié celsitudini humiliter nunciamus quod sortis humané conditio, nulli parcens, felicis memorié Matilldam de Monte Acuto, nuper nostri monasterii abbatissam ab hac luce subtraxit. Qua propter pedibus vestré majestatis prevoluté, dilectas sorores nostras, Mariam Dayrél, Sibillam de Felton et Margaretam de Saxham ad vestram regiam majestatem destinamus pro impetranda nobis licencia aliam eligendi in nostri monasterii abbatissam quam eis et nobis dignetur concedere vestra regia clemencia consueta. Diu regnare, ac triumphum de hostibus reportare, annuat vobis Christus.

Data in capitulo nostro, secundo die mensis Octobris, anno domini millesimo ccc^{mo} nonagesimo tertio.

(*Endorsed*:—Magnifico principi, domino nostro, domino Ricardo Regi Anglié et Francié et Domino Hibernié.)

[*Chancery Ecclesiastical Petitions, File* 35, *No.* 51.]

---

89. *Letters Patent* (*License*) *for the above Prioress and Convent to elect a suitable Abbess* (5 *October*, 17 *Richard II*).

De licencia eligendi, Berkyng. Rex dilectis sibi in Christo priorissé et conventui de Berkynge, salutem. Ex parte vestra nobis est humiliter supplicatum quod cum ecclesia vestra predicta per mortem boné memorié Matilldê de Monte Acuto, ultimé abbatissé loci illius, pastricis sit solacio destituta, aliam vobis eligendi in Abbatissam et pastricem Licenciam vobis concedere dignaremur ; nos precibus vestris in hac parte favorabiliter inclinati, Licenciam illam vobis duximus concedendam, mandantes quod talem vobis eligatis in Abbatissam et pastricem qué, Deo devota, ecclesié vestré necessaria, nobisque et regno nostro utilis et fidelis existat. In cujus rei, etc. Teste Rege, apud Westmonasterium, quinto die Octobris.

[*Patent Roll*, 17 *Ric. II, Pt.* 1, *M.* 21 (*Cal. p.* 317)].

---

¹ The Writ issued in compliance with this petition would have been enrolled on the Controlment Roll which is missing for this year.

90. *Letter from the above Prioress and Convent to the King, intimating the election of an Abbess* (7 *October* 1393).

Excellentissimo principi, *etc.* [*as in No.* 87], sué humiles et devoté priorissa et conventus de Berkynge orationum, *etc.* [*as in No.* 88] dominationi vestré presentibus literis intimamus quod boné memorié Matillda de Monte Acuto, nuper Abbatissa nostra, viam universé carnis ingressa, et concessa nobis a vestra magestate Licencia eligendi, nos, voluntate unanimi et consensu, dominam providam et discretam dominam Sibellam de Felton nobis elegimus in abbatissam et pastricem. Hinc est quod eandam presentamus celsitudini vestré, devotis precibus supplicando quatinus predicté electioni nostré regium assensum liberaliter inpendentes, Literas vestras super hoc domino episcopo Londoniensi dirigere vellitis. Valeat et vigeat vestra magnitudo regia per tempora longiora. Data apud Berkynge, in capitulo nostro, septimo die Octobris, anno domini millesimo ccc^{mo} nonagesimo tertio.

[*Original Letter, Chancery Ecclesiastical Petitions, File* 26, *No.* 2.]

---

91. *Letters Patent* (*Royal Assent*) *approving the above election for the information of the Bishop of London* (11 *October*, 17 *Richard II*).

De regio ssensu. Rex venerabili in Christo patri R[oberto], eadem gracia, Episcopo Londoniensi, Salutem. Sciatis quod electioni nuper facté in ecclesia conventuali de Berkynge de dilecta nobis in Christo Sibilla de Felton, moniali ejusdem domus, in abbatissam loci illius, regium assensum adhibuimus et favorem. Et hoc vobis tenore presentium significamus ut quod verum est in hac parte exequamini. In cujus, *etc.* Teste Rege apud Westmonasterium, xi die Octobris. *Per ipsum Regem.*

[*Patent Roll,* 17 *Ric. II, Pt.* 1, *M.* 20 (*Cal. p.* 319).]

---

92. *Certificate of the Bishop of London signifying his confirmation of the above election* (16 *November* 1393).

Excellentissimo in Christo principi et domino nostro, domino Ricardo, Dei gratia, Regi Anglié et Francié illustri ac domino Hibernié, Robertus, permissione divina Londoniensis episcopus, orationum suffragia et in Eo feliciter regnare, per quem reges regnant et principes dominantur. Excellencié regié majestati vestré, tenore presentium, significamus quod cum constaret nobis per literas vestras regias pridie nobis directas quod vestra regia celsitudo electioni nuper facté in monasterio monialium de Berkynge, nostré diocesis de religiosa muliere domina Sibilla de Felton, ejusdem monasterii moniali, in abbatissam loci illius electa, regium assensum adhibuit; pariter et favorem nobis significans per easdem literas ut facere possemus in hac parte et exequi quod est nostrum.   Electionem predictam, utpote concorditer et canonice factam, confirmavimus ac eidem electé et confirmaté regimen et administrationem omnium bonorum spiritualium ejusdem monasterii quatenus ad nos attinet plenarie impendimus cum omni solempnitate in ea parte debita et requisita.   Valeat et vigeat majestas vestré regié celsitudinis ad regnorum vestrorum gubernacula feliciter et longeve.   In cujus rei testimonium, sigillum nostrum presentibus duximus apponendum.   Data Londonié, die xvi^{mo} mensis Novembris, anno domini millesimo ccc^{mo} nonagesimo tertio, et nostré consulatus anno duodecimo.

[*Original Certificate, Chancery Ecclesiastical Petitions, File* 36, *No.* 8[1].]

93. *Letters Patent (Precept for Restitution of Temporalities) by the Escheator of Essex and Hertford, with writ* de intendendo *to the tenants of the Abbey* (17 *November,* 17 *Richard II*).

De restitutione temporalium. Berkyng. Rex Escaetori suo in comitatu Essexié et Hertfordié, Salutem. Cum venerabilis pater Robertus Episcopus Londoniensis electionem nuper factam in ecclesia conventuali de Berkynge, Londoniensis diocesis, de dilecta nobis in Christo Sibilla de Felton, moniali ejusdem domus, in Abbatissam loci illius, cui prius regium assensum adhibuimus et favorem, confirmaverit, sicut per litteras patentes ipsius Episcopi nobis inde directas nobis constat.   Nos confirmationem illam acceptantes, cepimus fidelitatem ipsius Electé, et temporalia Abbatié illius, prout moris est, restituimus eidem.   Et ideo tibi precipimus quod eidem Electé temporalia predicta, cum pertinentiis, in balliva tua liberes in forma predicta.   Salvo jure cujuslibet.   Teste Rege apud Westmonasterium xvii die Novembris.

Consimilia brevia diriguntur Escaetoribus subscriptis sub eadem data, videlicet [*list follows*].

Et mandatum est militibus, liberis hominibus, et omnibus aliis tenentibus de Abbatia predicta quod eidem Sibillé, tanquam Abbatissé et domine sué, in omnibus qué ad Abbatiam predictam pertinent, intendentes sint et respondentes, sicut predictum est.   In cujus, etc.   Teste ut supra.

[*Patent Roll,* 17 *Ric. II, Pt.* 1, *M.* 15 (*Cal. p.* 328).]

---

[1] This should also be found in the Bishop's Register.

II. INSTRUMENTS UNDER THE SMALLER SEALS

1. WRITS AND LETTERS MISSIVE

The evolution of these instruments is sufficiently indicated by the following specimens. A full account of their character and use is furnished by a recent work[1].

(a) *Occasional Forms*

94. *The Privy Seal substituted for the Great Seal.*—From the very beginning of the 13th century we find that a lesser seal in the shape of the King's 'Private' or 'Secret' Seal, or any form of Signet, might be substituted for the Great Seal. In such cases the reason of the substitution is explained in the sealing clause, and by some such phrase as 'because we have not our Great Seal with us.' In other cases, however, the King makes use of the seal of the Queen, the Justiciar or another of the principal 'curiales.' This casual use of the Lesser Seal may be contrasted with the systematic usurpation of the Edwardian period and the recognized practice in respect of Gascon instruments (No. 44).

95. *Letters Patent under the Privy Seal.*—The issue of a writ under the Privy Seal in the nature of an appointment to an Office would seem to be an extreme assertion of the sufficiency of instruments under the Smaller Seal which were extensively employed during the reign of Edward II for political and especially for fiscal business (Nos. 96 to 98). In the present case, however, it will be noticed that the Address is not general but to particular persons, whilst the Injunctive Clause contains specific directions. This points to a writ 'de intendendo' following the issue of formal Letters Patent of appointment and the latter will in fact be found on the Patent Roll dated the 3rd of May. The 'Privy Seal' (which has the appearance of the ordinary Secret Seal) is affixed to a tag.

---

[1] E. Déprèz, *Études de Diplomatique Anglaise* (1908). The following specimens were selected and annotated nearly two years before the appearance of this valuable essay, and circumstances did not allow of any use being made of the information contained therein for the purpose of the present work. A further account of these diplomatic forms will be found in the volume of 'Studies' previously referred to.

(*b*) General Forms

96. *Privy Seal Writ (French).*—The writ of Privy Seal, if not in fact of French origin, is more usually expressed in that language between the very end of the 13th and the beginning of the 15th century. In these instruments, which were fast usurping the functions of Writs under the Great Seal, we find usually an individual Address followed by an Injunction which, as in the specimen printed below, is merely a version of a common Latin formula. An Exposition, however, may be present, and there may be, as in the present instance, an explanatory Final Clause ('Qar nous avoms,' etc.) which somewhat resembles that found in the post-Conquest ministerial writs. The Dating Clause is uniformly simple. For reasons which are sufficiently obvious original missive writs under the Smaller Seals are rarely preserved, but many can be found enrolled in the Exchequer. Their occurrence in the Files of the Chancery Warrants for Issue, though anomalous, has doubtless contributed to their preservation.

97. *Privy Seal Warrant (French).*—This Writ of Privy Seal is practically a Warrant, such as was constantly issued from this time onwards in the vernacular (No. 88) as an authority for payments in the royal service. The heading ' De par le Roi,' serving as a departmental memorandum, and the Warrant formula in the Final Clause should be noticed. The former device, however, is especially associated with Letters under the Secret Seal or Signet in an epistolary style, and, in this aspect it may be regarded as a ' compendium ' for the formal superscription dispensed with in such formulas, as well as an indication of the authority for the Warrant. In later times the Privy Seal Letter retains the formal Superscription (No. 98).

98. *Privy Seal (English).*—The missive vernacular Writ of Privy Seal, now technically termed a Privy Seal Letter, was chiefly used during the later period as an authority for the issue of money or for some fiscal service, and for this purpose it supersedes almost entirely the ancient writ under the Great Seal. These Privy Seal Letters are entered in the Privy Seal Books of the Pells and Auditors' department of the Exchequer. At the same time executive instruments under the Privy Seal may be found in the Files of Warrants for Issues and many departmental instruments are entered amongst the Lord Chamberlain's Records and elsewhere, whilst some special forms will be described below.

99. *Signet Letter* (*English*).—Before the middle of the 15th century Letters Missive under the Smaller Seals (especially the Signet) are found in the vernacular. These in most cases are versions of the conventional French and Latin formulas in which a certain amount of originality may be discerned. Here the missive being addressed to a dignitary of the church is rogatory rather than mandatory in style, and this characteristic is also seen in the Final Clause. This specimen is taken from the Chancery Files of Warrants for Issue, but as it does not convey any direction to issue an appropriate instrument but rather points to some judicial action, it has been used as an example of a missive which is extremely difficult to find amongst the existing Records. In the 16th and 17th centuries Signet Letters relating to Irish affairs will be found entered in a series of Letter Books amongst the State Papers.

100. *Sign Manual Warrant.*—This type is especially associated with the increasing use of the vernacular from the reign of Henry V. The King's initials are usually affixed to the upper margin. The evolution of this practice may be clearly traced in the specimens selected and annotated by Sir H. Maxwell Lyte in the *Catalogue of the Museum of the Public Record Office.*

(c) *Special Forms*

101, 102. '*Benevolence*' (*Privy Seal*).—The use of the Privy Seal Writ for raising money by way of loan is well known in the case of the 'Benevolence' and of the similar instruments issued at a later date and known as 'Privy Seals' or 'Forced Loans.' Such writs were frequently issued, like the Papal Indulgences, as blank forms to be filled in for the locality concerned. In some respects this instrument may be regarded as corresponding to the writs of Assistance so frequently issued in the form of Letters Patent. The departmental directions appended to the draft of No. 102 for the information of the Chancery clerks are of interest in connexion with the formulas given in the following section.

103. *Commission of Array.*—Amongst the Warrants for Issues we occasionally find, besides royal requisitions to the Chancellor in connexion with his equitable jurisdiction, orders of a purely ministerial character, especially such as were executed under the Secret Seal. In this case the Chancellor is entreated to bring up armed forces to assist the King at the siege of Berwick. Possibly the fact

that the Great Seal was in the custody of a bishop possessing 'jura regalia' has not so much to do with the matter as the fact, indicated by the endorsement, that the Chancellor was then (1320) at York, the strategical base of an English army at Berwick. The contemporary Chancery Rolls show that no Letters under the Great Seal were issued in response to this missive. The Seal was affixed on the dorse securing a band with which the Letter was closed, as was usual in the case of instruments under the Secret Seal. It will be seen from the endorsement that this Letter was delivered and filed with other warrants for issue of the Great Seal.

Many Writs and Letters of this nature are preserved, some executed under the 'Privatum Sigillum,' the 'Privé Seal,' or 'Secré Seal' and others under the Queen's Seal, in the absence of the Privy Seal.

104. *Reference to the Council.*—Although Writs and Letters under the Smaller Seals addressed to the Chancellor were almost always in the nature of 'Warrants for Issue,' and therefore purely departmental, they are occasionally found to be of a ministerial character. In the interesting document printed below, the King refers a Petition to the Chancellor and other Councillors, not for the purpose of authorizing the preparation of an appropriate instrument, but for consideration and report. The result of this official action is recorded in the memoranda appended to the original Petition, which is annexed to the Writ.

This Writ is under the 'Secret' Seal, which was occasionally appended to a tag, though usually affixed to the dorse of the letter, as previously described.

----

94. *Letters Patent (under the Privy Seal) for the delivery of the Castle of Northampton (19 May, 18 John).*

Rex, Henrico de Nevilla, salutem. Mandamus vobis quod castrum Norhamtoné liberetis ubi dilectus et fidelis noster Falkesius de Breaute vobis dicet ex parte nostra. Et sciatis quod jam pridem illud vobis significavissemus nisi illud oblivioni tradissemus. Et in hujus, etc. Privato Sigillo nostro signatas, quia Magnum Sigillum nostrum nobiscum non habuimus, vobis inde mittimus.

Teste me ipso, apud Folkestane, xix die Maii, anno regni nostri decimo octavo.

[*Patent Roll*, 18 *John, Pt.* 2, *M.* 9 (*Rot. Litt. Pat. pp.* 183a).]

----

95. *Letters Patent* (*Writ* de intendendo) *to the tenants of the manor of Faxfleet, requiring them to be intendent to Joan, late wife of Alexander Comyn, to whom the King has committed that manor* (21 *May,* 4 *Edward II*).

Edwardus, *etc.* [*as in No.* 26], omnibus libere tenentibus et aliis de manerio Templariorum de Fraxlet in comitatu Eboracsiré ad quos presentes Litteré pervenerint, Salutem. Sciatis quod commisimus dilecté nobis in Christo Johanné, qué fuit uxor Alexandri Comyn, sorori dilecti et fidelis nostri Willelmi le Latimer, manerium predictum cum pertinenciis, tenendum quamdiu nostré placuerit voluntati. Et ideo vobis mandamus quod eidem Johanné in omnibus qué ad manerium predictum pertinent intendentes sitis et respondentes. In cujus rei testimonium, has Litteras nostras fecimus Patentes. Datum sub Privato Sigillo nostro, apud Berewicum super Twedam, xxi die Maii, anno regni nostri quarto.

[*Original Writ in P. R. O. Museum* (*Case No.* 76), *cf. Patent Roll,* 6 *Edw. II, Pt.* 2, *M.* 12 (*Cal. p.* 569).]

---

96. *Writ of* Levari facias (*Privy Seal*) *to the Sheriffs of London, concerning the levying of the debts of the Crown* (17 *November,* 15 *Edward II*).

Edward, par la grace de Dieu, etc. as viscountes de nostre cite de Londres, salutz. Nous vous mandons et chargeons, fermement enjoignauntz sur greve forfiture, que tutes les dettes que vous avez eu mandement de fere lever a nostre oeps deinz vos baillies par briefs ou par somons de nostre Escheqer, facez lever ove tute la haste et ove tute la diligence que vous unques pourrez, sanz desport ou soefferaunce fere a nuly de quele condicion q'il soit, s'il ne monstre aquitance, ou mandement vous viegne de nous de surfeer; et les deniers, sicom vous les ferrez lever, facez venir de temps en temps a nostre dit Escheqier et paer illoeques, sicome vous volez eschure nostre indignacion et vous meismes sauver de griefs damages; qar nous avoms estreitement chargez noz ministres du dit Escheqier q'ils facent reddement punir touz les viscountes q'ils en ceste chose troveront en lacheste ou en autre defaute. Donne souz nostre Prive Seal a Stratford atte Boghe, le xvii jour de Novembre, l'an de nostre regne quinzisme.

Et memorandum est quod consimilia brevia directa fuerunt singulis vicecomitibus Anglié eodem die.

[*L. T. R. Memoranda Roll, Mich.* 15 *Edw. II, rot.* 84d. *Madox, Hist. of Exchequer,* I. *p.* 358 *n.*]

97. *Privy Seal Letter (Warrant) for payment of wages due to Matthew de Gourney under an Indenture of War* (11 *May,* 1 *Richard II*).

De par le Roy.

Nous vous mandons que a nostre chier et foial Geoffrey d'Argenton chivaler, q'est demorez devers nous, par endenture, pur un an entier ovesque vynt hommes d'armes, le meismes acoutez, et vynt archers, a aler en nostre service devers nostre chier et foial Mayhu de Gourney, nostre seneschal d'Aquitaigne, pur nous servir en celles parties en la compaignie du dit seneschal, preignant le dit Geffrey de nous, pur lui et les ditz gentz d'armes, doubles gages et doubles regards acustumez, et pur les ditz archers doubles gages acustumez ; des queux gages il serra paiez avant la mayn, pur lui et les ditz gentz d'armes, pur un quarter du dit an, et des ditz regardz pur lui et les ditz gentz d'armes pur demy an ; et de semblables gages pur un autre quarter il serra paies a sa venue a la mier avant son passage, sicome en la dite endenture est plus au plein contenuz ; facez paier les ditz gages pur le dit primer quarter, et le regard pur le dit demy an, en la maniere avant dite. Et ces presentes vous en serront Garant. Donne souz nostre Prive Seal, a Westmester, le xj jour de Maij, l'an de nostre regne primer.

A noz bien amez William Walworth et Johan Philepot, Receivours de noz deniers pur la guerre.

[*Public Record Office Museum, Case No.* 79 (*Catalogue, p.* 33).]

---

98. *Privy Seal Letter (Warrant) to the Treasurer and Chamberlains of the Exchequer for payment of a certain sum to the person named therein* (27 *September,* 12 *Elizabeth*).

Willelmo Brymingham Generoso—ccli. Elizabeth, by the grace of God Quene of England, Fraunce and Ireland, defender of the faith, etc. To the Tresourer and Chamberlaynes of our Eschequer, greting. Wee will and commaunde you of our tresure at the Receipt of our said Eschequer to deliver, or cause to be delivered, unto our welbeloved William Brymingham, gent., or to his sufficient assignie, in consideration of such service as he hath done unto us in Ireland, the somme of twoo hundred poundes sterling over and above such other sommes of money as he hath had alredy, and besides such other benefitt as wee meane towardes hym for his said service. And theise our Lettres shalbe your sufficient Warraunt in this behalfe. Given under our Privie Seale, at our Castle of Windesore, the xxviith of September, the xiith yere of our reigne.

Ry. Oseley.

[*Exchequer of Receipt, Auditor's Privy Seal Book, No.* 1 *b, fo.* 1.]

---

99. *Signet Letter to the Archbishop of Canterbury for a certain case referred to his arbitration to be expedited* (9 *November*, 19 *Henry VI*).

By the King.

Right worshipful fader in God, right trusti and right welbeloved, we grete you wel. And forasmuch as we be enformed by oure welbeloved chapellain, maister Richard Chestre, that certain and divers maters of long time hanging betwix the Abbasse of oure monasteir of Syon and him, and in especial the title of right and possession of the chirche of Lancastre, by the agrement and compromise of either partye ben committed to be declared and demed by your laude and arbitrement; we prey you specially that ye wol, in al goodly haste as ye may, in the said maters yif youre arbitrement and make a final and a perpetual ende, so that oure said chapellain may the better attende on oure servise, and also the said Abbasse and convent of oure said monasteir of Syon and all the parisshoners of oure toune of Lancastre aforesaid may be sett in quiete and reste for ever; in the which thing doing ye shal, as we truste, deserve gret reward of God and do to us right singuler pleasur. Yeven under oure Signet, at oure manoir of Shene, the ix day of Novembre.

To the right reverend fadre in God oure right trusty and right welbeloved th'archbisshopp of [Canterbury] and primat of al England.

[*P. R. O. Museum, Case H, No.* 82 (*Catalogue, p.* 34), *cf. Patent Roll,* 19 *Hen. VI, Pt.* I, *M.* 12 (*Cal. p.* 493).]

---

100. *Warrant (Sign Manual) for an imprest at the Receipt of the Exchequer* (16 *October*, 13 *Henry VII*).

H. R.

For Perkin Warbeck's wife. Henry, by the grace of God, King of England and of Fraunce and Lord of Irelande, To oure trusty and welbeloved servant Thomas Stokes, oon of the tellers of oure Receipt, greting. We wol and charge you, for the diete of Katherine, daughter to th'erl of Huntlye, from Bodmen unto our derrest wife the Quene, wheresoever she bee, ye deliver unto our trusty servent Thomas Englisshe, sergeant of our pulterie, the some of 20 pounds sterlinges, upon a prest and rekenyng by him to be declared. And these our Lettres shall be your Warrant in this behalve.

Yeven under our Signet at our city of Excestre, the xvjth day of October, the xiijth yere of our reigne.

L. S.

[*Gairdner, Letters and Papers of Richard III, etc.* (*Rolls*) II. 73, *from the Original in the Public Record Office.*]

H. F.

101. *Privy Seal Letter ('Benevolence') referring to the King's necessities, to be further explained by the Commissioners appointed for this purpose, and requesting the loan of a considerable sum (20 July, 4 Henry VI).*

De par le Roy.

Chers et bienamez. Come pour la defense de nostre Royaume encountre noz rebeaux et ennemys et la brief expedition de noz guerres, nous conviendra necessairement avoir chevance et provision d'une grande somme de deniers, sicome plus au plain de par nous et nostre Conseil vous exposeront [*names of Commissioners follow*], lesqueux nous avons assignez, de l'avis de nostre dit Conseil, par noz lettres de Commission desouz nostre Grand Seal, pour communiquer et tanter ovec vous de et sur la chevance d'aucune somme notable par vous a apprester a nous en ceste nostre grande necessitee, et pour vous permettre pour et en nostre noun sufficeante seuretee de repaiement de tielle somme come vous nous vuillez en ce cas apprester. Si vous prions, tres cherement, q'en avancement de ceste besoigne, quel a l'aide de nostre Createur tournera au bien et transquillitee de nous, de vous, et de toute Christianitee, prendre vous vuillez le plus pres que vous pouvez en nous aidant a ceste foix par voie d'apprest d'une notable somme, tielle come par les sousditz commissioners de vous sera desiree, adjoustant nientmains a eux ferme foy et creance en leur relation a vous affaire de par nous et nostre dit conseil en celle partie. Donne sous nostre Prive Seal, a Westm[ester], le xxe jour de Juylli.

[*Original Letter in Exch. T. of R. Privy Seals and Letters Patent for Loans, Bundle* 1, *cf. Patent Roll,* 4 *Hen. VI, Pt.* 2, *M.* 9 (*Cal. p.* 355).]

---

102. *Privy Seal Letter (Draft) to serve as a Letter of Credence to the royal Commissioners for raising a forced loan, with a departmental direction as to the style of Address to be employed (21 July, ? 22 Edward IV).*

By the Kyng.

Trusty and Welbeloved, For asmuche as in certain matiers that gretely touchen and concernen the good weele and worship of us, our landes, lordships and subgitts, we have willed our Commissaries, berers herof, to commen with you, we woll, desire and pray you therfore hertely that in suche thinges as that thei or any of theim woll shewe, declare and sey unto you on our behalf, ye woll yeve unto hem and to eche of hem full faith and credence. And we pray you that ye leve not this as ye woll the goode weele and worship above-said. Yeven undre our Prive Seel, at Westminster, the xxj day of Juyll.

This style of ' trusty and welbeloved' may be direct to oon personne or to as many togider as shall lyke the said Commissioners. And it may serve for all maner men yif nede be, except Bisshops.

Item the said style of ' Trusty and Welbeloved' may serve for Citees, Towneships and Cominaltees after this tenur in the taile of the lettre. ' To our trusty and welbeloved, the thrifty men, notable persones and Cominalte of our Citee of .A. or of the towne of .B. and to everiche of theim.'

' To the Right dere in God and Dere in God,' everiche of thees styles may serve for Abbottes, Prioures, Denes, Archediacones. And, for nede, for thrifty persones.

Hamond.

[*Chancery, Warrants for Issue, (Ser.* 1), *File* 1326.]

---

103. *Writ under the Secret Seal to the King's Chancellor concerning the levy of the Yorkshire Fencibles for the siege of Berwick* (10 *September,* 13 *Edward II*).

Edward, par la grace de Dieu, Roi d'Engleterre, Seignur d'Irlande et Ducs d'Aquitaine. Al honurable piere en Dieu Johanne, par la meisme grace Evesque d'Ely, nostre Chauncellier, Saluz. Por ce que al besoign hom poet assaier ses amys, et nous, par commun assent de tous les grants qi sont pres de nous, avoms empris d'asseger la ville de Berewyk sur Twede ; purquoi vous avoms ordenez, come celui de qi nous nous fioms entierement, de faire lever et mesner a nous au dit siege totes les gentz deffensables du comitez d'Everwyk, aussi bien gentz d'armes come de pee et deinz franchise come dehors, sicome nous vous mandons plus pleinement par noz autres lettres ; vous prioms et chargeoms, tout especialment de cuer come nous pooms que, veues cestes lettres, totes autres choses lessees, entendez et purfournir en touz pointz le mandement que nous vous en fesoms par noz dites lettres, selonc la tenor d'iceles. Et ceste chose eiez tendrement a cuer et en nulle manere ne lessez, si cher come vous amez nous et la sauvete de nostre honur et le bon esploit de nostre guerre.

Donne sous nostre Secre Seal, al siege de Berewyk, le x jour de Septembre, l'an de nostre regne trezisme.

[Endorsed.] *Ista littera, cum ceteris litteris conligatis, venerunt ad Dominum apud Eboracum xv die Septembris.*

[*Chanc. Warr^{ts} etc. (Ser.* 1), *File* 1329/5070.]

7—2

104. *Writ under the Secret Seal to certain Councillors to consider and advise concerning the enclosed petition* (31 *June,* 17 *Edward II*).

Edward, *etc.* [*as in No.* 103]. A noz chers et foialx l'onorable piere en Dieu l'evesque d'Excestre, nostre Tresorier, et Mestre Robert de Baldoke nostre Chauncellier, Saluz. Nous vous enveoms ci dedeinz enclose une bille que nous feust baille par nostre chere cousine la countesse de Pembroke ; et vous maundons que, regardee la dite bille, et eu sur ce plener et bon avisement od ceux de nostre conseil, nous conseillez et avisez selonc ce que vous verrez que mielz fait a faire a nostre profite. Et facez auxint ordeiner od le conseil nostre dite cosine de l'enterrement son seigneur, selonc ce que vous verrez que soit a honeur de nous et de lui.

Donne souz nostre secre seal, a Rotherfeld, le xxxi (*sic*) jour de Juyn, l'an de nostre regne, xvij.

A nostre Seingneur le Roy prie Marie nadgers compayne Mounsire Aymar de Valence, Counte de Pembroke, q'il pleise a vostre haute seingeurie de ordener et dire ceo qe vous plest qe seit fet de sun enterrement, cest a saver, ou, quant, et en quele manere le cors deyt estre mene par chemyn ; kar ne semble mie a lui ne a cunseil que ele eyt que tele chose seit fete sauntz assent et commaundement de vous, a qui il fust si procheyn et vous ad servi si cum vous savetz.

Accorde est que le corps seit enterre a Westmester[1].

[*Chanc. Warr*[ts] *etc.* (*Ser.* 1), *File* 1329/6924/5.]

---

2. WARRANTS FOR THE ISSUE OF THE GREAT SEAL

(a) *Early Procedure*

The normal use of Writs or Letters of Privy Seal, Signet Letters and Sign Manual Warrants in the mediaeval period would seem to have been connected with the issue of Letters Patent, rather than with the administrative matters which were dealt with by the Missive instruments described above. On the other hand, it is probable that the rescripts or possibly the enrolments of the latter species no longer exist, though as we have seen a certain number of missive forms occur in the Files of original Warrants for Issue.

An attempt has been made here to show the sequence of these

---

[1] Other submissions, with the decisions thereon, follow. Cf. Lethaby, *Westminster Abbey*, p. 184.

instruments under certain conditions, distinguishing between the earlier and the later procedure as determined by the Statute of 1535.

Although the normal procedure, as indicated by the sequence of instruments printed below (Nos. 107—109 and 122), would seem to indicate that in both periods the first step in the direction of obtaining the grant of Letters Patent was taken by way of a Petition addressed to the Crown, the intervention of a Petition in all cases cannot be assumed. It will be inferred from the documents printed below that private instructions might be given for this purpose either verbally (No. 105) or by a private letter (No. 106).

Again it was sometimes enough that a petitioner should 'speak with' the Chancellor, Chamberlains or other courtiers; but in the interests of a new and increasing branch of royal revenue, it was considered desirable to treat a written petition as the basis of the departmental procedure for issuing the several seals. Thus it will be seen that the Petition when minuted for execution and despatched under the Signet or Secret Seal (No. 107) became at once a sufficient authority to the Keeper of the Privy Seal to despatch his warrant to the Chancellor (No. 108) for the issue of the Great Seal (No. 109). In the further sequence printed below (Nos. 110—112) the Petition itself has apparently no place, although it may nevertheless have been instrumental in procuring the Signet Letter (No. 110) which is the warrant for the writ of Privy Seal (No. 111) under which the Letters Patent (No. 112) were issued.

Again there appears to have been another procedure by which the Privy Seal only was employed as a Warrant for the issue of the Great Seal (Nos. 113, 114). Here a Draft of the instrument desired by the proposed Grantee (No. 115 *b*) was either enclosed with the Privy Seal Writ (No. 115 *a*) or else appended on the same sheet of writing (No. 116). The most frequent use, however, of the Privy Seal as an independent Warrant for the issue of the Great Seal was in the form of a Bill (Nos. 117, 118) which was distinguished from a formal Writ or Letter by the absence of a Superscription or Address. This instrument was chiefly used for Protections and Orders for Payment, and may be compared with certain Letters Missive under the Smaller Seals (Nos. 97, 101, 102).

The normal tri-lingual Warrant under the Signet (Nos. 119—121) was supplemented by other forms. Here either the Draft instrument itself was rendered, as it were, negotiable by the simple process of acceptance under the King's Sign Manual, with the addition of an official minute (which was a statutory requirement since 18 Henry VI, c. 1) for its due execution by the Chancellor, or the mere Petition (No. 122) was similarly accepted and despatched for execution. This perfection of the official procedure, however, which tended in the direction of producing an ' Immediate Warrant' was undesirable for fiscal reasons, and thus the whole procedure was elaborated and formalized under the well-known Act of 1535 (pp. 114—118), with the further noticeable innovation of the Departmental Docquet. This last device was perhaps the outcome of the official Memoranda found in early enrolments of Royal Charters and Letters under the Great Seal as well as appended to the original instruments. In the 17th century this Memorandum is expanded into a *précis* of the grant itself and it is also entered in an official Docquet Book.

Besides the above normal sequences and common types of Writs and Letters or Bills under the Smaller Seals, several special forms may be found in the mediaeval files of Warrants for Issues. Of these the *Fiat* (No. 123) is, as already mentioned, one of the commonest types, owing to its special use for the issue of Protections. Another special form is the Signet Letter (Nos. 124 and 125) or Signed Bill (No. 126) for the issue of the Privy Seal alone. In the last instance the document resembles the minuted Petition described above, the only distinction being that the date has been added to the body of the Petition itself in an official formula; but here nothing more than the issue of the Privy Seal was intended.

The issue of Letters Patent might also be authorized by a precept of the Regent or the Council during a minority such as that of Henry VI (No. 127).

The language of these instruments varies according to the date, some being in Latin, and others in French or English. It will also be found that this tri-lingual tendency has produced a conventional version of the typical formulas which can be rendered in Latin, French or English indifferently. Specimens of all three versions will be found below.

The Smaller Seals used in connection with these instruments were usually affixed on the back and were commonly kept in place by a band. The Signet and Secret or armorial Seals, however, were apparently used to secure the band of the letter and the external Address was usually written on this band. The Privy Seal was also affixed to the face of Bills of Protection, etc., *en placard*, immediately following the conclusion of the script. Only the outline of these seals can now be traced in the great majority of cases. It is scarcely necessary to observe that these instruments were in the form of writs, that is to say, they were written on narrow strips of parchment, though the draft instruments appended as a schedule might occupy a large membrane. In the case of the later instruments preserved subsequently to 1535 membranes of great size were frequently required, a form which is customary in the 17th century.

---

105. *Draft of Letters Patent with instructions, by the bearer, for due execution* (27 *Edward I*).

Rex universis presentes, etc., Salutem, in Domino. Noverit universitas vestra quod cum in sufferencia inter Regem Francié, suo et suorum, nos nostro et nostrorum nomine, super discordiis et guerris utrobique subortis, ad certum tempus inita et firmata, inter alia sit contentum [*etc.*]. Nos nobilem virum Gwydonem de Marchia, consanguineum nostrum, et alios quoscumque qui ad sui instanciam pro hominibus nostris, quos dominus Rex Francié captos tenet, manuceperint seu pro eis fidejusserint [*etc.*], promittimus, pro nobis et heredibus nostris, fideliter conservare ; ad hoc nos et heredes nostros ac omnia bona nostra, tenore presentium, obligantes. In cujus rei [*etc.*].

Eodem modo scribendum est pro domino Gwydone vicecomite de Tuart [*and many others*].

Fiant brevia super contentis in istis cedulis prout lator presentium vos inde plenius informabit.

[*Chanc. Warr^{ts} etc.* (*Ser.* 1), *File* 1394/1, *cf. Patent Roll,* 27 *Edw. I, M.* 17, 16 *July* (*Cal. p.* 427).]

---

106. *Mandate under the Secret Seal for the issue of Letters Patent* (30 *March,* 11 *Edward II*).

Edward, par la grace de Dieu, *etc.* [*as in No.* 103] a l'onurable pière en Dieu, J[ohan] par meisme la grace Evesque de Wyncestre, nostre Chauncelier, Saluz. Come nostre cher clerc Engelard de Warleye eit resigne la deanee de Tettenhale, q'est en nostre doneson, et Nous, a la queste nostre cher et feal monsieur William de Mountagu, cele deanee eoms donez a nostre bien ame William de Scheintone ; vous mandoms qe sur ce li facez aver son presentement en due fourme de nostre Graunt Seal. Donez souz nostre Secre Seal, a Thonderleye, le xxx jour de Marz, l'an de nostre regne unzisme.

[*Chanc. Warr^{ts} etc.* (*Ser.* 1), 1328/119, *cf. Patent Roll,* 11 *Edward II, Pt.* 2, *M.* 25 (*Cal. p.* 126).]

107. *Petition for the issue of Letters Patent minuted for due execution* (? *March,* 11 *Ric. II*).

Ista billa concessa fuit per Regem et liberata Cancellario exequenda.

A nostre tresredoute et tressoveraigne seignour, nostre s[eignour] le Roy; supplie vostre povere oratour Thomas Walworth, clerk, lui grauntier le prebende de Bugthorpe, en l'esglise d'Everwyk, quelle partient a vostre doigneson par cause de les temporaltees de l'ercevesque d'Everwyk esteantz en vos mayns; et ceo pur Dieu et en oevere de charitee.

[*Chanc. Warr*[ts] *etc.* (*Ser.* 1), *File* 1394/1505.]

108. *Writ of Privy Seal for the issue of Letters Patent ratifying the estate of Thomas de Walworth in the Prebend of Bugthorpe* (*co. York*) (19 *March,* 11 *Richard II*).

Ricardus, etc. [*as in No.* 20], venerabili in Christo, patri consanguineo nostro carissimo episcopo Eliensi, Cancellario nostro, Salutem. Cum nos, volentes securitati dilecti clerici nostri Thomé de Wallewurth, prebendarii prebendé de Bugthorpe in ecclesia cathedrali Eboracensi, providere, statum et possessionem quos idem Thomas habet in prebenda predicta, pro nobis et heredibus nostris, quantum in nobis est, acceptaverimus, approbaverimus, ratificaverimus et confirmaverimus; nolentes quod ipse super possessione sua prebendé predicté racione alicujus juris vel tituli, quod vel qui nobis competet, aut nobis vel heredibus nostris in futurum competere poterit, per nos vel heredes nostros aut ministros nostros quoscumque futuris temporibus impetatur, inquietetur, molestetur in aliquo, seu gravetur; vobis mandamus quod litteras inde sub Magno Sigillo nostro in forma debita fieri faciatis. Data sub Privato Sigillo nostro, apud Westmonasterium, xix die Marcii, anno regni nostri undecimo.

[*Chanc. Warr*[ts] *etc.* (*Ser.* 1), *File* 500/4724.]

109. *Enrolment of Letters Patent issued in accordance with the above mandate* (19 *March,* 11 *Richard II*).

De ratificatione. Rex, omnibus ad quos, etc., Salutem. Volentes securitati dilecti clerici nostri Thomé de Walleworth, prebendarii prebendé de Bugthorpe in ecclesia cathedrali Eboracensi, providere, statum et possessionem quos idem Thomas habet in prebenda predicta, pro nobis et heredibus nostris, quantum in nobis est, acceptamus, approbamus, ratificamus et confirmamus. Nolentes quod ipse super possessione sua prebendé predicté ratione alicujus juris vel tituli, quod vel qui nobis competit, aut nobis vel heredibus nostris in futuris competere poterit, per nos vel heredes nostros aut ministros nostros quoscumque futuris temporibus impetatur, inquietetur, molestetur in aliquo, seu gravetur. In cujus, etc. Teste Rege apud Westmonasterium, xix die Marcii. *Per Breve de Privato Sigillo.*

[*Patent Roll*, 11 *Ric. II*, *Pt.* 2, *M.* 30 (*Cal. p.* 412).]

---

110. *Signet Letter (Warrant) to the Keeper of the Privy Seal to make out a Warrant to the Chancellor for certain Letters Patent to be issued in due form* (26 *January*, 14 *Richard II*).

De par le Roy.

Trescher et bien ame. Come de nostre grace especiale eons grauntez a nostre ame vallet William Blythelowe, un de nos archers de la liveree de nostre corone, les gages de sys deniers le jour, a prendre annuelment a nostre Escheqer de Kermerdyn, par les mains de nostre Chamberleyn illeoques pur le temps esteant, a tout la vie du dit William, ou tan que nous eons autrement ordeignez pur son estat ; vous maundons que, par avys de nostre Counseill, faces faire sur cest nostre graunt noz Lettres de Warrant a nostre Chaunceller pur ent faire avoir au dit William noz Lettres Patentz desouz nostre Graund Seal, en due forme. Donne desouz nostre Signet, a nostre manoir de Wodestoke, le xxvj jour de Januar.

Macclesfeld.

[*Endorsed.*] A nostre trescher Clerc, mestre Esmond Stafford, Gardein de nostre Prive Seal.

[*T. of R. Warrants for Issue* (*Ser.* 1), *File* 1/6A.]

---

111. *Privy Seal Letter issued in accordance with the above warrant* (28 *May*, 14 *Richard II*).

Richard, par la grace de Dieu Roy d'Engleterre et de France et Seignur d'Irlande, a l'onurable piere en Dieu l'evesque de Wyncestre, nostre Chanceller, Saluz. Come, de nostre grace especiale, et pur le bon et agreable service quel nostre ame servant William Blithelowe nous ad fait et ferra, lui eons grantez d'estre un de valletz de la liveree de nostre corone, deinz la nombre des vynt et quatre archers de la dite liveree, pur terme de sa vie, preignant a nostre Eschequier sys deniers le jour par celle cause. Vous mandons que sur ce facez faire noz lettres desouz nostre grant seal en due forme. Don[ez] souz nostre Prive Seal, a Westministre, le xxviij jour de May, l'an de nostre regne, quatorzisme.

[*Chanc. Warr^{ts} etc.* (*Ser.* 1), *File* 525/7257.]

112. *Enrolment of Letters Patent issued in accordance with the above Privy Seal* (28 *May,* 14 *Richard II*).

Pro Willelmo Blithelowe. Rex, omnibus ad quos, etc., Salutem. Sciatis quod, de gratia nostra speciali, et pro bono et laudabili servicio quod dilectus serviens noster Willelmus Blithelowe nobis impendit et impendet infuturum, concessimus ei ad essendum unum vallettorum de liberata coroné nostré, infra numerum viginti et quatuor sagittariorum de liberata predicta, pro termino vité sué; percipiendo ad Scaccarium nostrum sex denarios per diem ex causa predicta. In cujus, etc. Teste Rege apud Westmonasterium, xxviij die Maii. *Per breve de Privato Sigillo.*

[*Patent Roll,* 14 *Ric. II, Pt.* 2, *M.* 8 (*Cal. p.* 420).]

---

113. *Privy Seal Writ* (*Warrant*) *to the Chancellor for the issue of certain Letters under the Great Seal in due form* (16 *October,* 22 *Edward III*).

Edwardus, *etc.* [*as in No.* 20], dilecto clerico nostro magistro Johanni de Offord, Decano Lincolnié, Cancellario nostro, Salutem. Cum, de gratia nostra speciali, concesserimus et licenciam dederimus, pro nobis et heredibus nostris, Kateriné qué fuit uxor Henrici Whisshe defuncti, qui de nobis tenuit in capite, quod ipsa maritare possit cuicunque voluerit, dum tamen ad fidem nostram existat; vobis mandamus quod eidem Kateriné litteras inde sub Magno Sigillo nostro, in forma debita, fieri faciatis. Data sub Privato Sigillo nostro, apud Westmonasterium, xvj die Octobris, anno regni nostri Anglié vicesimo secundo, et Francié nono.

[*Chanc. Warr^{ts} etc.* (*Ser.* 1), 334/19805, *cf. Patent Roll,* 16 *October,* 22 *Edw. III, Pt.* 3, *M.* 31 (*Cal. p.* 191).]

---

114. *Privy Seal Letter to the Chancellor for the issue of Letters Patent* (9 *June,* 2 *Edward IV*).

Memorandum quod xi die Junij anno, etc. secundo hoc breve liberatum fuit domino Cancellario Anglié, apud Westmonasterium, exequendum.

Edwarde, by the grace of God King of Englande and of Fraunce and lord of Irlande, to the reverent fader in God oure right trusty and welbeloved cousin George, bisshope of Excestre, our Chaunceller, gretyng. We late you wite that, for divers consideracions us moevyng, we of (*sic*) speciall grace have graunted unto our wel-beloved servaunt John Browne, rider of oure forest of Morff in our countee of Shrovesbury, for th' exercisyng and occupying of the same office, iiijd by the daye, for terme of his lyf, to be paied [*etc.*]; any acte [*etc.*] to the contrarie made notwithstanding. Wherefor we wol and charge you that, under oure Great Seale, ye doo make hereupon oure Letters Patentes in due fourme. Geven under oure Prive Seal, atte oure castell of Leycestre, the ixth daye of Juyne, the secunde yere of our reigne.

[*Chanc. Warr^{ts} etc. (Ser.* 1), *File* 791/977, *cf. Patent Roll*, 2 *Edw. IV*, *Pt.* 1, *M.* 10 (*Cal. p.* 191).]

---

115 a. *Privy Seal Letter to the Chancellor to prepare Letters Patent in due form according to the Draft enclosed herein* (12 *May*, 16 *Henry VI*).

Henri, *etc.* [*as in No.* 111]. A l'onurable piere en Dieu l'evesque de Bath, nostre Chanceller, Saluz. Nous volons et vous mandons que, selonc l'effet et purport d'une copie quelle nous vous envoions closee dedeins ycestes, faisants mencion d'une Marchée et trois Feires, lesqueux nous avons grauntez a nostre tres cher et tresame cousin, Johan, Sire de Beaumont, et a ses heirs, d'estre tenuz a ses manoirs de Hekington en le Countee de Lincoln et de Lughtburgh en le Countee de Leycestre, facez faire nos Lettres Patentes dessouz nostre Grand Seal en due forme.

Donne sous nostre Prive Seal, a nostre manoir de Kenyngton, le xij jour de Maij, l'an de nostre regne seszisme.

[*Chanc. Warr^{ts} etc. (Ser.* 1), *File* 712/4228.]

---

115 b. *Draft of Royal Charter enclosed in the above.*

Rex, universis et singulis archiepiscopis [*etc.*], Salutem. Sciatis quod nos, bonum et gratuitum servicium quod dilectus consanguineus noster Johannes Dominus de Bello Monte nobis ante hec tempora impendit, indiesque impendere non desistit, merito contemplantes, de gratia nostra speciali, consideratione servicii predicti, concessimus eidem Johanni quod ipse et heredes sui imperpetuum habeant unum mercatum [*etc.*] et duas ferias [*etc.*] ac etiam quandam aliam feriam [*etc.*] nisi mercatum illud et ferié illé sunt ad nocumentum [*etc.*]. Quare volumus [*etc.*]. Nisi [*etc.*], sicut predictum est. Hiis testibus [*etc.*]. Data [*etc.*].

Edmond.

116. *Writ of Privy Seal (Warrant) to the Chancellor to prepare Letters Patent in the following form* (25 *April,* 2 *Edward IV*).

Memorandum quod quarto die Maij, anno infrascripto, hoc breve liberatum fuit domino Cancellario Anglié, apud Westmonasterium, exequendum.

Edwardus, [*etc.*] [*as in No.* 20], Reverendo in Christo patri, dilecto et fideli consanguineo nostro Georgio, Exoniensi episcopo, Cancellario nostro, Salutem. Vobis mandamus quod, sub Magno Sigillo nostro, Litteras nostras Patentes fieri faciatis in forma sequenti.

Rex omnibus ballivis [*etc.*], Salutem. Sciatis quod, de gratia nostra speciali, perdonavimus, remisimus et relaxavimus, Ricardo Knotte [*etc.*], sectam pacis nostré qué ad nos versus ipsum Ricardum pertinet pro omnimodo prodicionibus [*etc.*] [*cf. No.* 67], per ipsum Ricardum ante datum predictum qualitercunque factis [*etc.*] et firmam pacem nostram ei inde concedimus. Ita tamen quod stet recto in curia nostra [*etc.*]. In cujus rei [*etc.*]. Datum nostro sub Privato Sigillo, apud Leycestriam, xxv die Aprilis, anno regni nostri secundo.

[*Chanc. Warrᵗˢ etc.* (*Ser.* 1), 791/909, *cf. Patent Roll,* 2 *Edw. IV, Pt.* 1, *M.* 17 (*Cal. p.* 185).]

117. *Privy Seal Bill (Latin) for the Issue of Letters Patent* (25 *July,* 17 *Edward III*).

Per Regem.

Cum dederimus et concesserimus dilecto clerico nostro Bartholomeo de Bourne Thesaurariam ecclesié Beati Petri Eboraci, vacantem et ad nostram donationem spectantem ratione alienationis advocationis predicté thesaurarié nuper sine licencia nostra facté, ut dicitur; vobis mandamus quod litteras sub Magno Sigillo nostro super hoc, in forma debita, fieri faciatis. Data sub Privato Sigillo nostro, apud Clarendon', vicesimo quinto die Julij, anno regni nostri Anglié decimo septimo, regni vero nostri Francié quarto.

[*Chanc. Warrᵗˢ etc.* (*Ser.* 1), 908/1, *cf. Patent Roll,* 17 *Edw. III, Pt.* 2, *M.* 33 (*Cal. p.* 109).]

118. *Privy Seal Bill (French) for the Issue of Letters Patent* (25 *July,* 17 *Edw. III*).

De par le Roi.

Nadgaires par noz Lettres Patentes grantasmes a Henri de la Panete la forestrie de Gaytscheles en Inglewode, a terme de sa vie, et puis nous, nient rementivez de cel grant, donasmes par noz semblables Lettres mesme la baillie a Adam de Brygthtone ; par qei vous mandons qe, veues leur Pàtentes, facez outre ce qe vous verrez qi soit affaire celle partie. Donne souz nostre Prive Seal, a Clarendon, le xxv jour de Juyl.

[*Chanc. Warr^{ts} etc.* (*Ser.* 1), 908/2, *cf. Patent Roll*, 19 *Edw. III, Pt.* 1, *M.* 21.]

---

119. *Sign Manual Warrant* (*Latin*) *for the Issue of Letters Patent* (13 *September*, 4 *Edward IV*).

Memorandum quod xv die Septembris, anno subscripto, ista billa liberata fuit domino Cancellario Anglié, apud Penley, exequenda.

E. R.

Per Regem.

Reverende in Christo pater, carissime consanguinee noster, Sciatis quod nos, pro certa pecunié summa, nobis per priorem et conventum Abbatié beaté Marié extra et prope muros civitatis nostré Eboraci pré manibus soluta, commisimus eisdem priori et conventui custodiam Abbatié predicté, per mortem boné memorié Johannis Cotingham, ultimi Abbatis loci illius, vacantis et in manu nostra existentis, habendum [*etc.*] absque aliquo inde nobis reddendo seu compoto faciendo ; salvis nobis et heredibus nostris feodis militum [*etc.*] ad Abbatiam predictam pertinentibus qué tempore vacacionis accidere contigerint. Et ideo vobis mandamus quatenus, sub Magno Sigillo nostro in custodia vestra existente, Litteras nostras super hoc, prout moris est, fieri faciatis in forma debita. Et hec Litteré nostré vobis erunt sufficiens inde Warantum. Datum nostro sub Signeto, in monasterio nostro de Reding, tercio-decimo die Septembris, anno regni nostri quarto.

Marpisfeld.

[*Chanc. Warr^{ts} etc.* (*Ser.* 1), 1378/20, *cf. Patent Roll*, 15 *September*, 4 *Edw. IV, Pt.* 1, *M.* 14 (*Cal. p.* 328).]

---

120. *Sign Manual Warrant* (*French*) *for the Issue of Letters Patent* (15 *November*, 13 *Richard II*).

De par le Roy.

Reverent pere en Dieu. Nous vous chargeons que vous bailliez nostre Grand Seel a un de noz feaux, cestassaver le Priour de Seint Johan, Piers Courtenay nostre Chamberlein, Nichel Sarnesfelde, ou a Edward Dalyngrugge, pour enseller un brief Patent et un autre

Clos, si mestier seit, de la tenour et sur la forme des lettres de nostre Grant Seel que vous mandez du proces par entre nos treschers et feaux le Comte de Salesbirs et Johan Montagu son fis, et parnez ariere nostre dit Seel en vostre garde. Et ce ne lessez. Donne a nostre manoir de Haverynge, souz le Signet de nostre compaigne la Roigne en absence de nostre, le xv jour de Novembre.

le Roy R.   S.

saunz departyr.

[*Public Record Office Museum, Pedestal No.* 5 (*Catalogue, p.* 47).]

---

121. *Sign Manual Warrant (English) for the Issue of the Great Seal* (2 *December*, 3 *Edward IV*).

R. E.   *By the King.*

Right reverend fadre in God, right trusti and entierly beloved cousin, we grete you welle. And for soo muche as we have been enfourmed that many indisposed personnes have of late secretly, by untrue feyned and subtile mayens, labored to provoke and excite simple people of oure Towne of Bristowe and cuntee therunto adjoynaunt to stirre and conspire meanes of commocions and insurrections, sewnyng ayenst oure honoure and estate, the comune wele of oure lande and oure lawes and peaixe. We therefore wol and desire you that, immediatly after the sight of thies, ye doo make oure commission of Oyer determyner directed to John Shipwarde, Maire of oure said town of Bristowe, Richard Cheek, one of oure Justices, Thomas Yong, oure serjiant at the lawe, William Canynges, William Godel, Philip Mede, William Howell, John Bagot, Thomas Kempson and William Spencer to th'entent that it may be proceded to the punicion of the said riottous personnes. And thies oure letters shall be unto you in that behalve suffisaunt Waraunt anenst us. Yeven under oure Signet, at oure Castel of Pountefret, the secunde day of Decembre.

Cosyn, yff ye thynke ye schuld have a warrant, thys our wryten that soffysse onto ye may have on made in dew forme. We pray you hyt ffayle not to be don.

[*Public Record Office Museum, Pedestal No.* 18. *Patent Roll,* 3 *Edw. IV, Part* 2, *M.* 11d (*Cal. p.* 139).]

---

122. *Sign Manual Warrant (Signed Bill) for the Issue of Letters Patent* (25 *February*, 1 *Edward IV*).

R. E.

Memorandum quod xxv die Februarii, anno regni Regis Edward quarti primo, hec Billa liberata fuit domino Cancellario, apud West-monasterium, exequenda.

Please it your Highnes to grant to your orator, John Thomson, viijl of ye pension of ye Priori of Monkenferley, to be perceptid to the sayd John, ȝerly, duryng his lyfe.

[*Chanc. Warr^{ts} etc. (Ser. 1), 1490/3759, cf. Patent Roll, 1 Edw. IV, Pt. 5, M. 21 (Cal. p. 139).*]

---

123. *Privy Seal Bill* (Fiat) *for the Issue of Letters Patent* (*Protection*) (8 *November*, 22 *Henry VI*).

Fiat protectio, cum clausula *Volumus*, pro Matheo de Gournay milite, qui in obsequium nostrum, in comitiva dilecti et fidelis consanguinei nostri Johannis marchionis Dorseté, locumtenentis nostri Acquitannié, ad partes transmarinas profecturus est, ibidem super salva custodia partium illarum moraturus ; per unum annum duratura. Data sub Privato Sigillo nostro, apud Westmonasterium, viij die Novembris, anno regni nostri vicesimo secundo.

[*Chanc. Warr^{ts} etc. (Ser. 1), 1080/241.*]

---

124. *Signet Letter* (*French*) *for the Issue of Letters under the Privy Seal only* (21 *November*, 1—2 *Henry IV*).

De par le Roy.

Tres chier et bien ame, pour ce que nous suymes enformez que parentre nos tres chers et bienamez les dean et chanoignes de nostre College dedens nostre Chastiel de Wyndesore, et nostre treschier et foial le Sire de Seymour, et noz treschers en Dieu les Abbe et couvent de Lilleshulle y est certein discensions de et sur le patronage de l'eglise de Northmolton en contee de Devenshire ; et nous ont suppliez aucunes de les dites parties q'ils pourront demonstrer devant nostre conseil les evidences touchant l'avoeson susdit. Si nous volons et vous mandons que, desoubz nostre Prive Seel, vous facez sur ce faire noz lettres en due forme a chescun de les dictes parties pour estre ovec leurs remembrances et evidences devant nostre conseil au tiel jour et lieu come de l'avys de mesme nostre conseil vous semblera estre resonable.

Et autres nos lettres desoubz nostre dit Prive Seel facez estre faites au reverent pere en Dieu l'esvesque de Wincestre, que toute ce que uncore est aderiere et a nous due dedens sa diocise d'une dysme jadys y grantee a nostre tres cher sire et cousin Richard, nadgairs Roy, nostre predecessour, mesme l'evesque face estre levez et paiez a nostre Tresorer a nostre oeps. Donne soubz nostre Signet, a nostre Chastiel de Hertford, le xxj jour de Novembre.

Soit fait lettre a l'evesque de Wircestre come dessus.

[*Endorsed.*] A nostre treschier et bieName clerc, maistre Richard Clifford, Gardein de nostre Prive Seel.

[*T. of R. Warrants etc. (Ser.* 1), 1/29.]

---

125. *Signet Letter (English) for the Issue of Letters under the Privy Seal only (20 November, 16 Edward IV).*

By the King.

Reverend fader in God, right trusty and welbeloved, forasmoche as we, of our special grace, in consideracion of the trew and faithful service whiche our welbeloved servant Robert Barker hath doon unto us, have yeven and graunted unto him the place of a felawe within our College called the Kinges Halle in our universite of Cambrige whiche ther shall next happen to be voyd by dethe, resignacion, or any other wise; to have and enjoy the same place to the said Robert, with all rights and dewtees therto apperteynyng, for terme of his lif; we wol and charge you that under our Prive Sele, being in your warde, ye do make our letters direct unto the maister of our said College, and in his absence to his substitute there, commaunding them by the same that into the forsaid place whiche there shal next voyde, withalle the said rights and deutes to the same belonging, they receyve and admitte the said Robert without delay; and theese our Letters shalbe your Warrant.

Yeven under our Signet at our paleis of Westminster the xxth day of Novembre the xvj yere of our reigne.

Robyns.

[*Endorsed.*] To the right reverend fader in God our right trusti and welbeloved the bisshop of Rowchestre, keper of our Prive Sele.

[*T. of R. Warrants etc. (Ser.* 1), 43/2226.]

---

126. *Sign Manual Warrant (Signed Bill) for the Issue of Letters of Privy Seal only* (15 *March, 2 Edward IV*).

R. E.

To the Kyng our liege lord,

Humylly besechyth your Heynesse your power scolar and oratour John Saucer to grante unto him, under your Letterys of Privat Seale, in dew forme to be made to the mastyr of the Kyngges Halle of Cambrygge, to be a felawe, and so to be admitted in the place of Thomas Cappys, a felaw of the same, the whyche levyt his place to that intent that your sayd supplyant may enjoy the same; whyth all manner of comoditeys and profettes to a felaw of the same Hall belonggyng and accustumyd. And he shall pray God for your most nobyll and ryall astatte. *Yeven, etc., atte Stamford, the xv day of Marche, the secunde yere of our reigne.*

[*T. of R. Warrants for Issues (Ser.* 1), 90/15.]

---

127. *Warrant of the Duke of Gloucester as Guardian of England, for the Issue of Letters Patent* (1418—22).

Le Duc de Gloucestre, Gardein d'Engleterre.

Reverend pere en Dieu, nostre trescher et tresentierement biename. Nous volons, a l'instance et priere du tres reverend pere en Dieu l'erchevesque d'Everwike, que a son cousin Henri Bowet, archediakne de Richemonde, qui desire grandement d'exercer son estudie a l'universitee de Boloigne pour greindre honour et meilleur apris, veuillez faire avoir un brief de passage soubz le Grant Seal en due forme, par force duquel brief il purra seurement passer, ovec sept homes a cheval en sa compaignie, hors du roialme pardevers la dite universitee, sans destourbance ou empeschement. Donne soubz nostre Signet, a Everwik, le viiime jour d'Aoust.

[*Endorsed.*] Au reverend pere en Dieu, nostre trescher et tres entierement bien ame l'evesque de Duresme, chancellier d'Engleterre.

[*Chanc. Warr^{ts} etc (Ser.* 1), 1537/4.]

(b) Later Procedure

(i) NORMAL PROCEDURE CONNECTED WITH THE ISSUE OF LETTERS PATENT UNDER THE GREAT SEAL SUBSEQUENT TO THE YEAR 1535.

1. *Memorandum by the Secretary of State of the Receipt of a Petition for Letters Patent* (1661).

"The Inhabitants of Conecticut in New England desire a charter to incorporate them."

[*S. P. Colonial* XVI. *No.* 13.]

---

2. *The Petition for Letters Patent (of Incorporation).*

To the high and mighty monarch Charles the Second, by the grace of God King of England, Scotland, France and Ireland, etc.

The humble Petition of John Winthrop in the name and behalfe of the Colony of Conecticut in New England.

Sheweth: That whereas your Peticioners for many yeares past since their possession and inhabiting the more westerly and inland parts of that Wilderness (of which there was lately an account presented to your Ma^ty in their humble address) have not had any opportunity, by reason of the calamities of the late sad times, to seek for and obtain such Letters Patents from your most excellent Ma^ty, their Soveraigne Lord and King, which might assure them of such liberties, priviledges and authorities as might incourage them to goe on through all difficultys and expences in soe great a worke of Plantacion [*etc.*] and whereas besides much that hath been expended by their Fathers [*etc.*], they have alsoe layd out a very Considerable summe [*etc.*]. May it therefore please your most excellent Ma^ty to grant and confirme to your Peticioners, your loyall Subjects of your said Colony of Conecticut, all and singular like powres, jurisdiccions, rights, liberties and privileges for your Peticioners' Plantacions, bounded [*etc.*], as were formerly granted to the other Plantacions of New England by your Maties Royall predecessors; to be held and enjoyed immediately from and under your most excellent Ma^ty by vertue of a Charter to be granted to your Peticioners; and that alsoe John Mason [*etc.*], being principall persons of the said Colony, bee those to whom the said liberties and priviledges be first granted on the behalfe of themselves and the said Colony.

[*S. P. Col.* XVI. *No.* 17.]

3. *Reference of the Petition to the Law Officers of the Crown.*

At the Court at Whitehall, the 12th of February, 1662.

His Matie is gratiously pleased to referre this Peticion to the consideracion of Mr Attorney Generall who is to advise and certifie what Powers, Priviledges, Estate and Interests hee thinkes fit for his Matie to grant unto the Peticioners.

Edw. Nicholas.

[*Ibid. (in dorso).*]

---

4. *Report of the Law Officers on the above Petition.*

May it please your most excellent Ma^ty.

In obedience to your Maties Refference upon this Peticion, I have considered thereof and of the papers hereunto annexed, and doe humbly conceave the powers therein conteyned may be granted as is desired, saving onely as to the freedome from Customes, the consideracion whereof I humbly conceave to be proper for the Lord Treasurer or others to whom the care of your Maties revenew belongs. All which I humbly submitt, *etc.*

G. Palmer.

[ ]¹ Feb. 1661.

[*Ibid. (in dorso).*]

---

5. *Docquet of the Sign Manual Warrant for a King's Bill to be prepared in due form.*

A graunte to incorporate Jn. Winthrop, John Mason and others, beinge the principall persons interested in the Colonye of Conecticutt in Newe England, into a Bodye politique, by the name of Governour and Companye of the English Colonye of Conecticutt in New England in America; graunting unto them and their successors such part of his Majesty's dominions there, and such powers and priviledges and advantages, as was directed to bee graunted by Warrant under the Signe Manuall, subscribed by Mr Attorney, procured by Secretary Nicholas.

Dated 28 Feb. 1662.

[*S. P. Dom. Docquets, Bundle 21, fo. 61. A draft of the Warrant is in S. P. Col. XVI. No. 27, and it is entered in the Warrant Book for April (S. P. Dom. Entry Bk., Vol. 5, fo. 255).*]

---

¹ The date is mutilated in the MS.

6. King's Bill for the same under the Sign Manual as an authority for the Preparation of Letters Patent in due form: with a Docquet (dated 5 April, 1662) at the foot (in the same form as No. 5 above) and the memorandum: *Expedita apud Westmonasterium decimo quarto die Aprilis anno regni Regis Caroli Secundi decimo quarto.*

[*H. O. Signed Bills, April,* 1662.]

---

7. (*a*) Signet Bill for the same (a transcript of No. 6).
[*Original deposited with the Keeper of the Privy Seal.*]

(*b*) Docquet (in the same words as No. 5).
[*Signet Office Docquet Book, April* 1662.]

---

8. (*a*) Privy Seal Writ for the same (a transcript of No. 6) counter-signed by S. Pepys, deputy of the Earl of Sandwich, with the date, 21 April 1662, filled in, with the memorandum: *quod vicesimo tercio die Aprilis anno regni Regis Caroli Secundi* 14°, *Billa ista deliberata fuit domino Cancellario Angliè apud Westmonasterium exequenda,* and at the foot the Chancellor's "*Recepi* 23 Apr. 1662."

[*Chanc. Warr^ts etc. (Ser.* 2), *April* 1662.]

(*b*) Privy Seal Docquet (in the same words as No. 5).
[*Privy Seal Docquet Book, April* 1662.]

---

9. (*a*) Letters Patent under the Great Seal, dated 23 April 1662 (in the same words as No. 6, with the Protocols completed).
[*Original despatched to the grantees: early copies in S. P. Col.* XVI. 46 *and* 47.]

(*b*) Enrolment of the above.
[*Patent Roll,* 14 *Chas. II, Part* 11, *No.* 10.]

(*c*) Patent Office Docquet (in the same words as No. 5).
[*Patent Office Docquet Bk. Vol.* 7, *fo.* 102 *d.*]

(ii) SPECIAL PROCEDURE FOR THE ISSUE OF LETTERS PATENT BY
IMMEDIATE WARRANT[1].

1. *Sign Manual Warrant for the preparation of a King's Bill for the purpose of a* Congé d'Élire.

Our will and pleasure is y^t you forthwith prepare a Bill for Our Royall Signature conteyning a *Congé d'eslire* directed to ye Dean and Chapter of Chester to impower them to elect a Bishop for that see, being void by the death of Dr Walton their late Diocesan. And our further pleasure is that you prepare a letter for Our Royal Signature directed to the dean and chapter recommending Dr Henry Herne, Dean of Ely, to be by them elected Bishop of ye Diocess. And for, etc. Given ye 3rd December, 1661.

To the Clarke of ye Signett attending.

[*S. P. Dom. Entry Bk. Vol. 6, fol.* 10.]

---

2. *Docquet of the* Congé d'Élire *and* Letter Recommendatory *prepared as above directed.*

January 23^d, 1661.

A *Congé d'eslire* to the Deane and Chapter of Chester to Elect a Bishop of that Sea, the same being void by the Death of Dr Walton, late Bisshop of that Diocesse: Subscribed by Mr Bere, upon signification of his Ma^{ts} pleasure under the Signe Manuall, procured by Mr Sec^{ry} Nicholas.

A Letter to the Deane and Chapter of Chester recommending Dr Ferne to bee Elected Bishopp of that Sea, the same being nowe voyd by the death of the late Bishopp there; procured upon significacon of his Ma^{ts} pleasure under the Signe Manuall, procured by Mr Sec^{ry} Nicholas.

[*S. P. Docquets, Bundle* 21.]

---

3. *King's Bill prepared according to the above direction and minuted to pass as an Immediate Warrant.*

M^d quod septimo die Aprilis, anno Regis Caroli Secundi quarto decimo, istud breve deliberatum fuit domino Cancellario Anglié apud Westmonasterium, in debita juris forma exequendum.

Carolus R.

Rex, etc. Dilecto nobis in Christo Decano et Capitulo Ecclesié

---

[1] The appointment of Law Officers, etc. was effected by another form of Immediate Warrant known as a Signed Bill.

Catholicé Cestrié, Salutem. Ex parte vestra nobis est humiliter supplicatum ut, cum Ecclesia predicta post mortem naturalem ultimi Episcopi ejusdem jam vacans et pastoris sit solatio destituta, alium vobis eligendum in Episcopum et Pastorem licentiam nostram fundatoriam vobis concedere dignaremur. Nos precibus vestris in hac parte cum favore inclinantes, alium vobis duximus concedendum, rogantes ac in fide et dilectione quibus nobis tenemini precipientes quod talem vobis elegatis in Episcopum et Pastorem qui Deo devotus nobisque et regno nostro utilis et fidelis existat. In cujus rei, etc.

Ex parte **W. Trumbull.**

This conteyneth your Majestie's Congé d'eslire unto the Deane and Chapter of Chester for electinge a Bishop for that See voide by the death of the last Bishop thereof.
Signified to be your Majestie's pleasure
under your Signe Manuall.

W. Trumbull.

Recepi 7 April 1662.

[Endorsed.]

Charles R.

Our will and pleasure is that this passe by Immediate Warrant.
Entered at the Signett Office the 4th of Aprill, 1662.

W. Trumbull.

Entered at the Privy Seale Office the 5th of April, 1662.

J. O. Cattle.

[*Chanc. Warr*ᵗˢ *etc.* (*Ser.* 2), *April* 1661.]

---

4. *Caveat, or protest, entred to delay the issue of Letters Patent in consideration of conflicting interests*[1].

A Caveat that no grant passe, to any person, of the Town Clerk's place of Leeds, in Yorkshire, till notice be given to Castilian Morris, of Leeds, the present Towne Clerke, or to Edward Copley, Esqʳ, at his chambers in Gray's inn, in Holborn Court.

9th March, 1688/9.

[*S. P. Dom. Entry Bk.* 73, *fo.* 3.]

---

[1] In another aspect the *Caveat* may be regarded as a Secretarial instrument (below, p. 149), or even as a Departmental Record (below, p. 164), since an independent series of these 'protests' is preserved in the Treasury Records.

3. DEPARTMENTAL WARRANTS FOR THE ISSUE OF THE GREAT SEAL

Warrants of a Departmental nature seem to have been filed amongst the Chancery 'Warrants for Issue,' and from an early period were accepted as a sufficient authority for the issue of Letters Patent which are stated to have been 'procured' by the respective Household officers (*per billam Thesaurarii Angliæ*, etc.).

Thus a Warrant might be submitted under the seal of the Lord Treasurer to the Lord Chancellor for the appointment of a revenue officer (No. 129), being presumably a matter within the jurisdiction of the former official. The personal seal was affixed on the face of the Warrant 'en placard,' and was sometimes secured by a slit in the parchment or by other devices. The Privy Seal was affixed on the dorse of the Warrant.

Similarly, Departmental Warrants were issued by the Treasurer of the Household to the Clerk of the Crown in Chancery (No. 130) in favour of a royal purveyor, to whom a Writ of Assistance had been granted since the 13th century. It will be seen that the language of this early Warrant is French, and the form of execution is noticeable. The later Writ of Assistance printed below (No. 131) is in Latin and is probably a draft submitted for expedition by the Chancery.

Amongst the earliest of such Departmental Warrants are those issued by the Chief Butler of England for the appointment of deputies to collect the dues comprised under the head of Butlerage (No. 128), and similar 'deputations' were made from an early date by the King's Ulnager (No. 132).

---

128. *Warrant of the King's Butler for the appointment of a Deputy to collect the Butlerage in the Port of London* (15 *Edward III*).

Reymundus Seguyn, Pincerna domini Regis, deputat sub se, in portu Londonié, Ricardum le Chaucer, ad ea qué ad officium Pincernarié pertinent, ac etiam ad colligendum et recipiendum, nomine suo, Custumam duorum solidorum de quolibet dolo vini per mercatores extraneos et alienigenos in dicto portu adductos, et duodecim denarios de qualibet pipa vini ; pro quo petit idem Reymundus quod fiant Commissiones ad dicta officia, nomine suo, in dicto portu exercendum et faciendum, quamdiu sibi placuerit.

L. S.

[*Chanc. Warr^ts etc. (Ser.* 1), *File* 1644/2.]

---

129. *Warrant of the Treasurer of England for the appointment of a Weigher in the Port of Boston* (9 *Edward III*).

Memorandum quod xxvj die Augusti, anno Regis Edwardii iij^tii post conquestum Anglié ix°, ista billa liberata fuit domino Cancellario Anglié, apud Westmonasterium, exequenda.

Fiant literé Domini Regis patentes ad constituendum Johannem Boston' tronatorem Tronagii et Pesagii in portu villé de Boston' et in singulis portubus et locis eidem portui adjacentibus. Habendum et occupandum officium illud quamdiu Regi placuerit ; percipiendo in officio illo feoda et vadia consueta, loco Nicholai de la Hay.

Domino Cancellario Anglié   *L. S.*   per Thesaurarium Anglié.

[*Chanc. Warr^ts etc. (Ser.* 1), *File* 1559/16; *cf. Patent Roll,* 9 *Edw. IV,*
  Pt. 1, *M.* 2 (*Cal. p.* 166).]

---

130. *Warrant of the Treasurer of the Household for a Commission for Purveyance to a yeoman of the Acatry* (4 *April,* 22 *Richard II*).

Soit fait comission an noum de Johan Baker, vallet, ordeignez pour faire Pourveance des boefs et moutons, pessons, et autres vitails et necessaries appurtenantz al office del Achat [*etc.*] : a durer pour dymy an. Escrit a Westmester, le quart jour de Aprille, l'an du regne nostre sieur le Roy Richard, second puis le Conquest, vint et secundo.

Johan Carpe, Tresorer de l'Oustiell nostre sieur le Roy.

L. S.

A James Byllyngsforde, clerk de la Corone.

[*Chanc. Warr^ts etc. (Ser.* 1), *File* 1648/4.]

---

131. *Warrant (Draft Signed Bill) by the Treasurer of the House-hold for a Commission for Purveyance* (25 *January*, 26 *Henry VI*).

Henricus, *etc.* [*as in No.* 20], dilecto sibi Thomé Strethend, Salutem. Scias quod assignavimus te ad pisces marinos pro expensis hospicii nostri, ubicunque inveniri poterint, tam infra libertates quam extra, feodo ecclesié dumtaxat excepto, pro denariis nostris in hac parte prompte et rationabiliter solvendis, capiendos et providendos. Et ideo tibi precipimus quod circa premissa diligenter intendas, et ea facias et exequaris in forma predicta. Proviso semper quod tu quic-quam contra formam Statutorum de hujusmodi provisionibus ante hec tempora editorum, colore presentis Commissionis nostré, non attemptes quovis modo. Damus autem universis et singulis vice-comitibus, majoribus, ballivis, constabulariis, ministris, ac aliis fidelibus et subditis nostris, tam infra libertates quam extra, tenore presentium firmiter in mandatis, quod tibi in executione premissorum intendentes sint, auxiliantes et assistentes in omnibus, prout decet. In cujus rei testimonium has Litteras nostras fieri fecimus Patentes, usque sextum decimum diem Julii, proximo futurum duraturas. Teste me ipso, apud Westmonasterium, xxv die Januarii, anno regni nostri vicesimo sexto. *Per billum Thesaurarii Hospicii ipsius Regis.*

Sturgeon.

[*Chanc. Warr^{ts} for Issues* (*Ser.* 1), *File* 1655 (*last document*), *Patent Roll,* 27 *Hen. VI, Pt.* 2, *M.* 28.]

---

132. *Warrant of the King's Ulnager for the appointment of a Deputy in the County of Bucks.* (16 *April,* 3 *Richard II*).

Willelmus Hervy, Ulnetor domini Regis per totum regnum, con-stituit et deputavit sub se, loco suo, Johannem Bedeford ad officium Ulnagii in comitatu Buckinghamscira, ad dictum officium excercen-dum. In cujus rei testimonium, presentibus sigillum suum apposuit.

L. S.

[*Chanc. Warr^{ts} etc.* (*Ser.* 1), *File* 1659/2; *cf. Patent Roll,* 3 *Ric. II, Pt.* 2, *M.* 3 (*Cal. p.* 430).]

III. DEPARTMENTAL INSTRUMENTS

These diplomatic documents differ from the two preceding classes inasmuch as, though executed under a departmental or personal seal, they were not merely subsidiary to the Great Seal itself. On the other hand they cannot be regarded as purely private Deeds. In some respects these instruments approach most nearly to the nature of the semi-official instruments cited below (Nos. 141—154), especially in the case of the Coket (No. 134), which was issued officially for use at the Ports. This is perhaps the best-known type of an interesting group of departmental seals, many early specimens of which have been fortunately preserved[1]. The departmental certificate, always known as the Debenture, has, through its connexion with the Wardrobe, to some extent the force of a Departmental Warrant, though it is not connected with the issue of the Great Seal. The form resembles that of a Privy Seal Bill, or the departmental memoranda on the Fine Rolls. In its connexion with the later "spending departments," the modern Debenture is associated with the class of Accounts or Vouchers (cf. No. 143). The execution of this instrument resembles that of the Departmental Warrant. By far the most extensive series of these official Certificates is connected with proceedings under the Edwardian Statutes of Merchants (11 Edw. I, 13 Edw. I (3)) and of the Staple (27 Edw. III (2) c. 9). These Certificates or Reports (Nos. 135—137) were made to the Chancery and were filed there.

The Licenses or Certificates of the Ecclesiastical Courts known as 'Dispensations' (No. 138) and 'Significavits' (No. 139) are regarded here as departmental instruments, because in the case of the former the subject-matter was regarded, even after the Reformation, as pertaining to the province of the primate in the place of the Pope, though a confirmation by royal Letters Patent was stipulated. These instruments were enrolled in the Chancery (Dispensation Rolls). The 'Significavit,' on the other hand, though an official

---

[1] British Museum *Catalogue* of Seals and *Matrices* exhibited. Other well-known types are connected with the Ulnage and Subsidy of Cloths and the inland Passes issued by the Commissioners for executing the Statutes of Labourers.

certificate rather than a personal petition (cf. No. 87), is of a decidedly professional character. The procedure in such cases was, however, amended by 53 Geo. III, c. 127.

Another quasi-departmental instrument, which is of common occurrence since the 15th century, is the Certificate or Diploma (with a professional Preamble and notarial Address) of an Officer at Arms (No. 140), usually known as a 'Grant of Arms.' This, like the Dispensation, was properly a license concurrent with Letters Patent. Chancery Warrants to procure such royal grants occur from the middle of the 15th century, the feature of these instruments, whether royal or departmental, being the technical description of the arms which are usually tricked on the original.

---

133. *Certificate (Debenture) for payment in the Wardrobe of an allowance to Yeomen of the Household* (12 *June*, 34 *Edward III*).

Debentur in Garderoba domini Regis Edwardi, tertii post conquestum, Johanni Northe et Roberto Ferrour, valletis Hospicii ipsius domini Regis, pro robis et calciatura suis, per compotum secum factum Londonié, xij die Junij, anno regni domini nostri Regis supradicti tricesimo quarto.

Triginta et sex solidos.

Farlee.   *L. S. Persolvitur, ut paret in pelle x die Junii anno xxxvi^{to}.*

[*Public Record Office Museum, Case H, No.* 91.]

---

134. *Letters Patent under the Coket Seal certifying the receipt of certain advances* (ex mutuo[1]) *over and above the Customs dues payable at the Port of Boston and promising repayment of the same at a certain date* (19 *October*, 1 *Edward III*).

Edwardus, *etc.* [*as in No.* 26], omnibus ad quos presentes Litteré pervenerint, Salutem. Sciatis quod de tribus saccis duodecim petris lané, de bonis Johannis Fox in portu de Sancto Botulpho debite custumatis et in navi Petri Raven carcatis, extra regnum nostrum educendis, recepimus ab eodem Johanne, ex mutuo, per manus

---

[1] Cf. Hall, *Hist. of the Customs Revenue*, II. 183.

Roberti But[te] et Johannis de Multone, collectorum et custodum custumé nostré in portu predicto, quatuor marcas duodecim solidos et decem denarios sterlingorum, videlicet de quolibet sacco lané predicté unam marcam, ultra debitam custumam nobis inde persolutam. De quo quidem mutuo, ad festum Sancti Michaelis anno Gracié millesimo ccc^{mo} vicesimo nono, predicto Johanni satisfieri faciemus. In cujus rei testimonium, has Litteras nostras fieri fecimus Patentes, sigillo nostro quod dicitur Coket signatas[1]. Daté apud Sanctum Botolphum, nonodecimo die Octobris, anno regni nostri primo.

[*Original Bond in O. L. P. Bundle* 5.]

135. *Certificate of the Deputy Clerks of the Recognizances at Norwich notifying the default of a certain debtor under the Statutes Merchant and requesting that Process may issue in accordance with those Statutes* (20 *October*, 43 *Edward III*).

Venerabili viro, ac domino illustri, domini Regis Anglié cancellario, sui Thomas de Bumpsted et Edmundus Rose, clerici ad recogniciones debitorum apud Norwicum accipiendas deputati, salutem cum omni reverencia et honore. Reverendé dominacioni vestré significamus, per presentes, quod decimo die Junii, anno regni domini Regis nunc tricesimo septimo, David de Strabolgi, comes Atcholl[ie], coram Rogero Verly et me prefato Edmundo, nuper ad recogniciones debitorum in eadem civitate accipiendas deputatis, recognovit se debere Johanni de Welburne de Norwico, Taverner del Cokrowe, jam defuncto, centum et quadraginta marcas quas ei solvisse debuit ad festum Pasché tunc proximo futurum, iuxta formam statuti apud Actonburnell et Westmonasterium editi et provisi. Et quia predictus David terminum sué solucionis non observavit, ut dicitur, reverendé dominacioni vestré supplicamus quatenus scribere jubeatis vicecomiti Norfolkié quod eundem David ad solucionem dicti debiti, Kateriné, que fuit uxor ejusdem Johannis de Welburne, Willelmo de Brook, Johanni de Corpesty, Willelmo de Welburne et Johanni Bacon, capellano, executoribus testamenti ejusdem Johannis defuncti, faciendam, juxta formam statuti predicti, compellat. Data apud Norwicum, xx die Octobris, anno regni ejusdem domini Regis nunc quadragesimo tercio.

In cujus rei testimonium, sigillum Officii de Recognicionibus debitorum presentibus est appensum[2].

[Endorsed.] *Norfolkia. Coram justiciariis de Banco, retornandum in xv^a Pasché.*

[*Chanc. Files (New Series), No.* 1435 (*in fine*).]

[1] The Seal is pendant on a strip inscribed on the face, *Pro Johanne Fox* and on the dorse [*iiij*] *Marcs xij solidi x d. Examinatur.*
[2] The Seal was attached to a strip but is now missing.

136. *Certificate of the Mayor of the Staple of Norwich notifying the default of a debtor under a recognizance and requesting that Process may issue according to the Statute* (10 *July*, 43 *Edward III*).

Venerabili viro ac domino illustri, Regis Anglié Cancellario, suus Bartholomeus de Appelyerd, major Stapulé civitatis Norwici ad recogniciones debitorum in eadem Stapula accipiendas deputatus, salutem, cum reverencia et honore. Reverendé dominacioni vestré significo quod xxx° die Junii, anno regni domini Regis nunc xl primo, Willelmus Marchal de Norwico, corczour, coram me recognovit se debere domino Thomé de Wentbrigge, parsoné ecclesié de Possewyke, decem marcas argenti, unde ei solvisse debuit quinque marcas ad festum Natalis Domini, tunc proxime futurum, et quinque marcas ad festum Annunciacionis Beaté Marié Virginis, tunc proxime sequens, juxta formam ordinacionum Stapulé Anglié pro huiusmodi debito recuperando in hac parte editarum et provisarum. Et quia predictus Willelmus terminos sué solucionis non observavit, ut dicitur, reverendé dominacioni vestré supplico quatenus scribere jubeatis vice-comiti Norfolkié et Suffolkié quod eundem Willelmum ad solucio-nem dicti debiti eidem domino Thomé faciendam, juxta formam ordinacionum Stapulé predicté, compellat. Data apud Norwicum in Stapula ibidem, x° die Julii, anno regni ejusdem domini Regis quadra-gesimo tercio.

[Endorsed.] *Norfolkia et Suffolkia. In Cancellaria. In quindena Pasché.*

[*Chanc. Files (New Series), No.* 1435 (*in fine*).]

---

137. *Certificate of the Mayor and Clerk of the Recognizances for the City of Coventry of a default as above* (20 *March*, 18 *George II*).

To the most excellent Prince, our Sovereign Lord George the Second, etc. Your humble and faithfull subjects and orators...present Mayor of your city of Coventry and...your Clerk assigned to take all Recognizances of Debts there for merchants and others, do certify unto your Chancery that upon the 10th day of October in the first year of your Majestie's reign...of the City of Coventry [*etc.*] came before...at that time Mayor [*etc.*] and...then your Majestie's clerk [*etc.*] and ac-knowledged to owe to...the sum of £40 [*etc.*] to be paid to the said...at the feast of the Annunciation [*etc.*] next ensuing [*etc.*] according to the form of the Statutes made and provided in the 11th and 13th years of the reign of King Edward I [*etc.*]. And we do further certify [*other defaults follow*]...

In witness whereof the Seales of our said Offices[1] are hereunto putt, at the City aforesaid, this 20th day of March in the 18th year [*etc.*], and in the year of our Lord 1744.

L. S.

[*Petty Bag, Cursitors' Records, Bundle* 1.]

[1] Official Seal (obv.) and Clerical Counter-seal (rev.).

138. *Dispensation (Faculty) for a Clerk in Holy Orders to accept a benefice vacant by the resignation of his father in his favour, with Ratification of the same by Royal Letters Patent* (5—6 *November,* 1595).

Dispensatio pro Midgeley. Johannes, providencia divina Cantuariensis archiepiscopus, tocius Anglié Primas et Metropolitanus, ad infrascripta authoritate Parliamenti Anglié legitime fulcitus, dilecto nobis in Christo Josepho Midgeley, clerico, in artibus magistro, et canonice admisso, salutem et gratiam. Exhibita nobis ex parte tua peticio continebat quod cum Ricardus Midgeley, pater tuus, ex cujus corpore, ut asseris, ex legitimo matrimonio procreatus existis, vicariam perpetuam ecclesié parochialis de Rachedall, diocesis Cestriensis, legitime obtentam, per annos aliquot retinuit, ac postmodum, ob certas causas, eandem vicariam in manibus Ordinarii dimisit ac resignavit, ut tibi genitori tuo in predicto beneficio liceat succedere dignaremur : Nos huic peticioni tué, satis honesté, multis de causis coram nobis expositis favorabiliter inclinati, tecum, ut predictam vicariam ecclesié parochialis de Rachedall, diocesis Cestrensis predicté, obtinere, et in eadem canonice institui ac investiri, ac in realem et actualem ejusdem possessionem induci, cum suis juribus, membris et pertinenciis universis, non obstante quod predictus genitor tuus proxime et immediate fuerit ejusdem ecclesié vicarius, auctoritate predicta, quantum in nobis est et jura regni patiuntur, tenore presencium graciose Dispensamus tibique pariter indulgemus, quibuscunque canonicis constitucionibus non obstantibus. Volumus etiam ut hé litteré tibi non proficiant nisi per Litteras Patentes regié majestatis debite fuerint confirmaté. Data sub sigillo ad Facultates, primo die mensis Novembris, anno domini millesimo quingesimo nonagesimo quinto, et nostré translationis anno decimo tercio.

Regina, etc. Omnibus ad quos, etc. Inspeximus quasdam Litteras Dispensacionis, presentibus annexas, quas, et singula in eis contenta, juxta quendam Actum, inde in Parliamento domini Henrici nuper Regis Anglié octavi, patris nostri, precharissimi editum, ratificavimus, approbavimus et confirmavimus, ac pro nobis, heredibus et successoribus nostris, ratificamus, approbamus et confirmamus per presentes. Ita quod Josephus Midgeley, clericus et in artibus magister, in dictis Litteris nominatus, omnibus et singulis in eisdem specificatis uti, frui et potiri valeat et possit, libere et quiete, impune et licite, secundum vim, formam et effectum earundem, absque impedimento quocunque. Eo quod expressa mencio [*etc.*] aut aliquo statuto [*etc.*] aut aliqua alia re [*etc.*]. In cujus rei, etc. Teste Regina, apud Westmonasterium, sexto die Novembris, anno predicto.

[*Chanc. Dispensation Roll,* 37 *Eliz.*]

139. *Certificate of the Archbishop of York signifying, as by law required, that an excommunicate is contumacious and invoking the secular arm according to the custom of the realm* (23 *June*, 1750).

To his most excellent Majesty and Sovereign Lord, George the Second, by the grace of God of Great Britain, France and Ireland, King, Defender of the Faith and so forth; Mathew by Divine Providence Archbishop of York [*etc.*]. Whereas the worshipful [*etc.*] officer of the [*etc.*], Archdeacon of the Archdeaconry of Nottingham [*etc.*] within our Cathedral [*etc.*], by his Letters, under the seal of the said Archdeaconry, bearing d[ate the] 19th June now instant, hath notified, signified and certified unto us :—That Sarah Roberts, the wife of Edward Roberts of the parish of Worksop, within the said Archdeaconry [*etc.*], hath been duly denounced excommunicate in the parish church of Worksop aforesaid for her contumacy and manifest contempt of the law and jurisdiction ecclesiastical [*etc.*]. In which sentence of excommunication the said Sarah Roberts hath stood and continued above the space of forty days, and doth still contumaciously stand, continue and persevere, contemning the keys of the Church. And whereas our Holy Mother the Church hath no further power in this case to repress the obstinacy and contempt of the said Sarah Roberts, the said official hath implored our aid and the assistance of our pastoral office, that we would Signify unto your most excellent Majesty (as the law requires) the state of the premises. We therefore humbly implore and intreat, according to the custom laudably observed within this realm, that your Majesty would vouchsafe to command the body of the said Sarah Roberts to be taken and imprisoned. That so those whom the fear of God does not restrain from evil, the severity of the Law may at length repress. And may the most High and Omnipotent Almighty preserve Your Majesty in safety. Given at York under the seal of our Office, 23 June, 1750.

Extracted by Jno. Shaw. *By Decree of Robt. Jubb,*
of Court Deputy Register.

[*Petty Bag, Cursitors' Records, Bundle* 1.]

---

140. *Official Diploma* (*Grant of Arms*) *by a Herald and King of Arms, by virtue of the authority given to him in his Office by the Crown* (14 *July*, 2 *Edward VI*).

To all nobles and gentles these present lettres readinge, hearinge and seinge, Thomas Hawley, alias Clarencieulx princypall heraulde and kynge of Armes of the southe East and West parties of this Realme of Englande, from the Ryver of the Trent southwarde, sendeth due and humble commendation and gretinge. Equyte willeth and reasone ordeyneth that men, vertuouse and of noble courage, be by their merites and good renowne rewarded, not onelye their parsons in this mortall lyff so breeff and transytorye, but allso after theim those that shalbe of their bodies discended, to be in all places of honour with other nobles and gentles accepted, reputed and taken by certeyn ensignes and demonstrations of honour and nobles[se], that is to saye, blason, helme and tymbre ; to th'ende that, by their ensamples, other may the more enforce theim selves to have perseveraunce to use their dayes in feates of armes and warkes vertuouse, to gett the renowne of auncyent nobles in their lyves and posteryties. And therefore I Clarencieulx Kynge of Armes, as abovesaide, not onely by the commen renowne, but also by the reporte and witnesse of dyvers worthie to be taken of worde and credence, am advertysed and en-fourmed that Robert Knyght of Bromley in the Countye of Kent, gentilman, is discended of a howse undefamed, and hath of longe tyme used himself so honestlye and discretelye so that he hath well deserved to be in all placys of honour admytted, nombred and taken in the companye of other nobles and gentles. And for the remem-braunce of the same, by the vertue, auctorytie and power attributed geven and graunted to me and to my Offyce of Clarencieulx Kinge of Armes by the Kynge our soveraigne lordes highnes by expressed wordes under his noble Great Seale, have devysed, ordeyned, geven and graunted to the saide Robert Knyght, gentilman, and his pos-terytie these armes and crest as foloweth, that is to saye [*etc.*]. To have and to holde to him and his posterytie and they it to enjoye for evermore. In witnesse whereof I the saide Clarencieulx Kynge of Armes, as abovesaide, have signed these presentes with my hande and sett thereunto the Seale of myne armes with the seale of my offyce of Clarencieulx Kynge of Armes. Yeven and graunted at London, the fourtenth day of July in the seconde yere of the reigne of our moste drade soveraigne lorde Edward the Sixt, by the grace of God Kynge of Englande, Fraunce and Irelande, defender of the faith and of the churche of Englande and also of Irelande in earth the supreme head.

Par moy Clarencieulx Roy d'Armes.

L. S.   *L. S.*

[*S. P. Dom. Misc. Box* 1, *No.* 5.]

IV. SEMI-OFFICIAL INSTRUMENTS

It was no part of the original design of the present work to present specimens of the great class of private 'Diplomata.' The adequate treatment of this subject would require a separate volume, whilst the classification and diplomatic description of these instruments have been dealt with in several important treatises and official editions[1]. But although a large mass of Ancient Deeds, as well as Manor Rolls, Accounts and Correspondence is now preserved amongst the Public Records, it must be insisted that these are merely fortuitous acquisitions. At the same time, however, we find many species of private diplomata entered in the Rolls of the Courts or in Books of Remembrance as a matter of precaution or favour. Moreover, the very forms of these private deeds were adapted to serve various royal or ministerial requirements and a very considerable number of such instruments are preserved both as originals and enrolments amongst the Exchequer and Chancery Records[2].

The semi-official instruments referred to above might be classified under the several denominations applicable to their legal or official character. Thus under the head of Conveyances we should find besides Deed Polls plentiful instances of Releases or Quit-claims (Nos. 141—144) amongst the Rolls and Registers of the Chancery, Exchequer and Bench. It may be observed, however, that 'Fines' or Final Concords, will be noticed in another volume dealing with the Records of Judicial Proceedings. Under the head of Contracts we should meet with a still larger number of Bonds and Recognizances (Nos. 145, 151), Oaths (Nos. 149, 150), Indentures (No. 146) and Assignments. Finally amongst very diverse forms of Certificates, special mention may be made of Notifications, Acknowledgments (Nos. 152, 153), Awards, Memoranda (Nos. 147, 148), and, in distinction to these purely official types, such personal Certificates as those relating to Musters, change of Residence and the Sacramental Certificates of a still later period (No. 154).

---

[1] E.g. Pollock and Maitland, *History of English Law*; Madox, *Formulare Anglicanum*; Round, *Ancient Charters* (Pipe Roll Society), *Facsimiles of Ancient Charters* (British Museum) and *Calendars of Ancient Deeds* (Rolls Series).

[2] Recognizances and other forms are also found amongst the Records of the King's Bench and other jurisdictions.

9

It has been found impossible to print more than a few specimens of the several types which have been referred to here, and of these it will be observed that some belong to the class of official Memoranda which are not actually composed in diplomatic form. It will also be noticed that the first of these semi-official instruments (No. 141) might be regarded as a letter under the Secret (or armorial) Seal. It has, however, been included here as representing the private financial enterprises of the Crown during the Edwardian period which were recorded 'specialiori modo' in certain famous 'Red Books[1],' just as the political expenditure of George III is recorded in a 'little Red Book' which, however, has never been in official custody[2].

141. *Acquittance by the King, under his Seal of the Griffon, of certain monies due upon the account of the Warden of a royal Castle (7 August, 15 Edward III).*

Edward, par le grace de Dieu, *etc.* [*as in No.* 111], a touz ceux qi cestes lettres verroient, Salutz. Sachetz nous avoir resceu en nostre chaumbre, par les meins nostre cher clerc Thomas de Hatfeld, de nostre cher et foial Monsieur Hugh Tirel, gardien de nostre chastel de Radenore en Gales, ove les membres, sesante et six livres, tresze soldes et quatre deniers de sterlinges en partie de paiement de ses arrerages en queux il nous est tenuz sur la parclose de son accompte, du temps quil estoit gardien de nostre chastel ove les membres avant-ditz. En temoignance de queu chose, nous lui avons fait faire cestes noz Lettres d'Aquitance. Donne souz nostre Seal de Griffone, a nostre Tour de Londres, le vij jour d'Augste, l'an de nostre regne d'Engleterre quinzisme et de France secound.

[*Record Office Museum, Case H, No. 77.*]

142. *Memorandum (bi-partite) recording the delivery of certain monies at the Exchequer (19 June, 4 Edward II).*

Memorandum quod die Sabbati xix die Junii, anno regni Regis Edwardi, filii Regis Edwardi, quarto, liberavit Marmaducus de Twenge, miles, Thesaurario et Camerariis de Scaccario, lx libras de denariis domini Walteri, Coventriensis et Lichfeldensis episcopi,

---

[1] Cf. No. 148, and the *Red Book of the Exchequer* (Fly-leaves).
[2] *Historical MSS. Commission 10th Report*, App. VI.

de arreragiis cuidam annué provisionis quadraginta librarum eidem domino episcopo per predictum Marmaducum annuatim concessé. In cujus rei testimonium, una pars istius Memorandi penes predictos Thesaurarium et Camerarios remanet, et altera pars penes prefatum Marmaducum.

Devery.

[*Chanc. Warr⁴ˢ etc. (Ser.* 1), *File* 1664.]

---

143. *Notification of the Receipt of a certain allowance of Cloth at the Great Wardrobe, by virtue of a Letter of Privy Seal* (16 *June*, 6 *Edward III*).

Pateat universis, per presentes, quod ego Philippus de Bastone, frater de ordine fratrum Carmellitarum, recepi Londonié, xvj die Junii, anno regni Regis Edwardi, tercii a conquestu, sexto, de magistro Willelmo la Zouche, clerico Magné Garderobé ipsius domini Regis, ad unum habitum pro me, per Litteram de Privato Sigillo, vj ulnas panni camel[ini] et vj ulnas panni burnetti. In cujus rei testimonium, presentibus sigillum meum apposui. Data Londonié, die et anno supradictis.

L. S.

[*Exchequer Proceedings, Bundle* 78, *File* 4.]

---

144. *Acquittance (Starr) by certain Jews to Adam de Stratton*[1] *of all claims in respect of divers lands* (15 *Edward I*).

Hereford. Elyas, filius Cressi, et Aaron, filius Isaac, recognoverunt per Starrum[2] suum quod acquietarunt Adé de Stratton sex acras prati et duodecim acras pasturé in Westerle in parochia de Oldesham, cum una acra et quarta parte cujusdam sepis quas predictus Adam tenet de Johane Tayleboys. Ita quod predicti Judei decetero neque-ant calumpniare super predictum Adam et heredes suos a Creatione, scilicet, usque ad Finem, quia acquietarunt omnino et pardonarunt predicto Adé.

Istud Starrum irrotulatum est in termino Sancti Hillarii anno regni Regis Edwardi xv.
Starrum Elyé filii Cressi, et Aaronis, filii Isaac, pro Ada de Stratton, irrotulatum (as above).

[*Ancient Deeds*, A 14894.]

---

[1] Deputy Chamberlain of the Exchequer (cf. *Red Book of Exchequer*, Vol. III. Preface).
[2] The Hebrew 'starr' is written on a schedule to the document.

145. *Memorandum of a Bond, with clause of defeazance, as security for the payment of certain rents to an official of the Exchequer* (51—52 *Henry III*).

Pro Ada de Stratton.

Idem venit coram Baronibus et recognovit, pro se et heredibus suis vel assignatis, et quibuscumque aliis qui decetero terras et tenementa sua in comitatibus Surrié et Kancié tenebunt, quod reddet singulis annis imperpetuum Adé de Stratton, clerico, et heredibus vel assignatis suis decem marcas ad festum Sancti Michaelis, pro terra de Retherhuthe quam idem Adam tradidit et dimisit predicto Thomé de Hegham et heredibus vel assignatis suis ad feodi firmam, prout plenius continetur in cyrographo inter ipsos super hoc confecto. Et nisi fecerit, concessit pro se et heredibus suis vel assignatis, sicut predictum est, quod Barones de Scaccario de terris, bonis et catallis suis dictos denarios non solutos fieri faciant [*etc.*].

[*Exch. K. R. Memoranda*, 51 *and* 52 *Henry III, Trin. M.* 27d.]

---

146. '*Indenture of War,' between William Fitz Ralph and the Crown for the provision and maintenance of certain men at arms and archers* (20 *September*, 1 *Richard II*).

Ceste endenture faite parentre nostre seignur le Roy Richard, d'une part, et monsieur William filz Rauf, d'autre part, tesmoigne que le dit William est demorez devers nostre dit sieur le Roy pur lui servir un quarter d'un an ovesque quarante homes d'armes et quarante archiers en un viage et armee de guerre, q'est ordenez a faire procheinement sur la meer, commenceant le dit quarter le jour que le dit William serra venuz au port de la meer ovesque sa dite retenue, par commandement de nostre dit seignur le Roy, prest pur eskypper et pur aler avant en dit viage. Et prendra le dit William pur lui et pur sa dite retenue gages de guerre acustumez, et pur lui mesmes et pur ses dits gentz d'armes regard acustumez et demy. Des queux gages et regard acustumez ils serront paiez pur le dit quarter avant le comencement du vit viage, et du demy regard il en a bon et covenable assignement d'en estre prestement serviz, le dit quarter finiz, sanz estre repellez. Et s'il aviegne que le dit William ovesque sa dite retenue demoerge en service de nostre dit seignur le Roy en dit viage outre le dit quarter, adonques il serra paiez, pur lui et pur sa dite retenue, pur le temps q'ils aront demorez en le service de nostre dit seignur le Roy, outre le dit quarter de autieux gages et regards come desus sont expressez. En tesmoignance de quele chose, a la partie de ceste endenture demorante devers nostre dit seignur le Roy, le dit William ad mys son seal. Don[ez] a Londres, le xx jour de Septembre, l'an du regne nostre dit seignur le Roy primer.

[*Exchequer K. R. Indentures of War*, 1 *Richard II*.]

147. *Indenture of the delivery of certain Exchequer Records by the King's Writ of Privy Seal (21 October, 37 Henry VI).*

This endenture made the xxj day of October, the year of the regne of King Harry the sext, xxxvii, betwene the Tresorer of England and the Chamberlyns of the Eschequer, on the one part, and the right wurshipfull and reverent Fader in God, Richard Beauchamp, Bisshop of Salisbury, on the other part, Witnesseth that the seid Tresorer and Chamberlyns, by vertu of a Pryve Seal beryng date the xx day of October, the xxxvii yeer of the regne of oure seid soverayne Lorde the Kyng, remaynyng in the files of Michelmesse terme in the xxxvii yeer of our seid soverayne Lord amonges other warrantes direct to the seid Tresorer and Chamberlynes, have delyvered to the seid Bisshop certeyn evydences and munnymentes concernyng convencions, communycacions, tretys, legues and trewes bytwis this Reawme and other landes and countrees, that ys to say [*etc.*].

[*Liber Memorandorum Scaccarii, fo.* 118 (*ed. Palgrave, Antient Kalendars etc. of the Exchequer, Vol.* II. *p.* 236).]

---

148. *Memorandum of the Delivery and Receipt of certain Exchequer Records (19—21 January, 14 Henry VI).*

Memorandum quod xix die Januarii, anno regni Regis Henrici sexti xiiii°, Thesaurarius et Camerarii de Scaccario, in presencia Domini Regis et aliorum Dominorum de Consilio, deliberaverunt custodi Privati Sigilli dicti Domini Regis duos libros, ligno ligatos et corio rubio coopertos, vocatos Libros de Remembrances, tangentes diversas bullas, papiras et litteras ac cartas diversorum dominiorum, terrarum et tenementarum, tam in partibus Anglié, Francié et Scocié, quam alibi, prout in eisdem libris continetur. Item, eodem die et anno, et in eadem presencia, deliberaverunt eidem Custodi Privati Sigilli unum alium Librum de Remembrance, coopertum cum uno albo suppello, continentem tractatus, privilegia, et alia munimenta Ducatus Aquitanié.

Qui quidem libri restituuntur per eundem Custodem Privati Sigilli xxi die Januarii proximo sequente.

[*Liber Memorandorum Scaccarii, fo. 79 b* (*ed. Palgrave, op. cit., Vol.* II. *p.* 157).]

---

149. *Form of the Oath of Office of the King's Justices (French, 14th century).*

Sacramentum Justiciariorum.

Le serment des Justices est : que bien et leaument serviront le Roi en office de la Justicerie, et dreiture a lour pouer fruont a touz, auxi bien as povres come as riches, et que pur hautesce, ne pur richesce, ne pur amour, ne pur haour, ne pur estat de nuly persone, ne pur bienfait, doun, ne p[ro]messe de nuly, qui fait lour seit ou lour pourra estre fait, autri dreiture ne destourberont ne respiterount, countre reson et countre les leis de la terre ; mes saunz resgard de nuly estat, ne de persone, leaument frount faire dreiture a chescun, solonc les leys usees ; et que riens ne prendrount de nuly saunz conge le Roi.......

[*Red Book of the Exchequer, fo. xiid* (*Report of Record Commissioners* (1800), *p.* 236).]

150.   *Oaths of Allegiance, Homage and Fealty taken by Scottish nobles* (28 *August*, 24 *Edward I*).

A tuz ceus qe cestes lettres verrunt ou orrunt, Johan de Swyneburn, Reÿnaud de Craunford del Conte de Are [*etc.*], Saluz. Pur ceo qe nous sumes venuz a la foy e a la volunte du tres noble prince e nostre chier seignour, Sire Edward, par la grace de Dieu Roy d'Engleterre, Seignour de Irlaunde, Duk de Aquytaigne, nous permettons, pur nous e pur nos heyrs, sur peyne de cors e de avoyr, e sur *quaunqe nous pussoms encore, qe nous ly servyroms bien e leaument contre totes genz qi purrunt vyvre e moryr totes les foyz qe nous* serroms requyz ou garniz de par nostre Seigneur le Roy d'Engleterre avauntdit ou par ses heyrs ; e qe nous leur dammage ne saveroms qe nous ne le desturberoms a tut nostre poer, e le lur faceoms a savoyr. E a cestes choses tenir e garder, nous obligeoms nous e nos heyrs e tuz nos biens ; e outre ceo avoms jure sur Seyntes Ewangeyles.

E puys nous touz, e chescun de nous par soy, avoms fet Homage a nostre Seignur le Roy avauntdit en cestes Paroles. "Jeo devenk vostre home lyge, de vie e de membre e de terrien honour, contre totes genz qe purrunt vivre e morir." E meymes cely nostre Seignour le Roy le ad resceu en ceste fourme. "Nous le receyvoms des terres dount vous estes ore seisi, sauve nostre dreyt e autry, e forprys les terres les queus Johan de Baillol qi fut Roy de Escoce vous dona puys qe nous ly eumes renduz le Reaume de Escoce, e forpris celes ensynk, les queus nous eumes seisi avaunt ceo qe vous feusez venuz a nostre pees."

Estre ceo nous touz, e chescun de nous par soy, avoms fet Feaute a nostre Seignour le Roy avauntdit en cestes paroles. "Je serray feal e leal, e foy e leaute porteray au Roy Edward, Roy d'Engleterre, e a ses heyrs, de vie e de membre e de terrien honour, contre totes genz qe purrunt vivre ou morir. E jammes pur nuly armes ne porteray, n'en conseyl, n'en eyde ne serray contre ly ne contre ses heyrs en nul cas qe peut avenir, e leaument reconusteray e leaument fray les servyces qe apartenent as tenemenz qe jeo cleym tenyr de ly, si Dieu me eyde e les Seynz."

En tesmoignaunce des queles choses nous avoms fet fere cestes lettres overtes, sealees de nos seaux. Donees a Berewyk sur Twede, le vynt utyme jour de Aust, l'an du regne nostre Seignur le Roy d'Engleterre, avauntdit, vyntyme quart.

[*Scotch Documents* (ed. *Palgrave, p.* 153, *No. xlvi*).]

---

151. *Recognizance entered into by William Giffard as security for good behaviour* (1216—24).

Omnibus Christi fidelibus presentem cartam inspecturis, Willelmus Giffard, Salutem. Noverit universitas vestra me spontanea voluntate mea pepigisse Domino meo Henrico, illustri Regi Angliè, filio Regis Johannis, quod ei et heredibus suis omnibus diebus vité meé constanter et fideliter serviam ; nec in aliquo tempore contra eos ero. Et ad majorem fidelis servitii mei securitatem, totam terram meam pono in plegiagium. Ita quod si forte contigerit quod a fideli servitio suo vel heredum suorum (quod absit) recesserim, tota terra mea, pro me et heredibus meis, erga ipsum Dominum Regem et heredes suos inquiratur et in usus eorum perpetuis cedat temporibus. Hanc autem cartam sigilli mei munimine roboravi ; hiis testibus [*etc.*].

[*Red Book of the Exchequer, Vol.* III. *p. cccx.*]

---

152. *Acknowledgement of disbelief in the doctrine of Transubstantiation* (1 *James II*).

I, A.B. doe solemnly and sincerely, in the presence of God, professe, testify and declare that I doe beleive that in the sacrament of the Lord's Supper there is not any transubstantiation of the elements of bread and wine into the body and bloud of Christ, att or after the consecration thereof by any person whatsoever ; and that the invocation or adoration of the Virgin Mary or any other saint, and the sacrifice of the masse, as they are now used in the Church of Rome, are superstitious and idolatrous ; and I doe solemnly, in the presence of God, professe, testify and declare that I doe make this declaration and every parte thereof in the plaine and ordinary sence of the words read unto me, as they are commonly understood by English Protestants, without any evasion, equivocation or mentall reservation whatsoever, and without any dispensation already granted me for this purpose by the Pope or any other authority whatsoever, or without thinking that I am or can be acquitted before God or man or absolved of this declaration or any parte thereof, although the Pope, or any other person or persons or power whatsoever, should dispence with or annull the same, or declare that it was null and voyd from the begining.

[*Chanc. Petty Bag, Oath Rolls, No.* 1, *Hilary*, 1 *James II.*]

153. *Acknowledgement by a Religious House of the Ecclesiastical Supremacy of the Crown (27 March, 27 Henry VIII).*

Quum ea sit non solum Christiané religionis et pietatis ratio, sed nostré etiam obediencié regula, domino Regi nostro Henrico Octavo, cui uni et soli, post Christum Jhesum servatorem nostrum, debemus universa non modo omnimodam in Christo et eandem sinceram, integram, perpetuamque animique devotionem, fidem et observanciam, honorem, cultum, reverenciam prestemus, sed etiam de eadem fide et observancia nostra ratione (quotiescunque postulabitur) reddamus et palam omnibus (si res postulat) libentissime testemur. Noverint universi ad quos presens scriptum pervenerit quod nos, Jana Meyns, mater sive matrona domus sive hospitalis jacentis extra portam borialem villé Calisié, vocatam le Lanteringate, fundaté et edificaté in honore beatissimé ac gloriosissimé Virginis Marié, Sancti Francisci, et Sancté Elizabethé, filié Regis Hungarié, pro sororibus tertii ordinis Sancti Francisci predicti et ejusdem loci consorores, uno ore et voce atque unanimé, omnium consensu et assensu, hoc scripto nostro, sub sigillo nostro communi in domo nostra capitulari dato, pro nobis et successoribus nostris, omnibus et singulis imperpetuum profitemur, testamur ac fideliter promittimus et spondemus nos, matrem sive matronem et consorores predictas et successores nostros, omnes et singulos, integram, inviolatam, sinceram, perpetuamque fidem observanciam et obedienciam semper prestituras erga dominum Regem nostrum Henricum Octavum et erga Annam Reginam, uxorem ejusdem, et erga sobolem ejus, ex eadem Anna legitime tam progenitam quam progeneranda, et quod hec eadem populo notificabimus, predicabimus et suadebimus ubicunque dabitur locus et occasio. [*Articles of acknowledgement follow concerning the ecclesiastical supremacy of the Crown, the denial of Papal jurisdiction, the doctrine of the Scriptures, and prayers for the royal family and church.*] Item quod nos, Jana Meyns, mater sive matrona et consorores, omnes et singulé predicté et successores nostri, consciencié et jurisjurandi sacramento nosmet firmiter obligamus quod omnia et singula predicta fideliter imperpetuum observabimus. In cujus rei testimonium, sigillum nostrum commune presentibus apposuimus. Data in domo nostra capitulari, xxvii die mensis Martii, anno domini millesimo quinquegesimo tricesimo quinto, et anno regni regis Henrici Octavi predicti, vicesimo sexto.

[*Signed*] **Janne Meins moeder van de suster van Calies**
[*and signatures of other sisters*].
L. S.

[*Docketted*]:—*Sorores Calesié.*

[*Exchequer T. of R. Acknowledgements of Supremacy, Box* I.]

154. *Certificate, attested by witnesses, of the Vicar and Church-warden of St Martin's in the Fields that George, Duke of Buckingham, received the Sacrament on the day preceding.*(5 *May*, 1673).

We, Thomas Lamplugh, Vicar, Minister of the Parish and Parish Church of St Martin in the Fields, in ye county of Middlesex and John Wilson, Church Warden of the same Parish and Parish Church, do hereby certifie that ye right Honorable George, Duke of Buckingham his grace, Master of the Horse to his Ma^ty, upon the Lord's day, commonly called Sunday, the fourth day of May, 1673, immediately after Divine Service and Sermon, did in the Parish Church aforesaid, receive the Sacrament of the Lord's Supper according to the usage of the Church of England. In witness whereof we have hereunto subscribed our Hands, the Fiffth day of May, in the Year of Our Lord, One Thousand, Six Hundred, Seventy and Three.

Tho: Lamplugh, Vic^r, Minister of the Parish and Parish Church of
St Martin's in the Fields.
John Wilson, Church Warden of the said Parish and Parish Church.

And Sr Nicholas Armour, knight, one of his Maties Equerries, and Thomas Sprat, Doctor of Divinity, Prebendary of the Collegiate Church of Westminster, do severally make oath that they do know the said Duke of Buckingham in the above written Certificate named, and who, now present, hath delivered the same into this Court, And do further severally make oath that they did see the said Duke of Buckingham receive the Sacrament of the Lord's Supper in the Parish Church of St Martin's in the Fields, in the county of Middlesex, in the said Certificate mentioned, and upon the day and at the time in the said Certificate in that behalf certified and expressed; and that they did see the Certificate above written subscribed by the persons abovenamed, vizt Dr. Tho: Lamplugh and John Wilson. And further they do say upon their respective oaths, that all other matters or things in the said Certificate recited, mentioned or expressed are true, as they verily believe.

Quinto die Maii, 1673.   Nic. Armorer.
Jurati et examinati in Curia.   Thomas Sprat.
     E.W. C.P.

[*Petty Bag, Sacramental Certificates, Bundle* 1 (*No.* 46).]

V. STATE PAPERS AND DEPARTMENTAL INSTRUMENTS

1. ROYAL LETTERS AND OFFICIAL CORRESPONDENCE

An epistolary style may be recognized in this country, as abroad, from a very early date, but at first the mediaeval letter must be regarded as a literary exercise rather than as a means of official communication. The dignified position of the feudal sovereign required the use of a more ceremonious style than that adopted by the polite letter-writer, and a convenient compromise was effected by means of the royal Writ. But although Writs of several kinds have been commonly included in printed collections of 'Royal Letters,' a distinction between the purely diplomatic and the epistolary styles may perhaps be suggested. Broadly speaking this distinction is seen in the transposition of the Superscription and Address, the omission of official Dispositive or Injunctive Clauses, and the substitution of a mere Valediction for a formal Attestation. It is true that the actual words of the diplomatic Superscription and Address are preserved in the modern letter, in which a conventional form of Notification and Exposition may frequently be recognized. Nevertheless, the distinction is at least of importance in respect of the transposition of the diplomatic formulas which was gradually effected between the 13th and 15th centuries.

In the earliest period, extending far into the 13th century, the only apparent distinction between the royal Letter and the royal Writ consists in a more familiar style of Address and Notification. An impersonal and vocative Address is rarely used, and then always in conjunction with the formulas of the diplomatic Superscription and Address, a Valediction being rare.

In the later period, from the close of the 13th century to the middle of the 15th, another style is gradually adopted, namely, an Address, in the dative case, which usually precedes the nominative Superscription. The Final Protocol also contains an important modification, the Attestation Clause being dispensed with. The Royal Letter is now 'dated' (or 'given') under one of the Smaller Seals though a Valediction is occasionally found in the style of the Anglo-Saxon writs.

From this stage it is only another step to the vocative style of the modern Letter in which the initial Superscription is brought down to form a Subscription, and the personal Address is superscribed or endorsed as a direction for delivery. The Letter now begins with an impersonal, vocative Address followed by a familiar Salutation and an impressive Notification. It concludes with the Dating Clause, described above, or with a simple Valediction, followed by a Subscription; or the Sign Manual may be affixed in lieu of a Superscription or Subscription. These innovations, however, are almost entirely confined to the French and English specimens of the tri-lingual correspondence of the 14th and 15th centuries, and the Valediction is chiefly found in the Letters addressed to the King or his ministers by the subjects. A further refinement may be observed in respect of the committal to a Holy keeping.

Finally, it should be noticed that snatches of several other ancient formulas may be traced, especially in the Address and Subscription of the modern Letter, whilst a curious recurrence of a diplomatic style may be easily recognized in the case of the letter written 'in the third person.'

In the State Papers of the 16th, 17th and 18th centuries, which are best known to us as 'Royal Letters' or 'official correspondence,' the devolution of the mediaeval Writ or Letter Missive can be clearly traced. The conventional forms of the mediaeval Chancery are still occasionally used in royal ceremony, diplomacy or the ordinary business of the State (Nos. 163—166), but for the most part a new style of correspondence, composed in the vernacular language and written in a cursive hand, obtains from the reign of Henry VIII (Nos. 167—171). The connection of this striking innovation with the Secretaryship of State, in its clerical aspect, under the well-known Act of 1535 may be easily surmised.

---

155. *Letter from Henry III to Hubert de Burgh (c. April* 1220).

Henricus, *etc.* [*as in No.* 80], dilecto et fideli suo Huberto de Burgo, justiciario Angliæ, Salutem.

Questi sunt nobis Leprosi de Lancastria, qui sunt de eleemosyna nostra, quod vicecomes, forestarii et servientes sui eis molestiam et gravamen injuste inferunt et eos, super eleemosyna illa, vexare non cessant, prout lator presentium vobis referre potest.   Quare vobis mandamus, rogantes, quatenus detis eis in mandatum, per literas nostras, ut de cetero ab hujusmodi molestia et vexatione desistant. Et quoniam Sigillum nostrum nobiscum non fuit, has literas sigillo dilecti et fidelis nostri W[illelmi] de Cantelupo fecimus sigillari. Valete.

[*Chanc. Ancient Correspondence*, I. 34 (*ed. Shirley, Royal and Historical Letters (Rolls), No. lxxxvii*).]

---

156.   *Letter from Henry IV to the Doge of Venice* (10 *August,* 1404).

Henricus, etc., magnifico et prepotenti viro, Duci Venetiarum, amico nostro carissimo, Salutem ac votivé dilectionis continuum incrementum.

Amice precarissime,

Scire velitis quod sumus in preparando nobis certas magnas naves quas munire intendimus fortibus et tutissimis paramentis.   Informatique sumus quod meliora cables et cordalia nullibi reperire poterimus quam in civitate vestra Venetiarum.

Quapropter vestram Magnificentiam predilectam, in qua specialissimam habemus confidentiam, ex toto corde rogamus quatinus [*Request for a supply of these cables, etc., follows*].

Habentes pro certo quod, cum gratia Altissimi, mercatoribus vestris premissa nobis aut nostris liberantibus, talis fiet et tam prompta solutio quod merito reputabunt se contentos : scituri pro firmo, amice precarissime, quod si onus tantilli negotii pro nobis [ad] presens subire volueritis, in singulis vestris agendis, etsi majora fuerint, erimus promptiores[1].

Precarissime amice, vos diu conservet in prosperis Trinitas Increata.

Datum etc. x die Augusti, anno, etc., quinto.

[*MS. Cott. Nero B.* VII. (*Royal and Historical Letters (Rolls), No. ciii*).]

---

157.   *Letter from a baron to the King* (1166).

Carissimo Domino suo, Henrico Regi Anglorum, Walterus filius Willelmi, ejus baro de Norhumberlande, Salutem.

Domine, sciatis quod isti sunt milites mei, feffati de veteri feffamento, scilicet.   [*List follows.*]

Et sciatis, Domine, quod feodum meum non debet vobis servitium nisi de tribus militibus.   Valete.

[*Red Book of Exchequer, fo.* 121 (*Roll Series, p.* 436).]

---

[1] Cf. No. 185.

158. *Letter from Henry IV to the Count of Hainault* (16 *Feb.* 1400).

Henri, *etc.* [*as in No.* 111], a nostre treschier et tresame Cousin le Duc Aubers de Bayune, Conte de Haynue, Holande, Zeelle, et Sire de Frize, Saluz et entier dilection.

Treschier cousin,

De vostre leesse en coer de ce que a estat roial de tous nostre poeple d'Engleterre sumes receuz, come voȝ bones lettres a nous par vostre conseiller et de vostre houstel, William, seignur de Dynsedore, chivaler, a nous presentees, purportant, et de ce aussi que par la grande affection que a nostre persone avez, vostre dit Chivaler avez pardevers nous envoiez pur nostre estat savoir, et vous ent la cer-teinetee reporter ; vous mercions de tresentier coer, tant come plus savons ou poons.

Si veullez savoir, treschier cousin, que a la faisance de cestes feusmes, Dieu merciez, tous sains et en bon point, esteantz tresjoious de vostre bon estat et sauntee, dount par voȝ dictes lettres nous avetz signifiez : vous empriantz que d'icel vous veullez certifier le plus souvent que bonement puvez, pur leese et confort de nous, et vostre bone voluntee et affection tout dys envers nous continuer, sur la grande affiance que en vous avons. Et si vous trouverez par tant prestz de faire, si Dieu plest, ce que a vous et lez voȝ tournir purra a honur et plaisir, sicome le dit William, vostre chivaler et le nostre, vous declarera pluis pleinement de bouche ; a qui veullez adjouster ferme foy et creance de ce q'il vous en dirra depar nous.

Treschier et tresame cousin, la Benoite Trinitee vous veulle tout dys ottroier joie et sauntee et treslong duree.

Donne souz nostre Prive Seal, a nostre Paleys de Westmoustier, le xvj jour de Feverer.

[*MS. Cott. Galb. B.* 1., *fo.* 127 (*Royal and Historical Letters* (*Rolls*), *No. ix*).]

---

159. *Letter from Morice Seigneur de Craon to Edward I.*

A tres haut et tres noble prince, son chier seigneur, mon seigneur d'Engleterre, par la grace de Dieu, Morice seigneur de Craon, son humble chevalier, bonneur et reverence, et soi touz jourz apparelli a son servise et a sa volente. Sire, je envoi a vous pour savoir vostre estat, que Dieu face bon ; si supploi a vostre hautece que il vos plese a le moi fere savoir ; quar je sui mout liz et mout reconfortez toutez foiz que j'em puis oir bones nouveles. Et je fusse a l'envers vous a ceste Pasque desraenement passee, se ne fussent granz besognes que je avois o le roy de Sezille, si comme frere Guy de la Marche vos dira. Si vos pri que vos m'en eyez pour excuse et, se il vos plest, si l'en creez de ce que il vos en dira de par moy. Comandez moi vostre volente que je sui tous jours desirant de la accomplir et de fere. Nostre Sire vos guart, l'ame et le cors, bien et longuement.

[*Endorsed.*]   A nostre Seignur Le Roy d'Engleterre.

[*Chanc. Ancient Correspondence*, XVI. 82.]

---

160.   *Letter from an official to the King* (7 *July*, 1403).

Mon tressoveraigne et tresgraciouse Seignur.   Je me recomande humblement a vostre roial Magestie.   Et pleise a vostre tressoveraigne Seignurie assavoir que yceste Samady, a noet, le vij jour de Juyllet, j'ay resceu certeines lettres de par Jenkyn Hanard moy adressez : lesquelles par le portour d'ycestes deinz ycestes closez j'envoie a vostre roial personne, que pleise a vostre trespuissant et tresdoute Seignurie d'ordener remedie, pur y resister et destruier les traitours que de jour en autre se enforceant, et grande mal et destruction a voz foialx de temps en temps faciont, sanz ascune resistance ; considerant, mon tresgraciouse Seignour, si aide en haste [*etc.*], tout; les chastelles [*etc.*] sont en grande peril et du poynt d'estre anientisez pour defaute de socour et de bone governance.

Mon tressovereign et tresgraciouse seignour, luy Tout-Puissant Dieu vous governe toutdys en vostres tresjoyeuses honours et bone prosperite, longe a durer.

Escript a Brechon, le vij jour de Juyllet, a l'houre de mid nyzt.

Le vostre simple Clerc et Oratour
Johan Faireford.
Recieviour de Brechan.

[*Endorsed.*]   Au Roy, mon tres [soverain] seignour.

[*MS. Cotton Cleo. F.* III., *fo.* 121*b* (*Royal and Historical Letters* (*Rolls*), *No. viii*).]

---

161.   *Letter from the King to his officers* (23 *June*, 1442).

Right trusty and welbeloved, we grete you wel.   And for as muche as our trusty and welbeloved squier for our body, Edward Hull, the which nowe late is commen unto us oute of our Duchie of Guienne, hath amonge other things reported unto us howe our ennemies and adversaires are comyng toward our cite of Bourdeaux to besiege hit, we late you wete that we kepe stille our said squier aboute our personne unto tyme that we have ordeined here our armee to goo thider for the helpe succor and defense of our said cite and of all our cuntreyes there ; of the whiche arme our cousin of Suffolk hathe told us that he and ye, oure Secretaire, have divers tymes communed before this tyme. Wherefore we wol that, for the comfort and encourageng of our true subgettes there, ye do this to be knowen amonge theym at your thider commyng as hit shal seme to your discrecons to be doon, wherin ye shal do to us good pleasir. Yeven under our Signet of th'Elge [*Egle*], at our Castel of Windesore, the xxiij day of Juyn.

Also our said Squier shal bringe certaine ansuere upon al ye matiers and articles that he hath brought at his said commyng thider. Yeven as above, etc.

[*Endorsed.*] To our right trusty and welbeloved knight, Sir Robert Roos, oon of our kervers, and Maister Th[omas] Bekynton our Secretaire, and to either of theym.

[*MS. Ashmol. M. 789, fo.* 174 (*Correspondence of Bekynton* (*Rolls*), II. 180).]

---

162. *Letter from Gerald Earl of Kildare to Henry VII* (5 *June,* 1489—93).

Most excellent Christen Kyng and my moost redoubted soveraine liege lord; in as humble and obeysaunt maner as eny subject can or may doo to his soveraine, I recommaund me to your moost noble and benyng grace:

Pleassed the same to be acerted that I have receyved your gracious Letters Myssives dated at your manere of Grenewich the xxviij day of Jullii last passed; wherby I have wele understand your gracious mynde that ye wold have me to your moste noble presaunce, that I mought ther by knowe your gracious mynd, and that ye mought have plenary comunicacion with me in alle suche thyngs as mought concerne the wele of that your said land, and that your subjectes of the same may be reduced to a good and lafull ordyr and obeisaunce, to the plesyr of Godd, wele and profite of the same your land, as in your said letters it doth appier more at large.

Gracious Lord I, accordyng to your highe commaundement, was in full mynd and purpose to have accomplisshed and performed your moost noble plesyr in the same, settyng apart all exscuses, till I was desyred by your true and feithfull subjects of this your land, and my cousynes in especiall th'Erle of Dessemond and the lord Bourk of Connaght, that I shold not depart. [*Excuses and professions of loyalty follow.*] And by the othe that I have doo onto your highnes, ther shold no thyng be to me soo grett a plesyr as oonly it mought be perfitly understaund to your grace what I have done for your honor and the wele of your subjectes of this your land. Moost excellent Christen Kyng and my moost redoubted soveraine liege lord, the blessed Trinyte preserve your moost noble grace to reigne moost roially, and of your enymies and rebelles to have the victory. Written at your city of Divelin, the vth day of Junii.

By your true and feithfull subject, Gerot, Erle of Kildare.

[*Endorsed.*]   To the Kyng, my soverayn liege Lord.

[*A. C. Vol.* LI. *No.* 122 (*ed. Gairdner, Letters of Richard III, etc. (Rolls)* I. 380).]

163. *Conventional Royal Letter of ceremony in a formal style* (*Latin*) (*27 October,* 1760).

Georgius Tertius, Dei Gratia, Magnæ Britaniæ, Franciæ et Hiberniæ, Rex, Fidei Defensor, Dux Brunsvicensis et Luneburgensis, Sacri Romani Imperii Archi-Thesaurarius et Princeps Elector etc., serenissimo et potentissimo principi domino Stanislao, eadem gratia regi Poloniæ, Magno Duci Lithuaniæ, Russiæ, Prussiæ, Mazoviæ, Samogitiæ, Kioviæ, Volhiñiæ, Podoliæ, Podlachiæ, Smolenciæ, Livoniæ, Severiæ et Czernichoviæ, Duci Lotharingiæ et Barii, Marchioni Mussipontis et Nomenii, Comiti Valdemontis, Albemontis, Sarwarden' et Salom' etc., fratri, consanguineo, et amico nostro carissimo, Salutem. Serenissime et potentissime princeps, frater, consanguinee et amice carissime. Quum, sic volente Deo Omnipotente, serenissimus et potentissimus princeps, Georgius Secundus, beatis̄simæ memoriæ Rex, avus noster honoratissimus, vicesimum quintum hujus mensis diem supremum obierit, atque in solium imperiale horum regnorum evecti simus ; Nos tametsi in summo moerore et luctu, haud intermittendam duximus tanti eventus notitiam, quam Majestati vestræ lubentiori damus animo, utpote persuasissimi ipsam iis quæ vel prospere vel secus nobis evenire poterint, sincere affectam fore. Quod superest, Majestatem vestram Supremi Numinis tutelæ commendamus. Dabantur in aula nostra apud Saville House, die vicesimo septimo mensis Octobris, anno Domini millesimo septingentesimo sexagesimo regnique nostri primo.

Majestatis Vestræ
Bonus Frater, consanguineus
et Amicus
Georgius R.[1]

[*Superscribed:*] Serenissimo et potentissimo principi domino Stanislao, Dei gratia Regi Poloniæ, [*etc.*] [*as above*].

[*F. O. King's Letters, Vol.* 16, *p.* 5.]

---

[1] A contemporary memorandum states "The words underlined [*i.e.* those italicized] were not wrote by the King." W. Pitt.

164. *Conventional Royal Letter of ceremony in a formal style* (*French*). (*The same tenor and date.*)

Très haut, très excellent et très puissant Prince, nôtre très cher et très amé bon frere et cousin: Ayant plû a Dieu tout Puissant d'appeller à lui, le 25ᵉ de ce mois, le serenissime et très puissant prince, le Roi George le Second, de très heureuse memoire, nôtre très honoré ayeul, et de nous élever à la couronne : Nous n'avons pas voulu, quoique dans la derniere affliction, différer de vous faire part d'un évènement si important ; étant persuadé que vous vous interessés sincerement à tout ce qui nous peut arriver, et nous nous servons de cette premiere occasion pour vous donner des preuves de nôtre amitié.

Sur ce nous prions Dieu qu'il vous ait, très haut, très excellent et très puissant prince, nôtre très cher et très amé bon frere et cousin, en Sa sainte et digne garde.

Ecrit à nôtre cour à Saville House, le 27ᵉ jour d'Octobre, 1760.

Vôtre bon Frere et Cousin,

George R.[1]

[*Superscribed.*]

A très haut, très excellent et très puissant Prince nôtre· très cher et très amé bon frere et cousin, le Roi très Chretien[1].

[*F. O. King's Letters, Vol.* 16, *p.* 2.]

---

165. *Conventional Royal Letter of ceremony in a familiar style* (*French*) (4 *September,* 1725).

Monsieur Mon Frere. J'ay appris par votre lettre du 19ᵉ d'Aoust l'heureuse nouvelle de la celebration de votre marriage faite à Strasbourg le 15ᵉ, et pour vous marquer plus amplement le joye très parfaite que j'en ressens, j'envoye extraordinairement auprès de vous mon très fidele et bien amé Jacques, Lord Waldegrave, un des Seigneurs de ma Chambre. Il aura ·l'honneur de vous feliciter en mon Nom, comme aussi Madame ma Soeur, votre nouvelle Epouse, sur l'accomplissement de cet evenement si desirable, qui fera comme j'éspere le bonheur de la France, et comblera de plaisir tous vôs veritables amis. Mon dit envoyé Extʳᵉ vous assurera de ma part des voeux très ardents que j'ai fait pour les suites de ce marriage les plus agreables que vous pouvés vous en souhaiter vous meme. Et il

---

[1] [Contemporary memoranda] "The King only wrote his name." W. Pitt.

"*The usual style to the Most Christian King is 'bon Frere, Cousin, et ancien Allié,' but the words 'ancien allié' were omitted in the letter of the other side, on account of the war between England and France.*"

H. F.

vous confirmera de bouche ce que je ne saurais repeter trop souvent, la sincerité de l'affection et de l'estime avec lesquelles je suis

Monsieur mon Frere,
Votre bon Frere,
George, R.

A Herrenhausen, le 4ᵉ Septʳᵉ 1725, N. S.

Au Roy très Chretien, Monsieur mon Frere.

[*F. O. King's Letters, Vol.* 15, *p.* 62.]

---

166. *Conventional Royal Letter of Ceremony in a familiar style* (*English*) (24 *May*, 1819).

To My Brother and Cousin.

My dear sister-in-law, the Duchess of Kent, having been early this morning safely delivered of a princess, I lose no time in communicating this happy event to your Imperial Majesty, being persuaded of the interest which you take in everything that concerns our Royal House. The friendly sentiments which your Imperial Majesty has always evinced towards me, induce me to hope that you will receive the intelligence with pleasure, as well as the assurances of the sincere attachment and distinguished consideration with which I am, Sir, My Brother and Cousin,

Your Imperial Majesty's
Good Brother and Cousin,
George, P. R.

Given at my Palace of Carlton House, the 24th day of May, 1819.

To my Good Brother and Cousin, The Emperor of Austria.

[*F. O. King's Letters, Vol.* 6, *p.* 196.]

---

167. *Official Letter in the King's name* (10 *October*, 1544).

After our most harty commendations. The Kinges Majeste having seen your letters, dated at Syttingborn, this morning, and taking your advertismentes signified by the same in verye good parte, hath wylled us, for awnswar, to signefie unto yow thatt His Majestes pleasure is ; thatt you shall [*etc.*].

And wher by your sayd letters it appereth thatt [*etc.*]. His Highnes hath commawnded us to wryte to [*etc.*] to tak order [*etc.*].

His Majeste is also pleased [*etc.*], for th'expedition wherof wee have att this present, by His Majestes commawndment, wryten to [*etc.*]. And thus we bydd your good Lordeshippes most hartely farewell.

From Otforde, the 10th of October att 3 of the clock att after-noone.

Your Lordeshippes assuryd
loving fryndes

(Signed)   **T. Cantuariensis.**   **W. Essex.**

               Tho. Westm[inster].   **Willm Petre.**

[*Superscribed.*]

To our very good lord, the Erle of Hertford, Greate Chamberlayn of England, and to our very loving frende, Sir William Paget, knight, oone of the Kinges Majestes two Principal Secretoryes.

[*Letters and Papers, Henry VIII.* (*Printed State Papers*, x. 108. *Cal.* XIX. (ii) 224.)]

---

168. *Official Despatch from Ministers to the King* (4 *June*, 1545).

Please it Your Majestie to b'advertised that, accordinglie to our last letters, dated from hens the 25th of Maye, by Nicholas your Majesties servaunt, th'ambassadours of the Protestantes wrote immediatlie to theire maisters of our conference with theim, and thei looke as soone as may be for answerr, which as soone as it cummeth to us, we shall diligently send it to your Majestie. [*Special information follows.*]

Other occurentes at this present, none that we know. God save Your Majeste. From Wormbs, the 4th of June.

Your Majesties moste humble
and bounden servantes,

Water Bucler.

Christophorus Mont.

[*Superscribed.*]   To the Kinges Majestie.

[*Letters and Papers, Henry VIII.* (*Printed State Papers*, x. 458. *Cal.* xx. (i) 437.)]

---

169. *Official Letter from a Secretary of State in the King's name* (6 *April*, 1689).

Hampton Court, 6 April, 1689.

My Lords,

It is His Majesty's pleasure that Sir William Gregory be constituted one of the Justices of the Court of Common Pleas in the place of Mr Ward, whom His Majesty (at his desire) is pleased to excuse from that office. It is perhaps now unnecessary to mention that the clause of *quamdiu se bene gesserit* is to be inserted in the Patent. I am,

your Lordships'
most faithful, humble servant,

Shrewsbury.

[*S. P. Dom. Entry Book, Vol.* 97, *p.* 61.]

170. *Official Letter from a Secretary of State (7 February, 1715).*

Whitehall, Feb. 7th, 1714/5.

Sir,

In answer to your letters of the 1st and 12th of February, I shall only say that I have truely acquainted His Ma^ty with the contents of them, as likewise with the justice done to you by the Earl of Stairs in all his dispatches.

I likewise represented to His Ma^ty in Council that it would be impossible for you to return home unless you were enabled to pay your debts, upon which His Ma^ty hath been pleased to direct that your demands as stated to my Lord Halifax be complyed with, and accordingly I have signifyed His Ma^ty's pleasure thereupon to Lord Halifax, who I am persuaded will be pleased to serve you. I assure you that I shall on all occasions be very glad of shewing you that I am with truth, Sir,

your faithfull, humble servant,
Ja. Stanhope.

Mr [Matthew] Prior.

[*F. O. King's Letters, Vol.* 14, *p.* 106.]

---

171. *Official Letter from a Government Department (26 June, 1837).*

Horse Guards, 26th June, 1837.

Sir,

I have the honor to acknowledge the receipt of your letter of the 12th ultimo, accompanying the General Monthly Returns which had been returned to you for signature, and in reply to that part of your letter wherein you state that you could not exactly ascertain how to affix your signature so as to authenticate them, unless you should be required to sign all the returns forming the documents entituled the 'Monthly Returns.'

I have to acquaint you that it is necessary that you affix your signature at the end of the nominal list of the staff in page 2, at the end of the nominal return of the troops in page 11, and at the end of the nominal lists of officers present and absent at page 19.

I have [the honour to be,
Sir,
Your most obedient, humble Servant,]
John Macdonald, A. G.

M. General Middlemore,
St Helena.

[*War Office, Commander in Chief. Letters to General Officers, Vol.* 91, *fo.* 113.]

2. ROYAL AND SECRETARIAL INSTRUMENTS

The official correspondence referred to above is best known to us in the shape of originals received by the King or his ministers (In-Letters); but it naturally includes the drafts or copies (Out-Letters) relating to this correspondence or to other business (Nos. 167 —171) and from one point of view these Out-Letters are of great importance to us, since the originals are not usually preserved in official custody.

At the same time we shall find side by side with these Out-Letters a large series of 'Entry Books' of Warrants, Commissions, Instructions, Passes, Proclamations, *Caveats* and other Secretarial instruments issued in the King's name (Nos. 172—179) or even on his own authority (Nos. 180—182) by the Secretary of State or some other of the great Household officers whose independent jurisdiction has survived from the mediaeval period (Nos. 195—199). Again, we may easily notice that, for the convenience of the despatch of public business, these instruments are connected with the conduct of Domestic and Foreign affairs respectively by the dual Secretariat of the 17th and 18th centuries. The Warrants and other forms mentioned above belong to the ancient jurisdiction of the Home Department of later times. In addition to this series, however, another will be found in connection with the business of the later Foreign Department, and here we have an interesting sequence of diplomatic instruments (Nos. 183—194) which are still used in principle in our own time.

(a) For Domestic Affairs

172. *Royal Proclamation revoking Privy Seals for a 'Forced Loan'* (1626).

[*Royal Arms, crest, supporters and motto.*]

By the King.

Whereas, sithence the late assembly in Parliament, wee did, for the raising of necessary summes of money to be imployed in the defence of the realme, direct our severall Letters and also sent by sundry Privie Seales into divers parts of this kingdome, of which wee had cause to expect a better returne than hath followed, which notwithstanding we impute not to any disaffection in our people, but to some miscarriage in that businesse, and the aversenesse of some not so well affected; and now, for that our intention is not to trouble our subjects many dayes at once, whatsoever the present necessitie of the common defence requireth, our will and pleasure therefore is, and we do by this our royal Proclamation signifie and declare, that such our Letters which required the free gift of our subjects, and also the Privie Seales issued sithence the last Parliament, shall be from henceforth remitted and discharged without any further demaund or payment to be had or made thereupon. And for such our loving subjects who have already given any money upon the said Letters or lent us money upon the sayd Privie Seales issued since the last Parliament, wee have given order how the same shall bee repayd unto them without delay.

Given at our Honour of Hampton Court, the 22 day of September, in the second yeere of our reigne of Great Britaine, France and Ireland.

God save the King[1].

Imprinted at London by Bonham, Norton and John Bill, Printers to the King's Most Excellent Majesty.

1626.

[*S. P. Dom. Proclamations, Vol.* i, *p.* 52.]

---

173. *Sign Manual Warrant (Passport) for an enemy's ship to leave an English port* (16 *July,* 1702)[2].

A. R.

Anne [*etc.*], To all our Admirals [*etc.*], Greeting. Whereas wee have been informed that the ship or vessell, called the Nonsuch of Challevette, arrived from Bordeaux in France in our port of Bristoll the 28th day of Aprill last past, being before our late declaration of warr, wee are therefore graciously pleased to grant our royall Passport to ye said ship or vessell to return into France; and accordingly our will and pleasure is, and wee do hereby strictly charge and require you and every of you (as wee do likewise pray and desire the officers and ministers of all princes and states in amity with us), to permit and suffer the said ship or vessell called the Nonsuch of Challevette, French built and owners, burthen about 30 tons and navigated by severall men hereafter mencõned, vizt. [*Names follow*], to sail from hence to ye said port of Bordeaux in France without any let, hindrance or molestacõn whatsoever; but on ye contrary affording such aid and assistance as may be necessary, any order, instruction or direction to the contrary notwithstanding. Provided nevertheless y^t this our Passport shall remain in force during this one voyage onely,

---

[1] In the original draft and in later imprints of these instruments the formula 'By His Majesty's Command,' with the counter-signature of the Secretary of State, is added.

[2] These Warrants are better known as 'Ship's Passes,' forming an extensive series of the State Papers Domestic. They were also issued by Consuls.

and no longer; y^t ye said ship carry on board no contraband goods nor any naval stores. Given at our Court at Windsor, ye 16th day of July, 1702, in ye 1st year of our reigne.

By Her Majesty's Command.

Nottingham.

[*S. P. Dom. Entry Bk. Vol. 72, p. 47.*]

---

174. *Sign Manual Warrant (Pass) for a subject to travel abroad* (2 *March*, 1674)[1].

Charles R.

Charles the Second, by the Grace of God, King of England, Scotland, France and Ireland, Defender of the Faith etc. To all admiralls, vice-admiralls, captains of our ships at sea, governours, commanders, souldiers, majors, sheriffs, justices of the peace, bayliffs, constables, customers, controllers, searchers and all others whom it may concerne, Greeting. Whereas we have thought fit to licence, and by these presents do licence our trusty and welbeloved Richard Bulkley Esqr, son and heire of our right trusty and welbeloved Robert, Lord Bulkley, to Passe out of this our realme into the parts beyond the seas for his better education and experience, with two servants to attend him, wee do hereby require and command you and every of you to suffer the said Richard Bulkley and his two servants to Passe by you out of our realme of England with twenty pounds in money and his and their wearing apparells and other necessarys without any lett hindrance or molestačon, as you tender our displeasure. And these our letters, or the duplicate of them, shall be as, as well unto you as unto the said Richard Bulkley, a sufficient warrant and discharge in that behalfe; provided always that the said Richard Bulkley do not make his abode in any popish colledge or seminary, nor use the company of any Jesuite, Romish priest, or otherwise evill affected to our state ; provided also that, notwithstanding anything in this our License, whensoever it shall seeme good unto us to recall the said Richard Bulkley home againe and shall signify the same unto him either by our own letters or by the letters of any four of our Privy Council by means of any of our ambassadors, that then it shall not be lawfull for him to remaine on the other side of the seas any longer time than the distance of his abode shall require and our laws do permitt. And our further pleasure is that when the said Richard Bulkley shall think fitt for his convenience, or shall be by us commanded to return into this our kingdome, you permitt him and his servants a quiet and peaceable passage by you into our said kingdome. Given at our Court at Whitehall, the second day of March, 1674, in the 27th yeare of our reigne.

By His Maj^ties command.

H. Coventry.

[*H. O. Precedent Bk. Vol. 1, fo. 54.*]

---

[1] Inland Passes were also granted to soldiers, etc.

175. *Sign Manual Warrant (Royal License) for change of Name, etc., countersigned by a Secretary of State (4 March, 1752).*

George R.

George the second [*etc.*], to our right trusty and right welbeloved cousin, Thomas, Earl of Effingham, Deputy to our right trusty and right entirely beloved cousin, Edward, Duke of Norfolk, Earl Marshall and our Hereditary Marshall of England, Greeting. Whereas our trusty and welbeloved William Peny Esqr and the Honble. Elizabeth, his wife, grand daughter and heir of Robert Sydney, late Earl of Leicester, deceased, have by their joint petition represented unto us their humble request that the issue of their bodies already had, or to be had, may at all times hereafter use, take and enjoy the name of Sydney, and also use and bear the coat armour of the said Robert, late Earl of Leicester, to them and their heirs for ever ; know ye that we, of our princely grace and special favour, have given and granted, and do give and grant, unto the issue now had, or to be had, of the bodies of the said William and Elizabeth his wife, full power, Licence and authority to assume and take upon them the said name of Sydney only, and to use and bear the coat armour of the said Robert, late Earl of Leicester, to them and their heirs for ever ; and that it is our further will and pleasure that you, Thomas, Earl of Effingham, Deputy to the said Earl Marshall, to whom the cognizance of matters of this nature does properly belong, do require and command that this our concession and declaration be registered in our College of Arms, to the end that our officers of arms and all others, upon occasion, may take full notice and have knowledge thereof, for which this shall be your Warrant. Given at our court at St James's the fourth day of March, 1752, in the twenty-fifth year of our reign.

By His Majesty's command.

Holdernesse.

[*H. O. Warrant Bk. Vol.* 25, *p.* 172.]

------

176. *Sign Manual Warrant (Royal License) for a subject to enter the service of a foreign state (29 April, 1763)[1].*

George R.

George the third, by the grace of God, King of Great Britain, France and Ireland, Defender of the Faith [*etc.*], to all to whom these presents shall come, Greeting. Whereas our trusty and welbeloved subject, Robert Alsop, Esqr, hath humbly represented unto us that he hath received some encouragement, and is desirous to enter into the service, at sea, of our good Sister, the Empress of all the Russias and praying us to grant him our Royal Licence for that purpose, we are graciously pleased to condescend to his request, and we do accordingly, by these presents, give and grant our full leave, licence and

------

[1] Cf. the License still required to receive foreign Orders.

permission to him, the said Robert Alsop, to enter himself into the service of our said good Sister, the Empress of all the Russias, and to continue therein until such time as we shall signify our pleasure to the contrary. Given at our Court at St James's, the twenty-ninth day of April, 1763, in the third year of our reign.

By His Majesty's command.

Dunk Halifax.

[*H. O. Warrant Bk. Vol. 29, p. 352.*]

---

177. *Sign Manual Warrant (Royal License) for the Lord Mayor of London to reside outside the city, for his health (12 March, 1733)*[1].

George R.

Right Trusty and Welbeloved, we greet you well. Humble suit having been made to us in your behalf for leave to remain or live sometimes during your mayoralty out of our City of London, for the recovery of your health, we are graciously pleased to condescend thereto, and we do accordingly, hereby, give and grant you full Licence and permission to remain or live out of our said city during your mayoralty, at such times and in such manner that your absence prove not prejudicial to our service; provided still that you return to our said city and there remain upon a signification of our pleasure to you by our Privy Council or either of our Secretarys of State. And so we bid you heartily farewell. Given at our Court at St James's, the twelfth day of March, 1732/3, in the sixth year of our reign.

By His Majesty's command.

Holles Newcastle.

To our right trusty and welbeloved John Barber, Esq[r],
 Lord Mayor of our City of London.

[*S. P. Dom. Entry Bk. Vol. 162, p. 239.*]

---

178. *Notification by the Secretary of State of a Pass granted for driving in the Park (17 March, 1716).*

Whitehall, 17 March, 1715/6.

My Lord,

I am commanded by His Majesty to signify to you his pleasure that the proper directions be given that her Grace the Dutchess of Newcastle be permitted to pass in her coach through the Horse Guards into St James's Park and out of it.

I am, etc.,

Holles Newcastle.

To the Gold Stick in Waiting.

[*H. O. Precedent Bk. Vol. 4, p. 24.*]

---

[1] Similar Licenses were granted to Lord Lieutenants and Sheriffs to quit their counties.

179.   *Warrant of a Secretary of State (in the King's name) for certain persons to appear before the Council (22 January,* 1688).

These are, in His Ma^{ty's} name, to require you forthwith to summon [*Names follow*] to appear befor His Ma^{ty} in Council upon the 3rd day of Feby next to answer to such matters of misdemeanour as shal be objected against y^{m}.   Given at ye court at Whitehall, ye 22nd day of Jan^{y}, 1687/8.

To Tho. Atterbury, one of His Ma^{ty's} Messengers [*etc.*].

[*S. P. Dom. Entry Bk. Vol.* 72, *p.* 217.]

---

180.   *Secretary of State's Warrant for the 'taking up' of the party named therein* (1715—16).

Charles, Lord Viscount Townshend [*etc.*].

These are, [in His Majesty's name, to will and require you to] search for...the wife of Col. John Haye, of whom you shall have notice, and her having found, seize and apprehend for suspicion of high treason, and bring her, together with her papers, in safe custody before me, to be examined and further dealt with according to law. In the due execution [*etc.*].

To His Ma^{ty's} Messengers in Ordinary.

[*H. O. Precedent Bk. Vol.* 2, *p.* 31.]

---

181.   *Secretary of State's Warrant* (Mittimus) *for the imprisonment of a person charged with High Treason* (1715—16).

Charles, Lord Viscount Townshend [*etc.*].

These are, in His Majesty's name, to will and require you to receive into your custody the body of Margery, the wife of Colonel John Hay, herewith sent you for high treason, and you are to keep her safe and close until she shall be delivered by due course of law. And for so doing [*etc.*].   Given [*etc.*].

To the Keeper of Newgate or his Deputy.

[*H. O. Precedent Bk. Vol.* 2, *p.* 33.]

182. *Protection by a Secretary of State from requisitions by the military power* (9 November, 1688).

Charles, Earl of Middleton, one of the Lords of His Ma^{ts} most honorable Privy Councill and Principall Secretary of State.

To ye officer commanding in chief any of His Ma^{ts} forces, and to all others whom it may concerne, Greeting.

The Countesse Dowager of Middleton, my mother, living at Kensington, and having only women in her family and no horses but what are necessary for her own coach, These are to request all His Ma^{ts} officers, civil and military, whom it may concerne, to exempt ye said Countess from having any soldiers quartered in her house and to save and spare her two horses from being pressed. Given at the Court at Whitehall, ye 9th of November, 1688.

Middleton.

[*S. P. Dom. Entry Bk. Vol.* 338, *p.* 133.]

(*b*) *Foreign Affairs*

183. *Instructions under the Sign Manual for a Minister to a foreign Court* (18 May, 1761).

George R.

Instructions for our trusty and wellbeloved Hans Stanley Esq., whom We have appointed our Minister to our Good Brother the most Christian King. Given at our Court at St James's the Eighteenth Day of May 1761, in the first year of Our Reign.

Whereas, in consequence of certain overtures relative to peace, made to us by our good brother the most Christian King, the Sieur de Bussy is to repair to our Court in quality of minister from the said most Christian King, and we, on our part, have appointed you to repair to the Court of France with the same character; and having already directed the several letters and memorials that have passed between the two Courts relative to these matters to be put into your hands, we have thought fit to give you the following Instructions for your conduct in the execution of the important trust thereby reposed in you.

1. You are, upon the receipt of these Instructions, together with our Full Power and Credential Letter to the most Christian King, to repair to Dover [*etc.*].
2. On your arrival at Calais [*etc.*].
3. On your arrival at Paris [*etc.*].

4. For your better guidance and direction in this important negotiation, we have judged proper to lay down [*etc.*].

5. With regard to any explanations which the Duc de Choiseul may give [*etc.*].

6. If the Duc de Choiseul shall touch the subject of the war [*etc.*].

7. Notwithstanding you are by our Full Power, authorized to conclude and sign anything, that may be agreed on between the two Courts: It is our express Will and Pleasure, that you do not...proceed to the signature of any act whatever with the Court of France, without first having our special orders for that purpose [*etc.*].

8. Whereas it is agreed between the two Crowns, that you and the Sieur de Bussy, shall respectively enjoy in France and in England, all the rights [*etc.*]. You are to be duely attentive to maintain our dignity in all things touching the same, and to take care that you be treated in the same manner as ministers of your rank [*etc.*].

9. You shall use your particular endeavours to inform yourself of the interior situation of the Court of France...and of all matters which may be of consequence, and worthy our knowledge; you shall constantly give an account to us by one of our Principal Secretaries of State, from whom you will receive such further Instructions and directions, as we shall think fit to send you, which you are to observe accordingly.

G. R.

[*H. O. Precedent Book, Vol.* 3.]

---

184. *Royal Letter* (*Credentials*) *for an Envoy to a foreign Court* (19 *May*, 1761)[1].

Monsieur mon Frere, ayant fait choix du Sieur Stanley pour se rendre à votre cour en qualité de mon ministre, je vous prie de donner une entiere créance à tout ce qu'il vous dira de ma part, et surtout aux assurances qu'il vous donnera de mon estime singuliere pour vous, et de mon desir sincere de voir heureusement retablir entre nous une amitié ferme et durable.   Je suis, Monsieur mon Frere

Votre bon Frere,
George R.

À St James ce 19 May, 1761.

[*Superscribed.*]
    Au Roi très Chretien, Monsieur mon Frere.

[*F. O. King's Letters, Vol.* 16, *p.* 14.]

---

[1] Re-credentials were also frequently issued.

185. *Sign Manual Letter (Pass) for a Minister to a foreign Court* (1 *September*, 1762)[1].

Georgius Rex.

Georgius Tertius, *etc.* [*as in No.* 163], omnibus et singulis ad quos præsentes literæ pervenerint, Salutem. Quando quidem prænobilis, perquam fidelis nobis, et predilectus consanguineus et consiliarius noster, Johannes, Dux de Bedford, Privati nostri Sigilli Custos, quem designavimus ad munus Legati nostri Extraordinarii ad serenissimum et potentissimum principem Ludovicum Decimum quintum, regem Christianissimum, bonum fratrem nostrum, jam Galliam profecturus sit ; quo destinatum iter tutius commodiusque conficiat, rogandos duximus omnes et singulos reges, principes, tam ecclesiasticos quam seculares, status, respublicas, ordines, liberas civitates, aliasque potentias nobiscum amicitia conjunctas, eorumque exercituum classiumque ductores, urbium et fortalitium præfectos, limitum custodes et, in universum, officiales ac ministros quoscunque, quod de subditis nostris quorum ullomodo intererit, firmiter injungimus ut prænominato Legato nostro Extraordinario una cum satellitis, famili[a] et sarcinis quibuscunque suis, liberum transitum permittant, ac in quovis loco commorandi, quantum ipsi libitum erit, potestatem faciant, ipsi novas Salvi Conductus literas, si res ita postulaverit, concedant ; eundemque omnibus aliis humanitatis ac benevolentiæ officiis excipiant, adjuventque. Quod nos grate agnoscemus, et pari vel alia data occasione, servata cujusque status et dignitatis ratione, vicissim reprensuri sumus. Dabantur in palatio nostro Divi Jacobi, die primo mensis Septembris, anno Domini millesimo septengintesimo sexagesimo secundo, regnique nostri secundo.

Ad mandatum Serenissimi Domini Regis.

Egremont.

[*F. O. King's Letters, Vol.* 16, *p.* 26.]

---

186. *Sign Manual Bill for Letters Patent (Full Power) for a Minister Plenipotentiary* (5 *May*, 1761).

Georgius Rex.

Georgius Tertius, *etc.* [*as in No.* 163], omnibus et singulis ad quos præsentes hæ Literæ, pervenerint, Salutem. Cum nobis nihil gratius accidere possit quam ut bellum illud, quod nos inter Regemque Christianissimum motum est, justis tandem pacis conditionibus finiatur ; cumque ea de causa virum quendam, tanto negotio parem, ad bonum fratrem nostrum Regem Christianissimum mittere decreverimus ; Sciatis igitur quod nos, fide, industria, ingenio et perspicacia

---

[1] This was not always necessary, *e.g.* in the case of Hans Stanley proceeding to Paris by special arrangement with the Court of France.

fidelis et dilecti nobis, Hans Stanley, armigeri, plurimum confisi, eundem nominavimus, fecimus et constituimus, sicut per præsentes nominamus, facimus et constituimus, nostrum verum, certum et indubitatum commissarium, procuratorem et plenipotentiarium ; dantes et concedentes eidem omnem et omnimodam potestatem, facultatem et authoritatem necnon mandatum generale pariter ac speciale cum ministro ministrisve ex parte prædicti Regis Christianissimi sufficienti authoritate instructo vel instructis, congrediendi colloquendique, ac de omnibus et singulis quæ quovis modo ad præmissa necessaria et opportuna judicaverit, conveniendi et concludendi, eaque omnia quæ ita conventa et conclusa fuerint, pro nobis et nostro nomine signandi, superque conclusis instrumenta quotquot et qualia necessaria fuerint conficiendi, mutuoque tradendi, recipiendique; spondentes et in verbo regio promittentes nos omnia et singula quæcunque a dicto nostro commissario, procuratore ac plenipotentiario, vi præsentium, transigi, concludi et signari contigerit, grata, rata et accepta, iis prorsus modo et forma quibus conventa fuerint, habituros.   In cujus rei testimonium hasce Literas fieri, manuque nostra signatas, Magno regni nostri Magnæ Britanniæ Sigillo communiri fecimus.   Dabantur in palatio nostro Divi Jacobi, decimo quinto die mensis Maii, anno domini millesimo septingentesimo sexagesimo primo, regnique nostri primo.

[*F. O. King's Letters, Vol.* 16, *pp.* 12—14.]

---

187.   *Sign Manual Warrant for Letters Patent (Commission) for the Secretary to an Embassy* (3 *July*, 1765)[1].

George R.

Our will and pleasure is that you forthwith cause our Great Seal of Great Britain to be affixed to an instrument bearing date with these presents (a copy whereof is hereunto annexed) containing our Commission constituting and appointing our trusty and welbeloved David Hume, Esqr, to be Secretary to our extraordinary embassy to our good brother the most Christian King.   And for so doing this shall be your Warrant.   Given at our Court of St James's, the third day of July, 1765, in the fifth year of our reign.

By His Majesty's command.

Dunk Halifax.

To our right trusty and right welbeloved cousin and councillor, Robert, Earl of Northampton, our Chancellor of Great Britain.

[*F. O. King's Letters, Vol.* 16, *p.* 111.]

---

[1] Like Commissions were issued for Consuls.

188. *Sign Manual Warrant (Protection) for a foreign Minister* (17 *December*, 1680).

[C. R.]

Charles the Second [*etc.*], to all our loving subjects whom it may concern, Greeting. Wheras our good brother the King of Spain has by a commission under his hand and seal bearing date yᵉ 12ᵗʰ day of Novʳ last past, constituted and appointed Don Philip de la Gu... to be his Agent in this Our Kingdom, and we have thereupon approved of the said Don P. de la Gu... as Agent of ye said King, our Will and Pleasure is, and we hereby require you to receive, countenance and, as theire may be occasion, favourably assist him in ye exercise of his said place, giving and allowing to him all ye priviledges, immunitys and advantages therunto belonging. Given at Whitehall, Dec. 17, 1680.

By [*His Majesty's Command*].

Sunderland.

[*S. P. Dom. Entry Bk. Vol. 72, p. 223.*]

---

189. *Official Letter (Pass) for the baggage, etc., of a foreign Minister* (23 *July*, 1723)[1].

Whitehall, July 23d, 1723.

Gentlemen,

Baron Schack, Envoy Extraordinʸ from the Duke of Lorrain, being upon his departure hence and having desired that his baggage and twelve couple of dogs, being a present from His Majᵗʸ to ye Duke, his master, may be put on board a ship on Thursday next without any hinderance or molestation, I am to desire that you will send some proper officer to ye house of ye sᵈ envoy in order to inspect his baggage and seal it up, and that you will shew him such further marks of civility and dispatch as may be necessary upon this occasion.

I am, *etc.*

R. Walpole.

To the Comptrollers of the Customs.

[*H. O. Precedent Bk. Vol. 2, p. 95.*]

---

190. *Royal Letter (Recall) summoning a Minister abroad to the King's presence* (27 *April*, 1753)[2].

George R.

Right trusty and right entirely beloved cousin and councillor, we greet you well. Whereas we have thought it for our service that you

---

[1] This Pass was also issued for consignments of wine and other goods to foreign ministers.
[2] The terms Recall and Revocation (No. 191) were sometimes used indiscriminately.

should repair to our presence to assist us with your counsel and advice, we do therefore herewith send you our Letters of Revocation for the Most Christian King and Queen, which you are to deliver to them, accompanying the same with such expressions of our esteem and friendship as you shall judge proper.   After which you shall make all convenient speed to return to us, assuring yourself of our favour and gracious acceptance of the service you have done us in that Court.   And so we bid you very heartily farewell.

Given at our Court at St James's, the 27th day of April, 1763, in the third year of our reign.

By His Majesty's command.

Egremont.

[*Superscribed.*]

To our right trusty and right entirely beloved cousin and councillor, John, Duke of Bedford, our Ambassador Extraordinary and Plenipotentiary to our good brother the Most Christian King.

[*F. O. King's Letters, Vol.* 16, *p.* 47.]

---

191.   *Royal Letter (Revocation) for the recall of a Minister to a foreign Court* (10 *September,* 1802).

George the Third [*etc.*], to the First Consul of the French Republic sendeth greeting.   We have thought proper to recall our trusty and wellbeloved Anthony Merry, Esquire, our Minister Plenipotentiary to the French Republic.   In communicating this our determination. to you, we have ordered our said Minister, when he shall have the honour of delivering this our Letter into your hands, to repeat to you our assurances of our constant and sincere desire to cement the union and good correspondence so happily re-established between us and the French Republic.   We have no doubt that the conduct of our said Minister during his residence at Paris has been perfectly agreeable to you, and that you will give him such testimonies of approbation on his taking leave as may entitle him to our favor upon his return into our royal presence.   And so we recommend you to the protection of the Almighty.

Given at our Court at St James's, this tenth day of September, 1802, in the forty-second year of our reign.

George R.

Hawkesbury.

[*F. O. King's Letters, Vol.* 18, *p.* 21.]

---

192. *Secretarial Certificate of an Envoy's Departure on his employment*[1].

These are to certify all whom it may concern, that [Sir John Norris], His Majesty's Envoy and Plenipotentiary to the Most Christian King, Czar of Muscovy, kissed His. Majesty's hand and departed out of His presence in order to that Employment, this present Saturday being the 6th day of July. Given at Whitehall, the 6th day of July, 1717.

[Sunderland.]

[*H. O. Precedent Book, Vol. 2, p. 95 bis.*]

193. *Secretarial Certificate of a Minister Plenipotentiary's Return from his Employment* (14 *October,* 1761)[1].

These are to certify all whom it may concern, that Hans Stanley, Esqʳ, His Majesty's Minister to the Most Christian King, returned into His Majesty's presence from that employment on Wednesday, the thirtieth day of September last past. Given at Whitehall, the 14th day of October, 1761.

Egremont.

[*S. P. For. Entry Bk. Vol.* 238, *p.* 53.]

194. *Secretarial certification of a Bill of Extraordinaries for a Minister abroad* (15 *October,* 1761).

Hans Stanley, Esqʳ, His Majesty's Minister Plenipotentiary to the Most Christian King, humbly craves allowance for his extraordinary disbursements in that service—   £500.

London, Oct. 13th, 1761.

H. Stanley.

Whitehall, 15 Oct., 1761.
I allow this bill, by His Majesty's special command.

Egremont.

[*S. P. For. Entry Bk. Vol.* 238, *p.* 53.]

---

[1] The object of this Certificate was to ascertain the exact period for which his allowance or diet was due (cf. No. **194**). In some cases (*e.g.* Hans Stanley) the diet was ante-dated by a special Warrant and no Certificate of Departure was therefore issued.

195. *Warrant of the Lord Chamberlain withdrawing his License for a Play* (26 *June*, 1682).

Whereas I did signifie His Maties pleasure in my Order dated ye 15th of June instant that a new play of Mr Crownes, called ,
should be lycens'd and acted at His Royall Highnesse Theatre, I doe now againe signifie His Maties pleasure that you forbeare acting ye said play untill further Order, at y^or perills. And this shall be yor Warr^t. Given und^r my hand this 26 day of June 1682 in ye 34th yeare of His Maties Reigne.

To Mr Beterton and ye rest of ye Comedians at His Royall Highnesse Theatre.

Arlington.

[Lord Chamberlain's Books (Ser. 1), *Vol.* 775, *p.* 83.]

---

196. *Warrant of the Lord Chamberlain for the arrest of parties charged with breach of the Privileges of the Household* (13 *June*, 1682).

Whereas   Ryley and   Osmond, bayliffs, have arrested, or caused to bee arrested, Sr Oliver Boteler, one of the Gentlemen of His Ma^ts most hono^ble Privy Chamber in Ordinary with fee, without my leave, which is a manifest breach of the priviledges of His Ma^ts houshold : These are therefore to require you to apprehend and take into your custody the bodyes of the said   Ryley and Osmond and them safely keepe untill they shalbe delivred by due course of law ; and all mayors, sheriffs, bayliffs, constables [*etc.*] are to bee ayding and assisting in the execucõn of this warrant. And this shalbe your warrant. Given under my hand and seale, this 13 day of June, 1682, in the 34th year of His Ma^ts reigne.

To Ralph Carter, Messenger in Ordinary of His M^ts Chamber.

[Lord Chamberlain's Books (Ser. 1), *Vol.* 775, *p.* 69.]

(c) *Royal Household*

197. *Warrant of the Lord Steward of the Household* (15 *September*, 1673).

These are to will and require you, to sweare and admitt the bearer hereof, William Cotton, into the place of Gentleman Harbing^r in Ordin^y to his Maj^ts Household, the same beeing become voyd by the death of Nicholas Woodgate, late Gent. Harbing^r, and to allow unto him the sayd William Cotton, the wages, board-wages, ffees, profitts, perquisites and advantages to the sayd place belonging. And for soe doeing this shall bee yor Warrant.

Clarendon House, the 15th of Sept^r, 1673.

Ormond.

To my very loveing freind,
    the Clerke of his Maj^{ts}
    Greenecloth attending.

[*Lord Steward's Records, Miscellaneous Books*, 329.]

---

198. *Warrant of the Lord Chamberlain for admitting an officer of the Household*[1].

These are to certify yt I have sworn, and Admitted Mrs Anne Wynyarde (*alias* Incledon) into ye place and quality of Keeper of ye Royall House of Westminster, within ye Palace of Westminster, in Ordinary to her Ma^{ty}. To have, hold, exercise and enjoy ye said place together with all rights, profits, priviledges and advantages thereunto belonging in as full and ample manner as any keeper of ye s^d Royall House hath formerly held, or of right ought to have held and enjoy'd the same. Given under my hand and Seal this 19th of October in ye first year of Her Maj^{ts} reign.

Jersey.

[*Lord Chamberlain's Books* (*Ser.* 1), *Vol.* 757, *p.* 95.]

---

199. *Warrant of the Lord Chamberlain to the Treasurer of the Household authorizing the payment of Bill-Money* (29 *August*, 1698)[2].

These are to pray and require you to pay or cause to be paid to Mrs Anne Wynyarde (otherwise Incledon) keeper of His Majestie's Pallace of Westminster the sume of eighty seven pounds, thirteen shillings and four pence for herself, her man, and six labourers, employ'd in making clean the said house and yards, for removing the forms and tressells and also for sweeping all the chimneys for the space of two hundred, sixty-three days from the 4th of November, 1697 to the 23rd of August, 1698 inclusive, att the rate of six shillings and eightpence a day as appears by the Bill annext. And for so doing [*etc.*]. Given [*etc.*] 29th day of August, in the tenth year of His Ma^{ts} reign.

Pere: Bertie.

To Lord Edward Russell.

[*Lord Chamberlain's Books* (*Ser.* 1), *Vol.* 756, *p.* 128.]

---

[1] See Nos. 200—3.   [2] See *Ibid.*

3. DEPARTMENTAL INSTRUMENTS

From a period not long posterior to the new Establishment of the Secretariat in the 16th century, we can trace the institution of Departmental Boards in place of the old hereditary or patent officers and casual agents or accountants of the Plantagenet *régime*.

The Records of these Boards or Commissions do not differ materially in character from the correspondence and instruments of the Secretariat itself. They possess one distinctive feature, however. which may be briefly referred to here. The In-Letter received by these bodies is forthwith dealt with in accordance with an official routine which has been preserved down to modern times. That is to say, the Letter in question is noted in a Register, previous to being read and considered. It may then be referred for the Report of some expert or a Minute may be forthwith made indicating the proceedings to be taken upon it (Nos. 200—203). These proceedings are recorded in the several forms of the simple Out-Letter (No. 189) or the more formal and ceremonious Warrants (No. 206), Commissions (Nos. 207 and 209), Orders (No. 204) and Instructions (No. 205). It should of course be clearly understood that these Out-Letters and Instruments may be issued independently of any In-Letter, whilst it would be found that many other miscellaneous instruments (Nos. 210, 211) are preserved amongst the Departmental Records.

---

200. *In-Letter* (*Memorial*) *to the Lords Commissioners of the Treasury* (*July*, 1701)[1].

The King's housekeeper of Westm^r having noe sallary (besides a small fee of sixpence a day out of the Exchq.) hath constantly been allowed 6s. 8d. a day upon bills exhibitted to the Lord Chamberlain of His Ma^{tys} household, and by vertue of his Lord^{ps} Warr^{ts} thereupon, for and in regard of the great charge, labour and trouble of himself (*sic*), his servants and others, in keeping, sweeping and cleaning the said house and yards, preserving the goods, sweeping all the chimneys and for mopps, brooms, brushes and other necessaries, and their continuall attendance thereon ; for the payment of which allowance all former Lords Chamberlains gave their warr^{ts} to the Treasurer of his Ma^{tys} Chamber. But the present Lord Chamberlain, having been

[1] See Nos. 198, 199.

pleased to suspend signing any for more then a year past, hath thought fitt lately to represent the same (amongst others) in a memoriall to his Ma^{tye} (which lyes before the Lords of the Treasury) for his Ma^{tys} direction. Whatever the case of others (who perhaps have large sallaries) may be as to bill-money, the housekeeper of Westm^r having noe other sallary, noe fees in Parliam^t, nor other advantages thereby and being now (especially by reason of the frequent and long sessions of Parliam^{ts}) at much more charge, care, trouble and attendance, then any former housekeeper there ever had (who neverthelesse received the same allowance) he humbly hopes and prays that the said allowance (being but a very reasonable reward and his whole subsistance) may be confirmed to him, either in the same method, or by such other means established as that he may receive what is already in arrear and be enabled for the future to perform his duty in the said office, with the same care, and dilligence for his Ma^{tys} service, as formerly.

[*Treasury Papers, Vol.* LXXV. *fo.* 206. (*Cal. p.* 519.)]

---

201. *Reference of the above Memorial for the Report of the Secretary to the Lord Chamberlain* (29 *July*, 1701).

Cockpitt, Treasury Chambers, 29th July, 1701.

The Lords Commissioners of his Ma^{ts} Treasury are pleased to referr this memoriall to Sr John Stanley, Bar., who is desired to consider the same, and certify their Lo^{pps} a true state of the matter therein contained, together with his opinion what is fitt to be done therein.

Wm. Lowndes.

[*Treasury Papers, Vol.* LXXV. *fo.* 206. (*Cal. pp.* 519—20.)]

---

202. *Report of the Referee upon the above Memorial* (4 *August*, 1701).

To ye Rt. Honble ye Lords Commissioners of his Maj^{ts} Treasury.

May it please your Lordships,

In obedience to your L^{dps} order of Reference, signify'd by Mr Lowndes the 29th of July, 1701, upon ye Memorial of Ann Whynyard, housekeeper of His Majesty's Palace at Westminster, I do humbly certify that ye s^d housekeeper is by vertue of her employment, oblig'd to keep ye s^d house and yards adjoining to it clean, to sweep the chimneys, etc., as is set forth in ye s^d memoriall. I do likewise certify that ye s^d housekeeper is by her Patent allow'd only a fee of sixpence a day payable in ye Excheq^r, and that I do find by the books of ye Lord Chamberlain's Office that ye s^d housekeeper has over and above had an allowance of six shillings and eight pence a day in consideration of ye s^d service, by Warrant from ye Ld Chamberlain, which allowance was continu'd to her till ye last day of March, 1699, when ye present Ld Chamberlain forbore granting his warrants for this, as well as some other services which have been formerly allow'd but are not expresst in ye establishment of ye Treasury of ye Chamber, till his Ma^{ts} pleasure were further known. And accordingly his Lord^p has mention'd ye s^d housekeeper's case, with ye rest, in a memoriall lately lay'd before his Majesty, in ye Treasury.

As to ye method of settling ye allowance which shall be thought fitt for ye s^d housekeeper, in consideration of her care and service, whether it shall be by way of salary upon ye establishment, or by warrant from ye Ld Chamberlain, as has been hitherto done, is most humbly submitted to your Lordships' great wisdom.

J. Stanley.

Lord Chamberlain's Office,
    August ye 4th, 1701.

[*Treasury Papers, Vol.* LXXV. *fos.* 204—6. (*Cal. pp.* 519—20.)]

---

203. *Treasury Minute in the above case.*

8 Aug^t, 1701.

To be considered before ye Establ. is finished.

[*Treasury Papers, Vol.* LXXV. *fo.* 206. (*Cal. p.* 520.)]

---

204. *Treasury Order.*

Order is taken this iiijth day of March, 1707, by virtue of Her Maj^{tys} letters of Privy Seale, bearing date ye 31st of Jan^{ry} last, 1707, that you deliver and pay of such Her Ma^{tys} Treasure as remains in y^r charge unto Charles, E. of Sunderland, Her Ma^{tys} principall Sec^{ry} of State or to his assignes the sum of £3000, without account, for Her Ma^{tys} Secret Service. And these, together with his or his assignes' acquittance, shall be your discharge therein.

Godolphin.
H. Boyle.
Examinatur per
Halifax.

[*S. P. Dom. Entry Bk. Vol.* 72, *p.* 203; *T. Order Bk. Vol.* 7, *p.* 118.]

---

205. *Royal Instructions, under the Sign Manual, for a Military Expedition* (12 March, 1695).

William R.

Instructions for our trusty and welbeloved Brigadier Genl. Wm. Steward, commanding our land forces going for Cadiz. Given at our Court at Kensington, the 12th day of March, 1694/5.

You are to embark with your own and three other reg^{ts} of foot which we have ordered to be sent to Cadiz according to such direction as we have given therein. At your arrival at Cadiz with the said four regiments, and during your continuance in Spain, you are to follow and obey such orders as you shall receive from time to time from our r^t trusty and welbeloved counsellor, Edwd Russell, Esqr, adm^l and captain gen^l of our fleet in the Mediterranean, or other commander in chief of our said fleet for the time being. When any vacancys shall happen of officers in any of the said regim^{ts} you are to take care that the said admiral of our fleet have notice thereof, to the end he may appoint others to supply the vacant commands, who are to be received and acknowledged accordingly.

And in whatever relates to our service to be performed by the said regiments or any part of them, you are to govern yourself and the said forces by such directions as shall be given you by the said admiral of our fleet, with whom we have entrusted the chief command of all our forces both at land and at sea in those parts.

By His Ma^{tys} Command.

Shrewsbury.

[*S. P. Dom. Entry Bk. Vol. 72, p. 309.*]

---

206. *Treasury Warrant* (2 March, 1679).

After [our hearty commendations]. Whereas it hath been represented to us by you, the Comptroller of His Maj^{ts} workes at Windsor, that foure black marble stones have lain a long tyme in Hen. ye viijths chappell in Windsor, and no use made of them, and we haveing spoken with Dr Durell, Deane of Windsor, who hath informed us that the sayd marble stones are His Maj^{ts}, and not belonging to the church; these are therefore to direct and authorise you to remove the sayd marble stones and to imploy them for His Maj^{tys} service towards makeing ye pedistall for His Maj^{ts} statue on horseback, cast in brass, to be set thereon, wch is to stand in the green yard in His Ma^{ts} Castle of Windsor; for wch this shalbe yor Warrant. Whitehall, Treasury Chambers, ye 2nd day of March, 1679.

L[aurence] H[yde]: J[ohn] E[rneley]: E[dward] D[eering]: S[idney] G[odolphin]: S[tephen] F[ox].

To Hugh May Esqr, Comptroll^r, John Ball Esqr, Survey^r of His Maj^{ts} workes at Windsor, and all others whom it may concerne.

[*Treasury Warrants (not money), Vol. 1, p. 158.*]

207.   *Form of a Military Commission* (1702—9).

Anne R.

Anne by the Grace of God, Queen of Great Britain, France and Ireland, Defender of the Faith etc., to our trusty and welbeloved   Esqr, Greeting.   We reposing special trust and confidence in your loyalty, courage and good conduct do by these presents constitute and appoint you to be Captain of that Company whereof Captain   was late Capt. in our regiment of foot commanded by our trusty and welbeloved   Esqr. You are therefore to take ye said company into your care and charge, and duly to exercise as well the officers as soldiers thereof in arms and to use your best endeavours to keep them in good order and discipline.   And wee hereby command them to obey you as their captain and you to observe and follow such order and direction from time to time as you shall receive from us, your Colonell, or any other your superiour officer according to the rules and discipline of war in pursuance of the trust wee hereby repose in you.   Given at our Court at   the   day of   170 , in the   year of our reign.

> *By Her Majesty's Command.*
>
> [   ]

[*S. P. Dom. Entry Bk. Vol. 72, p. 207.*]

---

208.   *Regimental Warrant (Letter of Service)* (12 *May*, 1725).

George R.

Whereas we have thought fit that an Independent Company be formed in the Highlands of North Britain, under your command, to consist of yourself, as captain, two lieutenants, three serjeants, three corporalls, two drummers and sixty effective private men.   These are to authorise you, by beat of drum or otherwise, to raise so many voluntiers in the Highlands of North Britain as shall be wanting to complet the said Independent Company to the above numbers.   And all magistrates, justices of the peace, constables, and other our officers whom it may concern are hereby required to be assisting unto you in providing quarters, impressing carriages and otherwise, as there shall be occasion.   Given at our Court at St James's, this 12th day of May, 1725, in the eleventh year of our reign.

> *By His Maj^{tys} Command,*
>
> **H. Pelham.**

To our r^t t[rusty] and w[ell-beloved] Simon, Lord Lovatt, Captain of an Independent Company of Foot ; or to the officer or officers appointed by him to raise voluntiers for that company.

[*War Office, Misc. Bks., Vol. 17, p. 49.*]

209. *Naval Commission* (14 *December*, 1714).

By the Comm^{rs} for executing the office of Ld High Admiral of Great Britain and Ireland [etc.]. And of all His Majesty's Plantations [etc.]

To Lieutenant Richard Morlen, hereof appointed Lieu^t of His Majesty's ship, the 'Fowey.'

By virtue of the power, and authority to us given, we do hereby constitute and appoint you Lieut. of His Majesty's ship, the 'Fowey,' willing and requiring you forthwith to go on board and take upon you the charge and command of Lieut. in her accordingly; strictly charging and commanding all the officers and company belonging to the said ship subordinate to you to behave themselves joyntly and severally in their respective imployments with all due respect and obedience unto you their s^d Lieut., and you likewise to observe and execute as well the standing instructions hereunto annexed, attested by our secretary, as what orders and directions you shall from time to time receive from your Captain or any other yor superior officers for His Ma^{tys} service. Hereof nor you nor any of you may fail, as you will answer the contrary at your perrills. And for so doing this shall be your Warrant. Given under our hands and the seal of the office of Admiralty, this 14th day of December, 1714, in the first year of His Majesty's reign.

By command of their Lordships,

J. Burchett	Orford	G. Byng
Geo. Dodington	J. Jennings	A. Shanyan
Geo. Baillie.		

[*S. P. Dom. Entry Bk. Vol. 72, p.* 323.]

---

210. *Cartel for Prisoners of War* (1 *January*, 1800).

By the Commissioners for conducting His Majesty's Transport Service, and for the care and custody of Prisoners of War.

We do hereby require and direct you to embark on board the 'St Clair,' Cartel vessel, Pollings Barber, master, now lying at Portsmouth, the 120 French prisoners named in the enclosed list, signed by M. Niou, who are released unconditionally, conformably to the 8th article of the Convention of Alkmaar. And you are to deliver the said list to the master, together with a copy thereof in the usual form and the instructions herewith sent you for your guidance.

Given under our hands, at the Transport Office, the 1st day of January, 1800.

R[upert] G[eorge].   A[mbrose] S[earle].
W[illiam] A[lbany] O[tway].

By command of the Commissioners.
Alex. McLeay.

To Mr John Holmwood, Agent for Prisoners of War, Portchester.

[*Admiralty, Medical Out-letters, Vol.* 318, *p.* 1.]

---

211. *Navy Board, Lieutenant's Passing Certificate* (*7 June,* 1708).

In pursuance of the directions of His Royal Highness, signified to us by letters from Mr Burchett of the 27th of May past, We have examined Mr Henry Fowke and find he hath gone to sea near nyne years in Her Ma⁸ ships undermenconed, in the quality there exprest, vizt.:

	y^r	m⁰	w^k	d^y
Shoreham, Volunteer per order...	3 :	11 :	2 :	5 :
Ditto, Midshipman	1 :	10 :	3 :	2 :
Jersey, do.	0 :	9 :	0 :	1 :
Royal Anne, do.	2 :	3 :	0 :	6 :
	8 :	8 :	3 :	0 :

He produceth a jurnall kept by him in Her Ma^{ts} ship, 'The Royal Anne,' and a certificate from Captain Dussenger of his good qualifications, behaviour, diligence, obedience to command and recommendation for preferment. He can splice, knot, reef a saile, work a ship in sailing, keep reckoning of a ship's way by plaine sailing or Mercator, observe by sun or star, find the variacōn of ye compass, shift his tydes, and is qualifyed to do the duty of an able seaman and midshipman.

Dated 7th June, 1708.

R. Haddock.   Tho. Hopton.   Tho. Coale.

[*Admiralty, Navy Board, Passing Certificates, Vol.* 2, *p.* 180.]

CAMBRIDGE: PRINTED BY JOHN CLAY, M.A. AT THE UNIVERSITY PRESS.

For EU product safety concerns, contact us at Calle de José Abascal, 56–1°, 28003 Madrid, Spain or eugpsr@cambridge.org.

www.ingramcontent.com/pod-product-compliance
Ingram Content Group UK Ltd.
Pitfield, Milton Keynes, MK11 3LW, UK
UKHW010046140625
459647UK00012BB/1653